Irvine Welsh

ID0953906

Manchester University Press

◉ Contemporary British Novelists

Series editor Daniel Lea

already published

J.G.Ballard Andrzej Gasiorek

Irvine Welsh

Aaron Kelly

Manchester University Press

Manchester and New York

distributed exclusively in the USA by Palgrave

Published by Manchester University Press
Oxford Road, Manchester M13 9NR, UK
and Room 400, 175 Fifth Avenue, New York, NY 10010, USA
www.manchesteruniversitypress.co.uk

Distributed exclusively in the USA by
Palgrave, 175 Fifth Avenue, New York,
NY 10010, USA

Distributed exclusively in Canada by
UBC Press, University of British Columbia, 2029 West Mall,
Vancouver, BC, Canada V6T 1Z2

British Library Cataloguing-in-Publication Data
A catalogue record for this book is available from the British Library

Library of Congress Cataloging-in-Publication Data applied for

ISBN   0 7190 6650 6   *hardback*
EAN   9780 7190 6650 4

ISBN   0 7190 6651 4   *paperback*
EAN   9780 7190 6651 1

First published 2005

14 13 12 11 10 09 08 07 06 05   0 9 8 7 6 5 4 3 2 1

Typeset
by Northern Phototypesetting Co Ltd, Bolton
Printed in Great Britain
by Bell & Bain Ltd, Glasgow

Contents

Series editor's foreword

Contemporary British Novelists offers readers critical introductions to some of the most exciting and challenging writing of recent years. Through detailed analysis of their work, volumes in the series present lucid interpretations of authors who have sought to capture the sensibilities of the late twentieth and twenty-first centuries. Informed, but not dominated, by critical theory, *Contemporary British Novelists* explores the influence of diverse traditions, histories and cultures on prose fiction, and situates key figures within their relevant social, political, artistic and historical contexts.

The title of the series is deliberately provocative, recognising each of the three defining elements as contentious identifications of a cultural framework that must be continuously remade and renamed. The contemporary British novel defies easy categorisation and rather than offering bland guarantees as to the current trajectories of literary production, volumes in this series contest the very terms that are employed to unify them. How does one conceptualise, isolate and define the mutability of the contemporary? What legitimacy can be claimed for a singular Britishness given the multivocality implicit in the redefinition of national identities? Can the novel form adequately represent reading communities increasingly dependent upon digitalised communication? These polemical considerations are the theoretical backbone of the series, and attest to the difficulties of formulating a coherent analytical approach to the discontinuities and incoherencies of the present.

Contemporary British Novelists does not seek to appropriate its subjects for prescriptive formal or generic categories; rather it aims to explore the ways in which aesthetics are reproduced, refined and repositioned through recent prose writing. If the overarching architecture of the contemporary always eludes description, then the grandest ambition of this series must be to plot at least some of its dimensions.

Daniel Lea

Acknowledgements

This book was written during my time as a Leverhulme Postdoctoral Fellow in Scottish and Irish Literature at the University of Edinburgh and I would like to acknowledge the financial support of the Leverhulme Trust and the care of Cairns Craig in his role as my mentor. I was also granted a Research Fellowship at the Institute for Advanced Study in the Humanities at the University of Edinburgh and I am indebted to the help of John Frow and Anthea Taylor during my time there. I am grateful to Dilys Rose and Robert Alan Jamieson for their discussions and insights into contemporary Scottish writing. Additionally, I would like to thank Duncan McLean for chatting with me about the Scottish literary scene in the late 1980s and early 1990s. I am greatly appreciative of Irvine Welsh for making time to be interviewed for this book and also thankful that he chose a pub as the location for our talk.

I want to thank the entire team at Manchester University Press for working on the production and publication of this book and I am gladly indebted to Daniel Lea, the series editor of Contemporary British Novelists, together with Kate Fox and Matthew Frost, for their patience, advice and encouragement during the writing process. David Salter read through the manuscript for me in a generous and diligent manner and I am eternally grateful to him for his efforts, his friendship and his kindness. My initial interest in Irvine Welsh's fiction was focused and further stimulated by numerous conversations with Patsy Horton and I would like to thank her for her warm and illuminating thoughts and work in this area. All the students on my Modern Scottish Fiction course at the University of Edinburgh have inspired me and helped me to think more deeply about contemporary Scottish culture and I would like to let them all know publicly how much I appreciate their insight, energy and views.

I am also beholden to the following friends or colleagues for their comments on my work, their guidance, encouragement or simply their friendship: Michael Allen, Nicholas Allen, Steffi Bachorz, Chris Bates, Eleanor Bell, Ester Carrillo, Noreen Doody, Alice Ferrebe, Leontia Flynn, Chris Frieze,

Sarah Gamble, Peter Garratt, Luke Gibbons, Alan Gillis, Colin Graham, Stipe Grgas, Stephen Hackett, Seamus Harahan, Martin Harvey, Stephen Harvey, Patsy Horton, Eamonn Hughes, Keith Hughes, Bob Irvine, Mark Jamieson, Daniel Jewesbury, Jim Kelly, Edna Longley, Willy Maley, Michael McAteer, Seán McKeown, Eoghan McTigue, Patrick Magee, Julie Marney, Chris Martin, Shane Murphy, Kate Nicol, Lisa Power, Emily Pritchard, Yassamin Sheel, Paul Smith, Allyson Stack, Randall Stevenson, Wendy Townsend, Lindsey Watson, Stuart Watson, Richard West.

Finally, this book is for my family, Jim, Greta, Philip and Sarah Kelly. As a meagre offering for all their love, this book is dedicated with all mine.

Abbreviations

For Eamonn Hughes

Introduction

Irvine Welsh and the 'long dark night of late capitalism'

Irvine Welsh was born in 1958 in Leith, an area of Edinburgh that largely grew out of its port and surrounding industries and which has always maintained an ambivalent relationship with the rest of the city.[1] His mother was a waitress and his father worked as a docker until ill health forced him to switch to the less strenuous job of carpet salesman. Whilst Welsh was still an infant his family moved to the then new housing scheme of Muirhouse, where he grew up. Muirhouse, like other outlying housing schemes, was part of a post-Second World War urban redevelopment programme in Britain that increasingly relocated working-class communities in socially engineered estates comprising highly concentrated agglomerations of prefabs, maisonettes and blocks of flats. Despite the heady optimism which informed much of the original planning, the future social problems of such housing schemes were foreshadowed by the fact that they were typically built on the peripheries of British cities: away, that is, from the main thoroughfares and centres of urban life, which were themselves being redeveloped as purely commercial spaces and tourist or consumer havens. As Welsh explained to a 1995 BBC2 documentary about his work:

> A place like Muirhouse – like fifteen years ago you'd go to Muirhouse and it'd be pretty much the same, sort of pretty drab housing schemes, not a lot there, but most people would have a bit of work and there'd be a chance of moving into something different and moving on or whatever. But that's just been completely cut off and it's become much more a kind of ghetto.[2]

Having left school and trained and worked in electrical engineering, Welsh moved to London where he was part of the punk music scene of the late 1970s and drifted through a series of jobs before working for Hackney Council, whose Manpower Services Commission sponsored him to gain qualifications in computing. During his time in London Welsh also made money through buying, renovating and then selling property, thereby taking advantage of both the Thatcherite entrepreneurial spirit and its housing boom during the 1980s. Welsh then returned to Edinburgh when he obtained a job with the City Council in the mid-1980s. Welsh's new employers also funded him to undertake a Masters in Business Administration at Heriot-Watt University from 1988 to 1990. It was during this period that Welsh began to write creatively and to embark upon work that would later form *Trainspotting* and *The Acid House*, including the reworking of jottings in diary and journal made during a trip across the United States in the early 1980s. Although Ron McKay asserts that 'a cynic might suspect that he had mythologised his life in order to conceal how embarrassingly straight he really was',[3] it is more often critics who have strained to make Welsh's biography as controversial as possible. This need to find Welsh's own life as shocking as those of his characters has extended to interpreting his cautioning by police for playing football in the street at the age of eight or his professed childhood fondness for inhaling the glue from model aeroplane kits as precursors of his dark and dangerous drugs past. Welsh was an intermittent heroin user for around eighteenth months but has always been keen to deflect any claims of long-standing addiction: 'What stopped me getting really bad was having crap veins'.[4] Subsequent brushes with the law, such as a night spent in custody in January 1996 in Glasgow after his arrest for being drunk and disorderly at a football match between Patrick Thistle and Welsh's beloved Hibernian, occurred once Welsh had been in the public spotlight as a writer and have retroactively encouraged critics to seek to mythologise his life as a so-called football 'casual' hooligan. Although Welsh has been viewed as a 'Scottish William Burroughs' since his first publication, his earliest disclosure of the lifestyle he led at the time of *Trainspotting*'s publication was much more modest than the déclassé aristocrat from St Louis whose opium-filled lifestyle in Tangiers was funded by his family's fortune:

> I'm basically Mr Straight from nine to five during the week. Maybe every other weekend I'll go to a rave. My finger isn't jammed on the self-destruct button any more but I'll give it a wee flick every now and then just for a bit of intrigue. Maybe once in about six months I'll go through

a miniature breakdown, and I'll disappear for a few days at a time; I'll vanish into this labyrinth of places in Edinburgh I never new existed, and come out of the other end.[5]

It is only since becoming a bestselling author that Welsh concedes: 'I basically do have the fucking Burroughs' lifestyle now cause now I have the money through the writing, whereas before I would have loved to have had the decadent lifestyle but I just played at it part-time cause I just didn't have the money'.[6]

Whilst working as a training officer for Edinburgh City Council's Housing Department Welsh developed HIV/AIDS awareness groups and male assertiveness workshops. The dissertation component of his MBA from Heriot-Watt University was written on Equal Opportunities, specifically for women in the workplace. By now, in a sense, Welsh's life had come full circle as he was working in a management capacity for the very same Edinburgh council Housing Department that planned and regulated schemes such as Muirhouse where he was once a resident. Due to an influx of cheap heroin into Scotland in the 1980s, housing schemes such as Muirhouse, which had already stagnated socially into ghettos through the de-industrialisation and mass-unemployment that characterised the late 1970s and 1980s, were now also blighted by further problems such as drug addiction, crime and the spread of HIV/AIDS. So whilst Welsh personally had enjoyed social mobility and become a management consultant – and had at one stage considered moving to Australia to set up a property development company – the overwhelming majority of people on housing estates like Muirhouse across Britain were trapped in their surroundings.

Welsh's own background, therefore, embodies a series of instructive social and cultural tensions and overlappings. With regard to social class Welsh's childhood on housing schemes must be considered alongside his entrepreneurial speculation in 1980's property development and rise as a management consultant. Although Welsh was once guest editor of *The Big Issue*, the magazine which helps homeless and poor people support themselves and provides a forum for their views, he also has commented: 'I'm always buying flats. I rent them through a property management agency. Edinburgh is a booming market, and I don't like to have too much cash . . . I get really schizophrenic about it. I didn't invent capitalism. It's not the best way of running things . . . But I'm not going to be a stupid martyr'.[7] In terms of gender, his associations with football casuals and

male subcultures, including writing a regular column for the largely
middle-class men's magazine *Loaded*, are juxtaposed with his MBA
dissertation on the disadvantages suffered by women in the workplace and his participation in men's self-help and awareness groups.
The issue of narcotics – for which Welsh's work is unfairly most
famous – maintains an antagonism in his writing between drug experiences as both individualised alienation and collective resistance.
This diverse personal experience is symptomatic of a broader British
historical context of shifting social and cultural forces from the 1970s
to the present. It is a context that impels the consideration of this
book's major themes: the decimation of traditional working-class
identities and community; the social opportunities and exclusions of
contemporary society; paradigm shifts in traditional forms of masculinity and gender relations due to de-industrialisation and a move
away from large, heavy industry to an economy of flexible accumula-
tion and service sector employment (a shift which entails the encom-
passing of a larger proportion of women in employment because they
are more poorly paid and more easily hired and fired). Welsh is keen
to set the ambivalences of his own background and his own politics in
precisely this context: 'You can't expect consistency from an individual in a world that's just full of inconsistency. I'm not into this personal political purity shite. You're a mass of contradictions. You just
try to work through these as best you can'.[8]

The conflicts of Welsh's background can also be traced in his readers, who include the art-house establishment, literati and academics,
fashion-conscious middle-class professionals, clubbers, people who
had never bought books before, drug addicts, football casuals and students, amongst whom Welsh often features as their favourite writer
in sociological surveys.[9] His work has taken hold amongst a diverse
range of people and has as a consequence been resident in bestseller
lists for nearly a decade. His first novel, *Trainspotting*, made the
Booker Prize last ten shortlist and also made the top ten of Water-
stones' 100 Greatest Books of the 20th Century. Welsh has become a
bestselling author and something of a literary and cultural phenomenon – critics now make reference to the '*Trainspotting* Generation'.[10]
Although Welsh has been embraced by contemporary style and fashion magazines – his books' covers are invariably adorned with *The
Face*'s description of him as 'the poet laureate of the chemical generation' – as a spokesperson for a new, diverse British culture located
around dance music, his views on drugs are also deeply embedded in

a fulmination against the deprivations of poverty and social exclusion. Indeed, in resisting accounts of a new multi-cultural Britain, Welsh maintains that class – and not sexuality or ethnicity – is still the main barrier to entry into the literary canon: 'It's more to do with class than ethnicity. They tend to accept ethnic writers as long as they're middle class. Hanif Kureishi is writing about middle-class suburban Asians, not Bradford or East London homeboys. Whereas, Caryl Philips is writing about the legacy of slavery, but it's acceptable because he went to Oxford'.[11] In terms of politics, Welsh has also written a regular column for the decidedly right-wing establishment newspaper, the *Daily Telegraph*, as part of its 2003 relaunch. Yet he has also used his new-found fame to highlight oppositional political causes neglected by the media and mainstream politicians, such as the case of Satpal Ram, who has fought his conviction for murder in June 1987 in an incident wherein he was defending himself from a racist attack. Similarly, Welsh has also supported the Liverpool Dockers' Strike which began on Monday 25 September 1995 when five workers were sacked at Torside Docks, causing a support strike and the subsequent dismissal of a further four hundred workers for refusing to cross the picket line. Welsh co-wrote a television screenplay about the strike with Jimmy McGovern and a dockers' writing group that was shown on ITV. On an album released to raise funds for the striking dockers and their families, Welsh provides the following introduction:

> In August 1989 the Tory Government abolished the National Dock Labour Scheme: this effectively ended job security for the dockers . . . The dockers remained on strike for twenty-eight months, receiving massive support from the public and the international community, but were not recognised by their own official trade unions or by the government. This album is dedicated to the strike and to workers struggling for their rights everywhere.[12]

Class and society in contemporary Britain

The Liverpool Dockers' Strike is highly significant in understanding contemporary British society and politics as it reflects the anti-union legislation instigated by the Thatcher government and its decimation of working-class communities and industries during the 1980s, but the period of the strike also bridges the transition from John Major's Conservative government to the New Labour administration led by Tony Blair that came to power in May 1997. The Blair government opposed the strike as vehemently as did Major's, and this hostility, together with the leadership of the British Trade Union Council's refusal to back the strike (and thus to confer upon it legitimacy), convinced many working-class people that the mainstream political hierarchy of British society, whether right-wing or supposedly left-leaning in the case of the Labour Party and the trade union leadership, did not represent them.

The reformist ideal that had structured British society after the Second World War – the belief that voting for mainstream political parties could ameliorate and improve one's society and position therein – whether One Nation Toryism or the social democracy of the Labour Party, which had produced measures such as the Welfare State and principles such as free health care and education, was fundamentally ruptured. The period comprising Welsh's life and work can be interpreted as signalling a disintegration of the postwar social settlement that precipitates a crisis of identity, society and political belief. It is perhaps best understood by Antonio Gramsci's theory of an 'interregnum':

> If the ruling class has lost its consensus, i.e. is no longer 'leading' but only 'dominant', exercising coercive force alone, this means precisely that the great masses have become detached from their traditional ideologies, and no longer believe what they used to believe previously, etc. The crisis consists precisely in the fact that the old is dying and the new cannot be born; and in this interregnum a great variety of morbid symptoms appear.[13]

Welsh's writing certainly diagnoses and details such 'morbid symptoms' emerging out of what one of his characters terms 'the long dark night of late capitalism' (A 240). For the Scottish working class 1979 was a crucial year as it marked the failure of a referendum on devolution (that would eventually be achieved in 1999). Moreover, that lack of democratic control over their future was compounded by Margaret Thatcher's British general election victory and her government's vigorous assault upon the organised labour of Britain's industrial heartlands – a campaign that was never endorsed by a democratic majority in Scotland (or for that matter Wales or large areas of working-class England).[14] Margaret Thatcher crystallised the ethos of her government and its neo-liberal economics with the proclamation: 'there is no such thing as society'.[15] The Thatcher government privileged individualism, the market and the making of profit above all else and afforded the advantages of its social Darwinism to a limited few at the cost of dismantling the Welfare State and its macro-economic management, of nationalised and state-owned industries, the National Health Service, free education and welfare provision for all. David Cannadine argues that Thatcher:

> attacked the trades unions, because they represented organised, collective, productive labour. She stressed the market, the public, the consumer and the individual, which undermined the language of social solidarity based on productive classes . . . As a result of her policies and rhetoric, Thatcher thus went a long way towards achieving her ambition of banishing the language of class from public discussion and political debate about the structure and nature of British society.[16]

It is important to stress that Cannadine's summary of Thatcherite objectives acknowledges that it was the *language* and class rather than its *reality* which was banished from society. The suppression of class terminology from mainstream political discourse was furthered by John Major's Conservative government, which superseded Thatcherism and espoused contemporary Britain as a 'classless society'. The New Labour government has not resisted but maximised this trend in its pursuit of what is deemed 'Third Way' capitalism, a supposedly equitable capitalist economy that benefits all and eschews the old ideological divisions of left and right. Anthony Giddens, who has worked in an advisory role for the New Labour government, defines the 'Third Way' as emerging from the proposition that capitalism and the market are not merely the preferable means by which to organise a society but the only one: 'No one any longer has any alternatives to capitalism'.[17] Hence, Roy in *Marabou Stork Nightmares* thinks about 'turning the other cheek and Christian forgiveness and all that sort of shite. But nobody believed in that crap anymair. It was just you against the world, every cunt knew that: the Government even said it' (*M* 165).

However, the New Labour government's sponsoring of the market and private finance should not be viewed as a radical departure. Any illusion that the leadership of the Labour Party were upholders of the cloth-cap socialist tradition from which the party emerged was dispelled when Jim Callaghan's government went cap in hand to the International Monetary Fund and the World Bank for economic assistance in the mid-1970s. This financial provision was granted on the basis of massive cuts in public spending, the gradual dismantling of the Welfare State and the promotion of market forces – all of which were strongly resisted by the working class. So the last Labour government of the 1970s actually anticipated and facilitated Thatcherism rather than being overturned by it. Welsh attests that the rise of monetarism and the market was not merely a New Right, Thatcherite initiative:

> All those things actually started in 1976, not 1979, when the Labour Government expressly went to the institutions of multi-national capitalism with a programme for the domestic economy based upon those principles. Now under Blair's leadership, they seem set to carry them forward with renewed vigour as the Tories have run out of steam. (*T&H* 8–9)

Notably, all the mainstream British political parties now couch their argument not in broadly political terms but in primarily economic ones. The policies of all the major parties in health, in education, in civil society, do not follow divergent political arguments but are instead determined by how such policies relate to the effective management of market-driven imperatives. Blair's election victory in May 2002 was achieved with around one million fewer votes than Neil Kinnock received in 1992 when he actually lost to John Major's incumbent Conservative government. There have been numerous lofty declarations by major politicians ruminating upon how they may arrest the growing apathy and depoliticisation of the British public. One of the points of this introduction, however, is to suggest that it is perhaps not ordinary people who are becoming depoliticised but mainstream politics itself. This point goes a long way to comprehending the falling numbers of British people, especially working-class people, who are willing to vote for these major parties. So when Welsh declares – 'I hate politics. I'm glad that hardly anyone voted in the British general elections'[18] – this should be understood in terms of an antipathy towards mainstream politics and the current parliamentary system rather than a wallowing apoliticism. In understanding the politics of Welsh's work, therefore, it is vital not to confine our definition of the political to the major parties and the parliamentary system and to instead enlarge its scope into the realm of ordinary people's lives and activities that have become increasingly disaffected from the major institutions of state and society.

And whilst contemporary Britain has been characterised by profound social change and the disruption of established class identities, the reconstitution of class is not synonymous with its disappearance. As Stuart Hall affirms: 'class relations do not disappear because the particular historic cultural forms in which class is "lived" and experienced at a particular period, change'.[19] Indeed, Welsh's own thoughts on being a writer corroboratively acknowledge shifts in class formation but affirm a mutable yet ongoing sense of oppression and inequality:

> It gives you more time to think about the injustices. It's that old story. If you're working nine to five you've not really got time to look. It is more external to me now. It's not intrinsic now. If I look back at the crap jobs I've had and sitting on the dole that's from memory now rather than a sort of feeling. The subtleties of the change as well; the sort of oppression is the same but the subtleties change from generation to generation.[20]

It is in this context of continued oppression and inequality – and a loss of faith in the capacity of the main institutions of society to ameliorate that plight – that the politics of Welsh's fiction and its concentration on drug addicts, thieves, misfits and an unemployed underclass must be placed. Welsh pitches his own work into what he identifies as a profound socio-cultural shift in contemporary Britain concerning drug use:

> in the Eighties the drug of choice for people changed from being alcohol and tobacco, sort of legal drugs, to illegal drugs – that was a major cultural sea-change in Britain that a lot of people, I think, failed to pick up on, that that was happening. And that's really what my books have been about, has [sic] been recognizing that there's a whole new chemical culture in Britain and the first kind of real manifestation of that was the heroin thing in the Eighties.[21]

Despite the claims of his detractors, Welsh's work is not interested in sensationalising drugs but is more acutely concerned with tracing the politics of different drugs and the communities and constituencies that assemble around such use, whether affirmative and constructive or alienating and destructive. In contextualising the drug use and violence in his work further, Welsh told *Spin* magazine:

> There is that whole kind of thing about society sort of disintegrating; all the institutions that hold society together, like the churches, the trade unions, the welfare state, the Labour Party, the whole idea of the extended family, and communities are all sort of gone. With the disintegration of society you have the attendant disintegration of the self as

well, because the reference points are gone. I think if you have an expo-
nential increase in that kind of really selfish, really violent, almost ant-
like behaviour, it's one of the few ways that people can integrate
themselves – through violence.[22]

Getting started

When Welsh began to write creatively in the late 1980s he relates that
it was mainly to alleviate the boredom of his management job and did
not have any concrete aims to begin with: 'the writing wasn't to get
me published, it was just a speculative thing'.[23] However, the work did
begin to get published in 1991 with 'The First Day of the Edinburgh
Festival' chapter of what would become *Trainspotting* appearing in
Scream, If You Want to Go Faster: New Writing Scotland, edited by
Janice Galloway and Hamish Whyte. Subsequently, further sections
appeared in the London-based fanzine, *DOG*, and in Duncan
McLean's Clocktower Press pamphlets (whose efforts would later be
anthologised by Jonathan Cape) and Kevin Williamson's Rebel Inc
(which would eventually become part of Canongate publishers).
McLean, Williamson and the Glaswegian Barry Graham were all part
of what Welsh terms 'a small cottage industry' of do-it-yourself style
publishing in the early 1990s in Edinburgh. Although this underground pamphlet culture did not start Welsh writing in the first
instance, he acknowledges that it did help move things along for him:

> I picked up that *New Writing Scotland* and I read a few things in it and I
> thought, 'Och, this is about fucking 99 per cent shite, I could do better
> than that', so I just banged it out. So there was Kevin and Duncan and
> Barry with all their little fanzines, and it was just like, 'Well, right I'll do
> this for this one, and that for that and so on'. And this was all before I'd
> finished *Trainspotting* for Cape, and it all just sort of happened. But I feel
> really terrible because there are brilliant writers in Scotland and they
> have trouble getting their stuff published, trouble getting their stuff out
> into the light, and there was no hassle at all for me . . . All I would say is
> that it was Kevin, Duncan and Barry with the pamphlets that really made
> everything happen.[24]

In early interviews Welsh fervently disclaimed any literary influence on his writing whatsoever and foregrounded instead its popular
cultural context. As John Walsh reports:

> 'I don't have any literary heroes at all,' he says, 'I don't take references
> from other writers, but from music lyrics, from videos and soap operas

and stuff. I try and keep as far away from "the classics" (he says the word with faint distaste, as one might say "the Government") as possible. Otherwise it becomes a self-serving thing and you start writing as a writer, rather than as a person or a cultural activist'.[25]

However, he is happy to concede that his influences are not so straightforward and are a shifting array of sources: 'It's the books that I'm into at the time. Anything I'm into at the time. I tell you something about *Trainspotting*, I don't know what the fuck I was into – I was so fucked up. It was a seven year gestation period writing that novel'.[26] Indeed, in contrast to his railing against the literary canon in his interview with John Walsh above, in Channel 4's television series *The Story of the Novel*, Welsh professed his admiration not only for Sir Walter Scott, but also the English novelists such as George Eliot, Jane Austen and Charlotte Brontë: 'They're still to me the greatest books ever written by English novelists. If you take it almost as a sort of canon, on the whole they've been such a powerful, devastating influence on literature, British literature, European literature'.[27] Welsh disclosed that the producers of the series wanted him to talk about William Burroughs and the Scottish addict writer, Alexander Trocchi, but he declined, and commented when being interviewed for this study: 'I think everyone is a big fucking kaleidoscope of feelings and emotions and things and it's like colouring in – you get your influences and they colour in and focus a part of you. I mean with Burroughs and Trocchi, I only got to know them after I started writing'.[28]

In terms of Scottish writing, Welsh acknowledges a tradition of literature with split or multiple selves, formal fracture and different modes and registers of voice that has filtered into his own work. He identifies a lineage stretching back from his avowed immediate precursors such as James Kelman and Alasdair Gray to the work of James Hogg: 'James Hogg's *Confessions of a Justified Sinner* is one of the best, most brilliant books ever written. In a way, that's where it all fucking starts from – all that Kelman, Gray stuff – that's where it starts from'.[29] Welsh remembers the importance and affirmation of reading Lewis Grassic Gibbon in school and pinpoints his reading of James Kelman's 1984 novel, *The Bus Conductor Hines*, as a key moment: 'Kelman was like Year Zero'.[30] He also cites William McIlvanney's *Docherty* (1975) as vital in stressing that literature did not have to be written in Standard English and deal purely with middle-class concerns: 'this is a fucking great writer using his own voice, and it's like James Kelman, to me, is doing that but just taking it one stage further.

And Alasdair Gray's taking it off in another direction. So it's always been there for me and I feel really lucky living at this time cause I've got McIlvanney, Kelman, Gray and Janice Galloway'.[31] What significantly affiliates the work of the Scottish novelists cited by Welsh – Lewis Grassic Gibbon, William McIlvanney and James Kelman – is a concern with voice and a concomitant effort to overturn the Standard English of the conventional novel, to infuse literature instead with the cadences and registers of working-class vernacular.

In addition to his fiction appearing in print, 1991 also witnessed less well-known publications for Welsh in the form of letters written to the *Scotsman* newspaper on the subject of Trevor Griffiths' play *Comedians* which was being performed in Edinburgh in October of that year. Welsh was incensed by members of the audience who had left the theatre on account of the play's content:

> Sir, – Last Saturday, I attended a matinee performance of the Trevor Griffiths play, *Comedians*, at the Royal Lyceum Theatre in Edinburgh. The play itself was performed to mesmerising perfection by a highly talented cast. Unfortunately, my enjoyment of this production was marred by the constant whinging of other members of the audience, a large number of whom created further disturbance by leaving during the play. While I accept that some narrow-minded types will be upset by explicit language, it is unfortunate that such people cannot suspend their prejudices for a few hours. Their behaviour was unsettling to other members of the audience and an insult to the highly gifted actors on the stage.[32]

On the same letters page was a missive from one of those 'whingers' complaining about the play, by a (Mrs) E. M. Bogie, who Duncan McLean claims was actually a spurious persona adopted by Welsh himself:[33]

> Sir, – Why did your drama critic fail to warn your readers that the play *Comedians*, at present running at the Royal Lyceum, was not only a rather dull and boring play but one in which the characters used foul, obscene and profane language throughout? Some of the sentiments expressed in the play were also insulting, to Jews, black people and the Irish. Surely an ordinary audience could only have a feeling of shame that such a degrading play could be produced and supported by so many illustrious bodies representing Edinburgh.[34]

Whether the sequence was deliberately set-pieced by Welsh, the Bogie letter spurred the following riposte from him a week later:

Sir, – Mrs E. M. Bogie, in a letter today on the subject of the play
Comedians, at Edinburgh's Lyceum Theatre, manages to illustrate the
points I made about the knee-jerk reaction of the narrow-minded to
explicit language. More importantly, she displays a great misunder-
standing of the message and sentiment of the brilliant play by Trevor
Griffiths. The play is an attack on the ugly racism and sexism which
underpin mainstream British humour, and the collusion of the audience with such racist and sexist attitudes. What the response by many
people to this play illustrates, is the problem of the lack of advance information as to its content. Many people obviously inferred from the title
that this was some genteel comedy of manners, or equally unchalleng-
ing farce. For a play such as this to work it requires an audience with a
level of sophistication which enables them to see the evils of racism and
sexism without colluding in them, but at the same time not reacting to
the explicit language, which is used for illustrative and authenticity purposes. The Royal Lyceum may have to examine its publicity for events
such as this, if only to encourage the moaners to stay away, and refrain
from boring us all to tears.[35]

The letters disclose a number of things about Welsh's own aesthetic:
as with Griffiths' approach, Welsh's work is highly politically engaged
and seeks to confront issues such as racism and sexism that he perceives as structuring the dominant political and cultural landscape of
Britain. However, it avoids sloganeering and simple moralism and
instead journeys into the very core of such reactionary attitudes in
order both to comprehend and to critique them fully. Yet this political
confrontation which pulls no punches is also driven by an artistic
dynamic that is not only committed politically but also sensitive to the
importance and aesthetics of form. Hence, those theatre-goers and
professionals who were so berated by Welsh as a precious bourgeois
elite when his own plays – *Headstate* and *You'll Have Had Your Hole*
– were performed, may be surprised to learn that in the early 1990s it
was Welsh who was demanding a 'sophisticated' theatre audience
who did not disrupt the performance of plays with inappropriate
behaviour. Nonetheless, Welsh's sense of Griffiths' own perspective
– confronting political issues yet doing so through the directives and
tenets of an artistic form – does inform his central method: 'You
should write about what's actually happening but it should be fun and
enjoyable – and that's my fucking two standards'.[36] If Welsh was the
author of the Mrs Bogie letter, then the whole exchange also anticipates Welsh's capacity in his fiction to parody different registers of
language, to mock and deride the authority and sanctity of supposedly

polite and refined discourse, to switch between linguistic codes and to construct masks with which to disguise himself and to manipulate for political and artistic purposes.

Decentred fictions

Standard appraisals of Welsh's work – such as 'the barbarous north-of-the-border irruption that is the fiction of Irvine Welsh'[37] – enthrone English history and culture as a harmonious continuity whilst permitting the British peripheries agency only in so far as they sporadically trespass that order. Such a view recapitulates the dominant narrative paradigms of British history outlined by Cairns Craig, wherein a normative, seemingly self-contained English exemplar simultaneously situates and marginalises obtrusive provincial forms: 'In the history of England, Scottish or Irish issues will be relevant only when they destructively intrude into the otherwise continuous domain of English narrative . . . England has a history; [Scotland] will only acquire a history once it comes into the orderly and progressive world imposed upon it by England'.[38] It is highly significant that when *Trainspotting* was published many critics and reviewers, including those who surveyed it favourably, either demurred or flatly refused to confer upon it the status of a novel. John Hodge, who rewrote *Trainspotting* as a screenplay for Danny Boyle's 1996 film version, describes it as a 'collection of loosely related short stories about several different characters. Only towards the end does it take on a continuous narrative form . . . the characters, each with a distinctive voice, are defined by internal monologue as much as anything, and the language is uncompromisingly specific to a time and place'.[39] For Jason Cowley *Trainspotting* is a 'collection of stories', whilst Sarah Hemming deems it 'a series of unrelated episodes', and Lucy Hughes-Hallett discusses a work 'broken up into fragments'.[40] Similarly, Michael Brockington finds it 'hard to call it a novel, more a ragged accretion of short stories'.[41] All of these readings of *Trainspotting* conveniently concentrate upon how the novel fails to meet their own expectations of a novel's form and function rather than considering whether it is precisely those expectations which fail *Trainspotting*. So given that the fragmentary form of *Trainspotting* and much of Welsh's other novels and collections of shorter fiction is conventionally regarded by mainstream critics as a literary drawback, this study seeks to shift the critical emphasis from failed novels to decentred fictions. In other words, mainstream metropolitan criticism often mistakes as a failed or underdeveloped version of itself a writing that is actually the site of radical difference. The inability or unwillingness of critics to regard *Trainspotting* as a novel is directly related to its refusal to mirror and endorse a standard model of what a novel should be and should do. As Welsh himself notes: 'This medium, literary fiction, is a middle-class plaything, so you're analysed, dissected and defined by people who have come from a certain cultural viewpoint. They are looking into a world that they don't have direct first-hand experience of so they rely on intuitive views and prejudices which may or may not be appropriate'.[42]

It is not a question therefore of why Welsh's work falls short of an already agreed and universal standard, but one of why that standard fails to justify its own claims to universality and typicality. The task is to determine why the ideology of the conventional novel holds such sway and also why it is in such need of thorough interrogation. By way of an answer, the novel emerged concomitantly with the historical rise of the middle class and the nation state.[43] Resultantly, the novel has traditionally served as one of the cultural arenas wherein bourgeois society ratifies itself and bolsters its own self-identity and hegemony. In particular, bourgeois society tends to view itself as the culminated and harmonious fruition of historical progress and development: hence, bourgeois society is self-affirmingly a normal society. The conventional novel and its ordered aggregation of social classes have become the yardstick by which a society is adjudged to be normal, healthy and historically mature. The implication is that nations, peoples, individuals or classes which do not produce novels in this normative form are not merely different but abnormal, aberrant and, according to the bourgeois narrative of historical development, immature or not fully formed social subjects or constituencies.

There is a temptation to regard fracture in the Scottish novel as an example of Scotland's oddity or unusualness, its status, in David McCrone's terms, as a stateless nation displaced by its incorporation within a dominant and English-dominated British identity. McCrone formulates Scotland's peculiarity thus:

> In terms of its structural position in the historical development of the capitalist world economy Scotland is doubly unique. Britain as a whole was the first state to have a thoroughgoing capitalist revolution; second, Scotland's capitalist revolution occurred within a country lacking the political and institutional structures of statehood. Further . . . such a

transformation occurred before the ideological input of nationalism
which was to inform the political and economic features of capitalist
industrialisation in much of Europe ... Scotland crossed 'the great
divide' to become an industrialised society without the benefit or hin-
drance of nationalism, which usually acted as a political or ideological
vehicle for much of the European bourgeoisie. Further, Scotland's economy was rarely if ever self-contained and independent. It was an open
economy, reliant on external capital and technology, and subject to the
vagaries of the broader economic and political environment, whether of
Britain or a wider European capitalist economy.[44]

So, according to the teleological narrative of this argument, where
England developed and matured organically, Scotland retarded and
splintered. Tom Nairn, for example, perceives Scotland's as an anomaly outside the norms of historical progress and concludes that 'an
anomalous historical situation could not engender a "normal" culture'.[45] Under such analysis, the fracture and splitting of works, such
as James Hogg's *Confessions of a Justified Sinner* (1824) or Robert
Louis Stevenson's *Dr Jeckyll and Mr Hyde* (1886), together with the
contemporary fiction of Welsh and others, becomes reducible to a
fraught and irregular recalcitrance to normal and progressive forms.
Nairn comments: 'The opposite of mature all-roundedness is pre-
sumably infantile partiality, or fragmentariness'.[46] In a confirmation
of the bourgeois narrative underpinning the progressive model of historical development, the insinuation ghosting such pronouncements
is that Scotland would have been normal if only it had evolved a
mature and well-rounded middle class.

Hence, for Edwin Muir even a writer such as Sir Walter Scott was
torn between disparate dialects and the contradictory polarities of a
Scottish culture that never developed as itself but instead remained
pinioned between Englishness and Britishness. Muir insists that for
Scotland to become truly Scotland it must adopt the wholly and organically unified normalcy represented by England's development and its
cultural products:

the pre-requisite of an autonomous literature is a homogeneous language. If Shakespeare had written in the dialect of Warwickshire,
Spenser in Cockney, Raleigh in the broad Western English speech
which he used, the future of English literature must have been very different, for it would have lacked a common language where all the
thoughts and feelings of the English people could come together, add
lustre to one another, and serve as a standard for one another.[47]

Notably, Muir peculiarises what he regards as the disintegration of Scottish culture and society in contradistinction to a unitary English tradition that harmonises the nation. Yet his references to various English dialects, regions and classes in fact divulges the very exclusions and hierarchies upon which that supposedly common and shared standard English national language and literature are founded. So Muir's own valorisation of a unitary and organic English literature actually discloses the relations of power through which its alleged normativity is constructed. The conventional novel is not a direct reflection of social consensus and normality but is rather a form that seeks to repress the social conflict, the suppressions and antagonisms that are constitutive of its very production. The inability of the dominant metropolitan account of history and culture to view otherness as anything more than a miscarried version of itself attests not to the actual inferiority of less powerful peoples but to the inadequacies of that hegemonic model. It reveals the necessary exclusions upon which a dominant culture's imaginary unity is based. Moreover, the fantasy of a 'homogeneous' national language and culture signals not historical development and maturity but contested processes of hierarchisation, marginalisation and disenfranchisement. The purpose of this brief account of the novel has been twofold. Firstly, it has sought to destabilise an acceptance of the conventional novel as verification of social unity and to uncover it instead as a structure of dominance empowering a standard discourse and worldview whose fantasy consensus seeks to elide its exclusion of otherness and oppositional voices. Secondly, it also instructs that the formal innovation and dissonance of Welsh's work is not due to some unitary national condition but rather is propelled by the very dynamics of class and resistance that characterise the novel as a form no matter how much its hegemonic model would strive to curb them.

Bakhtin and the novel

Edwin Muir's advancement of a homogeneous national language is an espousal that can be contextualised by what Mikhail Bakhtin terms *monologism*: the ideology of an impossibly unified and common language equitably shared by all. As Bakhtin conveys, this ideology of a monologic, unitary language is a hegemonic process that entails the 'victory of one reigning language (dialect) over the others, the supplanting of languages, their enslavement, the process of illuminating them with the "True Word", the incorporation of barbarians and lower social strata into a unitary language of culture and truth, the canonization of ideological systems'.[48] For Bakhtin, language is fundamentally *dialogic*: a continual struggle over meaning and of resistance by those deemed 'barbarians' and 'lower social strata' to their incorporation within and subjugation by a standard language of power. For the ideology of Standard English not only denotes a supposedly standardised language that is equitably accessible to all but also one that sets the standard, so that any other speech or discourse is, by definition, substandard, deviant and inferior. This hierarchy constructed by Standard English is encased in the conventional novel as a form. The superintending and authoritative register is in Standard English: it is the language of power and objectivity, a language that can be trusted. Working-class or regional dialects and accents never assume narrative control and where they do appear in the conventional novel it is only as a character's speech, which can be regulated by the Standard English of the main narrative and safely cordoned off with quotation marks that prevent it from assuming the elevated level of thought or intellectual complexity. In Welsh's work the demotic becomes a mode for thought, agency and consciousness rather than a behavioural trait whose ultimate meanings are decided by an overarching Standard English omniscient register. As Welsh contends:

> If you look at the way that working-class people are treated in literary and serious fiction, even by supposedly hip writers like Amis or McEwan, the working-class characters are seen as oafs to laugh at and are denied any kind of inner life, the kind of life that middle-class people have. Middle-class people are in power, they are in control and they are the main voices who are pontificating, analysing, and evaluating.[49]

So Welsh's characters are people who are, to appropriate the words of John Strang in *Marabou Stork Nightmares*, usually 'not fuckin quoted' (*M* 149) in the conventional novel, erased from its standard construction of human agency. There is another sense in which they are 'not fuckin quoted', in that Welsh – as with James Kelman before him – refuses to place the speech of his characters in quotation marks. Where working-class characters are permitted to speak in the conventional novel the quotation marks around their words helps cordon them off from the authoritative Standard English of the main narrative and its reflective, interpretative power. Welsh, like Kelman, dissolves this narrative hierarchy by placing the speech of his characters on an equal register with that of the narrative itself to produce a democracy of voice.

Welsh's subversion of the novel's standard language is neatly illustrated in Bakhtin's terms: 'authoritative discourse permits no play with the context framing it, no play with its borders, no gradual and flexible transitions, no spontaneously creative stylizing variants on it'.[50] Welsh's fiction undermines precisely the position of a singular authoritative discourse to fix itself in language by flouting it, in Bakhtin's terms, with a polyphonic *heteroglossia* of multifarious meanings and voices. However, it is important to stress that there is a political and class dynamic to all of this experimentation: it is not merely the 'play' of a vacuous postmodern plurality that is actually designed to mystify concrete social and economic inequality through its deadening cultural relativism. The fracture of late capitalism's social upheaval necessitates Welsh's effort to construct new representational strategies for textualising social experiences and identities that are denied not only by the conventional novel but also by the main institutions of contemporary social life. Notably, in Welsh's phonetic rendering of speech, 'I' is figured as 'ah' – which not only approximates its sound in working-class Edinburgh demotic but resonates on a textual level. 'Ah' can also signify on the page, variously, a pause or hesitation, the postponement of meaning and significance rather than its usual assertion with the annunciation of the first person singular, and also an expression of pain, or of disapproval. These submerged levels of meaning in what appears only a phonetic figure convey the splintering of selfhood and identity faced by many of Welsh's characters.

Furthermore, gender fractures the supposedly homogeneous fabric of the nation as much as the class tensions in Welsh's work. It is also perhaps the most contentious component of Welsh's fiction. It is noteworthy that in discussing the disruption of industrial and working-class community in contemporary Britain, Welsh links this disempowering crisis in class solidarity with a crisis in masculinity in his reference to 'the emasculation of the collective'.[51] This conflation of working-class power and male power is dangerous in its erasure of the agency of women from this context of disenfranchisement – in fact, it almost makes women culpable for this disempowerment, this 'emasculation'. So as this study moves through Welsh's fiction and its avowed effort to afford Edinburgh's working-class people an interior-

ity and complexity that they have been denied in conventional literature, it will also question whether that interiority and complexity is
also accorded to women. For example, Ellen Raïssa Jackson and Willy
Maley point to 'a lacuna in Welsh's work, the question of female
agency'.[52]

In terms of masculinity and the paradigm shifts of late capitalist de-
industrialisation and fracture, it is worth observing, as Michael
Kimmel does, that masculinity is not an immutable biological state
but instead 'a constantly changing collection of meanings that we
construct through our relationships with ourselves, with each other,
and with our world. Manhood is neither static nor timeless, it is
historical'.[53] Kimmel continues that:

> The hegemonic construction of manhood is a man *in* power, a man *with*
> power, and a man *of* power. We equate manhood with being strong, suc-
> cessful, capable, reliable, in control. The very definitions of manhood we
> have developed in our culture maintain the power that some men have
> over other men and that men have over women.[54]

Welsh's fiction is strewn with working-class men who struggle to
embody the myths of masculine power propagated by patriarchy that
are ultimately irreconcilable with their daily lives. Yet Welsh's many
disempowered male characters do still seek to assert control over
others that they perceive to be weaker than themselves, whether they
are women, homosexuals, ethnic others and so on. The tendency
amongst some of Welsh's characters who are themselves oppressed
to oppress others as a means of asserting some form of beleaguered
power – whether through sexism, homophobia or racism – is an
example of what Peter Stallybrass and Allon White term *displaced
abjection*: 'the process whereby "low" social groups turn their figura-
tive and actual power, *not* against those in authority, but against those
who are even "lower"'.[55] To that end, Welsh considers his own work as
focusing on 'the idea that pain is passed on. It takes a strong person
to deal with it, let go of it, without passing it on again in some way. It's
usually not directed at the person who gave you the pain in the first
place, but to some other innocent person. And people do rise above it,
and do sort of get beyond it'.[56]

Common language

Although Matthew Hart argues of Welsh that 'no other Scottish writer . . . has gone so far as to upset common perceptions of Scotland as a land of heather and history', there are other equally prevalent stereotypes of Scotland for the metropolitan imagination.[57] For the doctrine of metropolitan progress does not merely produce stereotypes of Scotland's touristic quaintness in the form of romantic and Kailyard (literally meaning 'cabbage patch') literature. Simultaneously, Scotland's supposed exclusion from the development of metropolitan history produced a discourse representing Scottishness as a backward and unenlightened place of uncouth barbarism. Although both sets of stereotypes at first glance appear contradictory – and indeed they are – their ultimate function was purposively singular: to banish Scottishness from the teleology of progressive development structuring English, and by extension, British culture and society. As Robert Crawford notes, in the second half of the eighteenth century, according to Olivia Smith, 'Civilization was largely a linguistic concept, establishing a terrain in which vocabulary and syntax distinguished the refined and civilized from the vulgar and the savage'.[58] There emerged a tension between an eighteenth-century concern to treasure the inheritance of Lowland Scotland and its Scots poetry and another desire after the political union of the Scottish and English parliaments in 1707 to play a full part in the cementing of Britishness wherein Standard English was the language of power and progress. Consequently, there followed an attempt to remove supposed 'Scotticisms' from polite, educated and empowered discourse, as exemplified by James Beattie's *Scotticisms Arranged in Alphabetical Order, Designed to Correct Improprieties of Speech and Writing* (1787). Scots deviations from Standard English became bywords for non-literariness, viciousness, inaccuracy and inarticulacy. Perhaps the most notable member of the English literary canon to demonise the Scottish as the site of an infernal and subterranean vulgarity is Samuel Taylor Coleridge. His views on the 'Scotch' (and his reasons for insisting upon referring to the Scottish thus will become apparent below) are worth quoting in full as they distil all the major assumptions of a rabidly dehumanising metropolitan discourse on Scotland's monstrous deviation from Anglicised civility and development:

> A Scotchman = an HYPANTHROPE, or a Sub-human. On this subject, or miserable object (Punicè, that is, in the Carthaginian dialect, a Sub-

Jack, or Hop-Jack) I have . . . [this] to record: . . . that Sawney Benè was
a Scotchman – I humbly beg his pardon – a *Scotsman* I should have said
. . . that he no sooner passes the threshold of that Pandemonium (*id est*,
Caledonia) but Alexander shrinks up into Sawney: . . . that of the overseers of the Slave-plantations in the West Indies three out of four are
Scotsmen, and the fourth is generally observed to have suspiciously
high cheek-bones: and on the American Continent the aforesaid Whip-
pers-in . . . are either Scotchmen, or (*monstro monstrosius!*) the Ameri-
canized Descendents of Scotchmen; . . . that I have detected the reasons
why the Trans-tweedians, in defiance of all grammatical analogy, do,
one and all, affect to call themselves Scotsmen, instead of Scotchmen.
Guilt is ever on the Look-out, quick-nosed, far-sighted walks on as if it
had befouled itself and looks as if it smelt it. Now just cast your eye on
the finals, tch, in Walker's rhyming Dictionary – Bitch, Botch, Blotch,
Ditch, Grutch (sometimes spelt, grudge) crutch, clutch, Witch, Scritch
. . . Letch, Pitch (what sticks to you and defiles you) . . . To these add
Wretch . . . Penultimately, *nota bene*, SCRATCH, and OLD SCRATCH,
by the Prophet Issaih said to dwell and reign in *the* NORTH, and by him
called LUCIFIER or Lightbearer . . . the very name of Old Scratch's
(Lucifer's) septentrional Abiding-Place, *Scotia*, & that of his Children,
Scotos – evidently, from the Greek . . . Darkness, and (tho' omitted from
most Lexicons) . . . Land of Darkness . . . the Literatuli of the Scotch
(and the Scotch are Literatuli, hollow Sepulchres with one coating of literary White-wash!) forever pretend to illuminate the age, & throw Light
in a circle on the omne scibile, they either resemble Phosphorus . . . and
shine only in the Dark for those who can see nothing else, make a mar-
vellous Shew yet display themselves only, or like the Stellæ tenebricosæ
of Theophrastus Bombastus Paracelsus, that eradiate positive Cold and
Darkness, they blankly and downrightly bedarken us . . . *scotizing* thro'
eternal Quartos . . . For myself, I forsee that I shall be accused of carrying candour to excess, and liberality to a faulty extreme; but I willingly
admit to this censure rather than be even suspected of a feeling so opposite to my principles, so alien from my habits & very nature as that of
NATIONAL PREJUDICE: displays of which I as much dislike in the
matter of an Essay, as I do digressions and successive parentheses in the
Style.[59]

Coleridge's end rhymes associate the 'Scotch' with defiling 'Pitch',
with wretchedness, lechery, with primordial evil ('Witch') and the
Devil ('Old Scratch'), and cultural failure and underdevelopment
('Botch'). He also traces *Scot* etymologically back to the Greek for
darkness so that *Scotia* or Scotland is the land of darkness. The Scottish are, for Coleridge, a low, debased people who shame the more

sophisticated English through their inability to rise to the standard of British civility. But equally, where British civilisation harmfully excels itself – in this instance through the slave trade – it is the Scottish who are to blame for its worst excesses.[60] Therefore, when Elizabeth Young claims that 'Welsh is the voice from the pit', and Boyd Tonkin terms Welsh 'a voice, out of Edinburgh by way of Hades', although both critics are attempting to do justice to the social deprivation suffered by many of Welsh's characters, such comments also reactivate this long-sedimented discourse exoticising the Scottish as dark, infernal and demonically uncivilised.[61] Thus, Giles Gordon, writing in *The Scotsman*, accuses Welsh and other novelists such as James Kelman of actually pandering to another set of metropolitan stereotypes that are equally as powerful as those of kilts and heather: '*Trainspotting* (and James Kelman's Booker Prize-winning novel *How Late it Was How Late*) present the Scots as the English like to see them: drunken or drugged, aggressive, illiterate, socially inept, boorish'. *Trainspotting*, for Gordon, should be renamed as *Brainrotting*.[62]

However, the supposed lowness, defilement and 'bad' language of writers such as Welsh or Kelman can also be placed in a more radical Scottish context, an assertion of 'common language' not in the sense of low vulgarity but of democratic commonality. Nicholas M. Williams deems combination of Scots and obscenity in Scottish writing to be a kind of *scotology*[63] – a pun which is compounded by the phonetic rendering of Iggy Pop's pronunciation of Scotland as 'Scatlin' in *Trainspotting*. Willy Maley also discerns the co-existence in Scottish writing of the scatological and the philosophical, the excremental and the existential:

> Welsh's influences, or effluences, range across contemporary film, music and television rather than resting on the canon. He excels at that potent blend of the excremental and the existential, 'keech and Kierkegaard', that is all the rage in new Scottish writing, a social surrealism that takes its cue from cinema and dance as much as literature.[64]

In addition to contemporary popular culture, the mutual articulation of an engaged philosophical and intellectual voice in a form that is supposedly low or improper can be attached to a long-standing Scottish popular-democratic tradition brilliantly traced by George E. Davie's *The Democratic Intellect* (1961), particularly its chapter 'The vernacular basis of Scottish Humanism'. Davie uncovers a dissenting

Scots tradition that sought to raise the vernacular to the level of the supposed civilised language of Latin and the classics, to demonstrate that the vernacular could be a literary and philosophical language.[65] This democratic intellectualism exists both in and beyond the university and counters an elitism that not only prioritises a dominant language of power but also enthrones it exclusively as the only mode through which advanced and complex thought can be expressed. This tradition that radically refuses cultural hierarchies flows through the eighteenth and nineteenth centuries and filters into the work of Lewis Grassic Gibbon, Tom Leonard, James Kelman and Irvine Welsh.[66] All of these writers refute Standard English's claim to a monopoly upon thought, consciousness and intellectual reason by allowing the voice of the vernacular to drive their narratives. Welsh explains that when he began writing the process was propelled by an oral and spoken vernacular dynamic: 'I had all these voices in my head and I wrote them down. I thought, I can't write this book in "proper" English'.[67] It is perhaps fitting, then, for a writer whose prose is so often driven by orality that his popularity is in part due to word of mouth. As Welsh comments: 'It's a good thing that the books are so available among the club audience because in a way it makes the heavyweight critics' view of them superfluous, because they are being sold mostly through word of mouth to people who don't normally read fiction'.[68] Indeed, Welsh places himself in the context of attempting to regalvanise literature with the oral and demotic voices that its standard forms have attenuated, inferiorised or expurgated completely:

> I grew up in a place where everybody was a storyteller, but nobody wrote. It was that kind of Celtic, storytelling tradition: everybody would have a story at the pub or at parties, even at the clubs and raves. They were all so interesting. Then I'd read stories in books, and they'd be dead. I got thinking that had a lot to do with Standard English . . . I wanted to capture the excitement of house music, almost like a four-four beat, and the best way to do that was to use a language that was rhythmic and performative.[69]

In fact the intersection of an oral tradition and dance music culture and technique is central to the method informing Welsh's polyphonic fictions. Contemporary dance music, its sampling and juxtaposition of sources and materials, together with the skill with which DJs mix tracks in and out of one another in clubs, all provide structural analogues for Welsh's own avowed fusion of styles and voices:

It's like bringing out a DJ bag and taking a couple of different records and mixing them together creates a different sound, and it's the same principle with stories – you're mixing different genres like science fiction and urban realism and this kind of stuff . . . the skill of the DJ is to produce something that's continuous, and I think what I'm trying to do is to produce something out of these different, disparate kind of elements that still has a continuous feel to it.[70]

For Welsh 'the bass is the fucking story line and you've always got to respect the bass; you can mix your different voices over it'.[71] Indeed, Welsh's contemporaries remark that one of the things that was immediately apparent from his earliest publications with Rebel Inc and the Clocktower Press was his ability as a compelling storyteller amidst this diffusion of voices to which his ear was also sharply tuned.[72]

The interplay of a multiplicity of voices in Welsh's work fully embodies Bakhtin's concept of *heteroglossia*. Welsh's writing revels in what Bakhtin calls *grammatica jocosa*, the transgression of conventional grammatical order and the revelation of erotic, obscene, punning or resistant counterpoints and over-turnings of received meanings.[73] Welsh's writing is *revolting* language in two senses. It delights in transgressing the sacrosanct pieties of conventional literary discourse, offending and revolting the guarantors of its aesthetic and ethical codes. In doing so, it is also a language in revolt, a mutinous democratic intellectualism that sunders the proprieties and values of those conventional literary codes and their monopoly on intelligence and complexity rather than merely reinforcing them by accepting their terms. Alan Sinfield argues that in Welsh's writing 'what is accomplished specifically is that English people and other literary readers are prevented from supposing that they can readily assimilate Scotland, as if it were merely an extension of Englishness, or merely a tourist theme park'.[74] Welsh's work, therefore, resists the obliteration of Scottish literature's difference and its incorporation as an appendage to a dominant English culture that is typified in T. S. Eliot's refutation of the very existence of Scottish literature:

The first part of the history of Scottish literature is part of the history of English literature when English was several dialects; the second part is part of the history of English literature when English was two dialects – English and Scots; the third part is something quite different – it is the history of a provincial literature. And finally, there is no longer any tenable distinction to be drawn for the present day between the two literatures.[75]

Nevertheless, given the focus of this introduction on issues of class as well as nation, indeed its stress on the necessity of not subsuming such class dynamics within the supposed unitary fabric of the nation, it should be emphasised that democratising the novel does not just entail the rapprochement of national literatures as already agreed and homogeneous entities. Hence, Lewis Grassic Gibbon observes that for middle-class Scotland, too, Scots as a language 'is not genteel. It is to the bourgeois of Scotland coarse and low and common and brutish'.[76] It is in Welsh's depiction of Edinburgh that the class fractures of a supposedly homogeneous nation are brought into focus.

Edinburgh

One of the major achievements of Welsh's work has been its redress of the absence of working-class Edinburgh from literary representation, just as William McIlvanney and James Kelman had done for the Glaswegian and West Coast working class in Scotland. The anger impelling Welsh's depiction of a previously silenced Edinburgh working class is primarily directed at two prevailing and hegemonic constructions of Edinburgh – bourgeois Edinburgh and tourist Edinburgh:

> It was listening to a fellow MBA student from the Home Counties and a middle-class Glaswegian student telling me about what kind of a city Edinburgh was that made me think about its image. That image was a lie: it was at best just a small constituent part of the culture of that city. That of the middle-class, festival city. Yet it had a hegemony over all the other images of this urban, largely working-class but multi-cultural city. Other realities existed, had to be shown to exist.[77]

Yet it should be stated that Welsh has never claimed his representation of the city as the only one: 'As far as I'm concerned, the festival has to happen somewhere and it may as well happen in Edinburgh. That's fine, as long as you recognise the plurality of the cultures in the city. To have Edinburgh defined by festival culture or Muriel Spark culture or even *Trainspotting* culture for that matter, is wrong'.[78] The Edinburgh Festival, which began in August 1947 as the Edinburgh International Festival of Music and Drama, now serves as an umbrella term for five separate festivals: the International Festival, the Fringe, the Film Festival, and the Jazz (from 1980) and Book Festivals (1983 onwards at which Welsh often reads). The Festival

period attracts well over half a million visitors per year, making Edinburgh Britain's second largest tourist attraction after London. However, Welsh argues that this event only serves to provide a fantasy
space that disavows Edinburgh's real hollowness and deprivations:
'The festival is only here because the city has a kind of vacuum for a
heart, so it desperately tries to find a role for itself'.[79] Here Welsh's
remarks about Edinburgh echo those expressed by Edwin Muir, the
Scottish writer and critic, in his *Scottish Journey*, which was originally
published in 1935 and found the city's inhabitants living in 'a sort of
vacuum'.[80] Muir also adumbrates Welsh's polemic against bourgeois
Edinburgh and its marginalisation of the working class. Muir
observed of the social divisions of Scotland's capital city and its veneer
of civility: 'it is a city of extraordinary and sordid contrasts [. . .] The
entire existence of Edinburgh as a respectable bourgeois city depends
upon that fact'.[81] Muir finds in the bourgeois tea-rooms of the day
a metonym for the city's wider hypocrisy: 'The effect that these
places are designed to produce is one of luxury, and the more select
of them strive for an impression of adroitly muffled silence, silence
being in an industrial civilization, which is the noisiest known form
of civilization, the supreme evidence of luxury because the most
difficult thing to achieve'.[82] It is a quietude that also depends upon
the silencing of the working class, its banishment from this urbane
idyll. Welsh's work articulates that repressed experience that is actually constitutive of the city's continued functioning, its repressed
economy of toil, oppression, unemployment, disadvantage and
crime.

For Muir Edinburgh's position as Scotland's capital city was also
highly inappropriate as he adjudicated it to have displaced an essential Scottishness and the continuity of its history:

> although Edinburgh is Scottish in itself, one cannot feel that the people
> who live there are Scottish in any radical sense, or have any essential
> connection with it. They do not even go with it; they look like visitors
> who have stayed there for a long time. One imagines that not very long
> ago the real population must have been driven out, and that the people
> one sees walking about came to stay in the town simply because the
> houses happened to be empty. In other words, one cannot look at Edin-
> burgh without being conscious of a visible crack in historical continuity.
> The actual town, the houses, streets, churches, rocks, gardens, are still
> there; but these exist wholly in the past. The past is a national past; the
> present, which is made up of the thoughts and feelings and prejudices

of the inhabitants, their way of life in general, is as cosmopolitan as the cinema. This is not universally true; but it applies to the populace, rich and poor, the great multitude who have been Anglicised and American-ised, whether by the film, the Press, the radio, the lending library, or the public schools.[83]

Under Muir's analysis, the Edinburgh working class is not just writ-ten out of history and culture by capitalist oppression but also here, in his own terms, by Muir's nationalist construction of what a people should be too. Edinburgh's urban working class is no longer a 'real' Scottish people but phantasmal interlopers and usurpers who threaten the supposedly authentic and concrete Scottishness of Edin-burgh's architecture and landscape with their haunting modernity. Hence, Edinburgh's working class has conventionally been doubly excluded and marginalised. Firstly, by the social exclusions and eco-nomic inequalities of capitalism – the 'tarting up' of the gentrified city centre for bourgeois consumer culture – and secondly, within a nationalist paradigm, by the 'tartaning up' of that same city centre – the concomitant tourist culture of Scotland as a national heritage site. The Edinburgh of romantic or puritanical nationalism myth has no imaginative or social space for an urban working class. Thus, many of Welsh's characters are trapped in the drug addiction and poverty of Edinburgh's peripheral and forgotten housing schemes that prevent them from intruding upon the bourgeois and tourist centre – out of sight and out of their minds.

In a thought-provoking review of James Buchan's *Capital of the Mind: How Edinburgh Changed the World* (2003) in the *Guardian*, Welsh acknowledges the cultural, scientific and philosophical flower-ing in Edinburgh during the Scottish Enlightenment. However, Welsh avers that increased squalor, poverty and social exclusion were 'the real cost of the Scottish Enlightenment':

> In James Craig's New Town, Edinburgh created the world's first suburb, where, along with George Square across the city, the great and the good could discuss matters of import in a convivial setting. However, by seg-regating the upper middle classes from the 'mob', it inadvertently gave birth to its poorer sister, the ghetto. Edinburgh, then, was the first city to render most of its citizens invisible. This process continued after the second world war, with the building of peripheral housing schemes, and moves on at pace today with developments for the moneyed forcing the cost of housing and inner-city living up. But capitalism will constantly find ways to satisfy aspirational groups while further disenfranchising

the masses. In some ways the Edinburgh of Walter Scott is the prototype
for the tourist industry in all British cities.[84]

So rather than interpreting Edinburgh's cultural, scientific and archi-
tectural richness and its poverty and disenfranchisement as incon-
gruities, Welsh saliently reads both as constituent parts of the same
historical process, the ascent of one dependent upon the disadvantage
of the other. It is a verification of Walter Benjamin's dictum that
'there is no document of civilization which is not at the same time a
document of barbarism'.[85] Bourgeois and tourist Edinburgh obviously
have strongly vested economic interests in obliterating the traces of
their own constitutive barbarism: 'Tourists want to come to the
Athens of the North rather than the HIV capital of Europe . . . and the
people who suffer from HIV [are] deemed implicitly detrimental to
tourism . . . So the schemies are taken out of existence'.[86] This point
also helps explain why there is a strongly existentialist voice in
Welsh's work, for it sets about representing and foregrounding
people whose daily existence is denied continually by power, by the
major political parties, by tourism, by conventional literature and by
urban planning.

So although a devolved Scottish parliament has been in place since
12 May 1999, such an event should not be regarded as the culmination of a struggle for Scottish democracy. It is rather merely the insti-
gation of a forum where the politics of class, gender and conflictual
social demographics may be aired and contested. Catherine Lockerbie, for example, the Director of the Edinburgh International Book
Festival, argued that the work of writers such as Kelman and Welsh
will become less relevant because 'now that devolution has been
achieved, people don't have to prove they are Scottish writers any-
more'.[87] Lockerbie's analysis is notably pitched at a national level –
subsuming problematics such as class and gender. Certainly the work
of writers such as Welsh and Kelman can be understood in terms of
Robin Robertson's comment that 'for years Scots have felt left out and
put down. They have been denied political and cultural representation. When that happens, people find new ways to express who they
are'.[88] However, this introduction has sought to indicate that the
assertion of voice in Welsh's work and that of his contemporaries is
not a homogenous national one but instead is socially and culturally
specific in an oppositional manner that the national narrative will
continue to seek to stratify and exclude. Indeed, speaking in an inter-

view at the moment of devolution, Welsh also resists viewing the
Scottish parliament as the attainment of a unitary Scottish freedom,
preferring instead to concentrate upon how power and inequality
persist:

> The worst-case scenario is that the parliament will be crap . . . You
> always get an oligarchy that creams it off for themselves. There is such
> a moribund infrastructure of deadbeats and con-men in the Labour
> Party that has dominated politics in central Scotland for so long. I'd be
> absolutely astonished if these people didn't manage to push their noses
> in the trough and dominate. Hopefully not. But as someone who has
> worked for local authorities in Scotland, you always live in fear that will
> happen.[89]

In moving chronologically through Welsh's published work, this
study will attend itself to the key contextual frameworks established in
this introduction. It will attest to Welsh's resistance to accepted narratives of national and regional identification and his investigation of
the voices produced from the margins of contemporary social fragmentation. An assessment of the development of Welsh's work
necessitates an engagement with the social and political change and
convulsion which determine and inspire it. Most particularly, the
guiding themes of this study are class fracture, the dissolution of traditional, industrial communities, the attendant unsettling of established paradigms of masculinity and a period of intense flux in gender
relations and identifications, and, ultimately, a confrontation with the
mechanics and logic of consumer capitalism. Equally, the material
embroilment of Welsh's work in those very consumerist dynamics of
commodification, the mass-marketing of his work and his elevation
in some circles to, by turns, voguish drug cultural guru or respected
cultural commentator, are all directly relevant to any clear sense of the
changing shape and nature of his published work over the last decade.
But what is evident, across the shifting social and cultural contexts
that span his work, is Welsh's edgy and uncompromising desire to
give a voice to the voiceless, to tap into the consciousnesses and experiences of characters pinioned between the ravages of contemporary
social decay and de-industrialisation and the enticements and seduc-
tions of commodity culture.

Notes

1 Leith had been a separate municipality until its official incorporation within the city of Edinburgh in 1920 – despite the overwhelming opposition to the move expressed in a popular plebiscite.

2 *In Your Face. Irvine Welsh: Condemn More, Understand Less*. BBC2. Broadcast 27 Nov 1995.

3 Ron McKay, 'Would the real Irvine Welsh shoot up?', *Observer*, Review (4 Feb 1996), 9.

4 Cited in Mary Riddell, 'Irvine Welsh interview', *New Statesman* (3 May 1999), 22. For further accounts of Welsh's past see McKay, 'Would the real Irvine Welsh shoot up?', 9, and John Walsh 'The not-so-shady past of Irvine Welsh', *Independent*, Weekend Section (15 Apr 1995), 25.

5 Cited in Kenny Farquarson, 'Through the eye of a needle', *Scotland on Sunday* (8 Aug 1993), 4.

6 Cited in Aaron Kelly, 'Irvine Welsh in conversation with Aaron Kelly', *Edinburgh Review* 113 (2004), 8.

7 Cited in Andy Beckett, 'Irvine Welsh: the ecstasy and the agony', *Guardian* (25 July 1998), 6.

8 Cited in Farquarson, 'Through the eye of a needle', 4.

9 K. Wishart, 'Drugs and art meet on campus', *Times Higher Education Supplement* (30 May 1997), 18.

10 Jonathan Romney, '*The Acid House* – bleak house', *Guardian* (1 Jan 1999), 7.

11 Cited in Jennifer Berman, 'An interview with Irvine Welsh', *Bomb Magazine* 56 (1996), 61. For Welsh's views on how a homogeneous Britishness is spurious, especially in terms of race and class, see his 'Foreword' to Phil Vasili, *The First Black British Footballer. Arthur Wharton 1865–1930: An Absence of Memory* (London: Frank Cass, 1998), xi–xiii.

12 *Rock the Dock*. Creation Records 1998. CRECD240.

13 Antonio Gramsci, *Selections from the Prison Notebooks*. Ed. and trans. Quintin Hoare and Geoffrey Nowell Smith (London: Lawrence and Wishart, 1996), 275–276.

14 The profound resistance and resentment towards the dismantling of Scotland's industries was evidenced most fully in the British general election of May 1997 when no Conservative MPs were returned in Scotland.

15 Cited in Scott Lash and John Urry, *Economies of Signs and Space* (London: Sage, 1994), 34.

16 David Cannadine, *Class in Britain* (London: Yale University Press, 1998), 14.

17 Anthony Giddens, *The Third Way: The Renewal of Social Democracy* (Cambridge: Polity Press, 1998), 43.

18 Cited in Alexander Laurence, 'Irvine Welsh: Scottish and still alive', *Free*

Williamsburg 13, www.freewilliamsburg.com/july_2001/interviews/html (July 2001).

19 Stuart Hall, *The Hard Road to Renewal: Thatcherism and the Crisis of the Left* (London: Verso, 1988), 212.

20 Cited in Steve Redhead, *Repetitive Beat Generation* (Edinburgh: Rebel Inc, 2000), 145–146.

21 *In Your Face.*

22 *Spin Magazine*, 'Scots, drugs and rock'n'roll: an interview with Irvine Welsh', www.spin.com/new/poplife/author.html (Sep 2002).

23 Cited in Kelly, 'Irvine Welsh in conversation with Aaron Kelly', 7.

24 Cited in Kelly, 'Irvine Welsh in conversation with Aaron Kelly', 7–8.

25 Cited in Walsh, 'The not-so-shady past of Irvine Welsh', 25.

26 Cited in Kelly, 'Irvine Welsh in conversation with Aaron Kelly', 8.

27 *The Story of the Novel.* Channel 4. Broadcast 20 July 2003.

28 Cited in Kelly, 'Irvine Welsh in conversation with Aaron Kelly', 8.

29 Cited in Kelly, 'Irvine Welsh in conversation with Aaron Kelly', 9.

30 Cited in Kelly, 'Irvine Welsh in conversation with Aaron Kelly', 9.

31 Cited in Kelly, 'Irvine Welsh in conversation with Aaron Kelly', 9.

32 *The Scotsman* (18 Oct 1991), 14. I am grateful to Duncan McLean for making me aware of the existence of these letters and to Randall Stevenson for furnishing me with the exact dates in which Griffiths' play was produced in Edinburgh.

33 Thanks to Duncan McLean for discussing the matter with me in an interview on the 20 March 2003. Welsh himself denies that he was the author of the Mrs Bogie letter.

34 *The Scotsman* (18 Oct 1991), 14.

35 *The Scotsman* (25 Oct 1991), 16.

36 Cited in Kelly, 'Irvine Welsh in conversation with Aaron Kelly', 10.

37 *Private Eye, Literary Review* No.1061 (23 Aug–5 Sep 2002), 24.

38 Cairns Craig, *Out of History: Narrative Paradigms in Scottish and British Culture* (Edinburgh: Polygon, 1996), 101.

39 John Hodge, *Trainspotting and Shallow Grave: The Screenplays* (London: Faber, 1996), xi.

40 Jason Cowley, 'Prickly flower of Scotland', *The Times* (13 Mar 1997), 33; Sarah Hemming, 'Grim wit in a drug wasteland', *Financial Times* (21 Dec 1995), 11; Lucy Hughes-Hallett, 'Cruising for a bruising', *Sunday Times* (15 Aug 1993), 6.

41 Michael Brockington, 'Poisoned haggis', *Vancouver Review* (Fall/Winter 1995), www.sfu.ca/~brocking/writing/phaggis.html (Aug 2003).

42 Cited in John Mulholland, 'Acid wit', *Guardian*, G2T (30 Mar 1995), 8.

43 For a comprehensive overview of the novel form see Ian Watt, *The Rise of the Novel* (London: Pimlico, 2000). Benedict Anderson also offers an

account of the role the novel played in cementing the bourgeois nation state in his *Imagined Communities: Reflections on the Origin and Spread of Nationalism*. Second Edition (London: Verso, 1991).

44 David McCrone, *Understanding Scotland: The Sociology of a Stateless Nation* (London: Routledge, 1992), 35.

45 Tom Nairn, *The Break-Up of Britain: Crisis and Neo-Nationalism* (London: Verso, 1981), 155.

46 Nairn, *The Break-Up of Britain*, 157.

47 Edwin Muir, *Scott and Scotland: The Predicament of the Scottish Writer* (London: Folcroft Library Editions, 1971), 19–20.

48 M. M. Bakhtin, *The Dialogic Imagination: Four Essays*. Ed. Michael Holquist. Trans. Caryl Emerson and Michael Holquist (Austin: University of Texas Press, 1981), 270.

49 Cited in Mulholland, 'Acid wit', 8.

50 Bakhtin, *The Dialogic Imagination*, 78.

51 Irvine Welsh, 'City tripper', *Guardian*, G2 (16 Feb 1996), 4.

52 Ellen-Raïssa Jackson and Willy Maley, 'Birds of a feather? A postcolonial reading of Irvine Welsh's *Marabou Stork Nightmares*', *Revista Canaria de Estudios Ingleses* 41 (2000), 193.

53 Michael Kimmel, 'Masculinity as homophobia: fear, shame, and silence in the construction of gender identity' in Harry Brod and Michael Kaufman, eds, *Theorizing Masculinities* (London: Sage, 1994), 121.

54 Kimmel, 'Masculinity as homophobia', 125.

55 Peter Stallybrass and Allon White, *The Politics and Poetics of Transgression* (London: Methuen, 1986), 53.

56 Cited in Berman, 'An interview with Irvine Welsh', 59.

57 Matthew Hart, 'Substance abuse: *Glue*', *Postmodern Culture*, 12: 2 (2000), 158.

58 Olivia Smith, *The Politics of Language 1791–1819* (Oxford: Clarendon, 1984), vii, cited in Robert Crawford, *Devolving English Literature* (Edinburgh: Edinburgh University Press, 2000), 18.

59 Kathleen Coburn, ed., *The Notebooks of Samuel Taylor Coleridge Vol. III, 1808–1819* (Princeton NJ: Princeton University Press/London: Routledge & Kegan Paul, 1973), note 4134. I am greatly indebted to the kindness of Dr Will Christie of the University of Sydney for hunting down this reference and for his thoughts on the subject.

60 The implication in Coleridge's idea that three out of four slave overseers are Scottish and the fourth has 'high cheekbones' is that the fourth is actually also Scottish – his mother having had extra-marital sex with a Scot, hence the base and uncivilised physiological features.

61 Elizabeth Young, 'Blood on the tracks', *Guardian* (14 Aug 1993), 33; Boyd Tonkin, 'A wee Hades: *Marabou Stork Nightmares*', *Observer*, Review (23 Apr 1995), 20.

62 Giles Gordon, 'Pandering to the English view of Scotland the drugged', *The Scotsman* (13 June 1997), 19.

63 Nicholas M. Williams, 'The dialect of authenticity: the case of Irvine Welsh's *Trainspotting*' in T. Hoenselaars and Maruis Buning, eds, *English Literature and the Other Languages* (Amsterdam: Rodopi, 1999), 225.

64 Willy Maley, 'Subversion and squirrility in Irvine Welsh's shorter fiction' in Dermot Cavanagh and Tim Kirk, eds, *Subversion and Scurrility: Popular Discourse in Europe from 1500 to the Present* (Aldershot: Ashgate, 2000), 192.

65 See George E. Davie, *The Democratic Intellect: Scotland and Her Universities in the Nineteenth Century* (Edinburgh: Edinburgh University Press, 1961), 203–221. Also useful is Davie's *The Scottish Enlightenment and Other Essays* (Edinburgh: Polygon, 1991).

66 For a concise and useful account of the recent explosion of Scottish fiction see Ian Bell, 'How Scotland got the write stuff', *Observer* (19 Nov 1995), 17.

67 Cited in Kelly, 'Irvine Welsh in conversation with Aaron Kelly', 16.

68 Cited in Mulholland, 'Acid wit', 8.

69 Cited in Dave Welch, 'Irvine Welsh', www.powells.com/authors/welsh.html (Sep 2002).

70 *In Your Face.*

71 Cited in Kelly, 'Irvine Welsh in conversation with Aaron Kelly', 15.

72 The contemporaries in question are Robert Alan Jamieson and Duncan McLean and I would like to acknowledge my gratitude to both for sharing their thoughts on Irvine Welsh's emergence.

73 See M. M. Bakhtin, *Rabelais and his World*. Trans. Hélène Iswolsky (Cambridge, Mass: MIT Press, 1968).

74 Alan Sinfield, *Literature, Politics and Culture in Postwar Britain* (London: Athlone Press, 1997), xvii.

75 T. S. Eliot 'Was there a Scottish literature?', *The Atheneum* (1 Aug 1919), cited in Douglas Dunn, ed., *The Faber Book of Contemporary Scottish Poetry* (London: Faber, 1992), xvii.

76 Lewis Grassic Gibbon, 'Literary lights' in Gibbon and Hugh MacDiarmid, *Scottish Scene, or, The Intelligent Man's Guide to Albyn* (London: Hutchinson, 1934), 165.

77 Welsh, 'City tripper', 4.

78 Cited in Mulholland, 'Acid wit', 8.

79 Cited in Iain Grant, 'Dealing out the capital punishment', *Sunday Times* (5 Sep 1993), 14.

80 Edwin Muir, *Scottish Journey* (Edinburgh: Mainstream, 1979), 28.

81 Muir, *Scottish Journey*, 9, 11.

82 Muir, *Scottish Journey*, 22.

83 Muir, *Scottish Journey*, 24–25.

84 Irvine Welsh, 'Flower of Scotland', *Guardian*, Review (23 Aug 2003), 11.
85 Walter Benjamin, *Illuminations*. Trans. Harry Zorn (London: Fontana, 1992), 248.
86 Welsh, 'City tripper', 4.
87 Quoted by Alan Massie, 'Sir Walter Scott's literati', *Scotland on Sunday* (16 June 2002), 23.
88 Cited in John Arlidge, 'Return of the angry young men', *Observer* (23 June 1996), 14.
89 Cited in Riddell, 'Irvine Welsh interview', 22.

1

Trainspotting (1993)

Given that Welsh's debut novel has now sold around one million copies in the United Kingdom alone, it is worth stating that its original print run was only three thousand. Although Welsh is often criticised for cynical, bestselling populism, Duncan McLean relates how he had offered to help Welsh negotiate a better advance from the publisher, Secker and Warburg – around £500 more than the £1000 he did receive – but that Welsh was more concerned with simply getting the novel published than making money.[1] McLean also recalls how his earlier publication of materials from *Trainspotting* with his Clocktower Press imprint was far from a marketing coup: 'Our slowest seller was undoubtedly *Past Tense: Four Stories from a Novel* by Irvine Welsh . . . In those days, to write about heroin addicts on a run-down Edinburgh estate was far from the easy commercialism critics often accuse Irvine of having adopted. Quite the opposite: only a few folk shared my enthusiasm for what he was doing'.[2] So it is misleading to confuse the success of Danny Boyle's 1995 film version of *Trainspotting* with the early reception of Welsh's work and the initial limited pressing of the novel does disclose the publisher's insecurities about its potential market and literary success. Nonetheless, the novel had sold around 100,000 copies by the release of the film version and Secker and Warburg did from the outset afford *Trainspotting* heavy promotion – arranging for a pre-release feature in the *Literary Review* and having Welsh read from the novel in a well-publicised event on 30 August 1993 at the Edinburgh Book Festival, which also featured Duncan McLean.

As discussed in the introduction, *Trainspotting* took shape in the late 1980s and incorporated some journals that Welsh kept in the early part of the decade. In particular, the novel confronts not only the decimation of working-class areas of Edinburgh through the influx of cheap heroin in the 1980s but also the related spread of HIV infection through the practice of needle sharing in the 'shooting galleries' where users injected the drug. The transmission of HIV was exacerbated by the refusal of the authorities at both state and municipal levels to provide clean needles for addicts lest this be viewed as a softening of drugs policy. In fact, it was left to charities such as Oxfam to distribute clean needles to addicts on the housing schemes for much of the decade. Eventually a clean needle exchange was set up and from 1988 methadone, which was to be taken orally, was officially prescribed to heroin addicts in Edinburgh in an effort to regulate drug usage and to curb the rate of HIV infection. Welsh explains how the writing of *Trainspotting* was directly impelled by the devastation of the working-class Edinburgh where he had grown up:

> The motivation for writing *Trainspotting* was because there were so many people that I'd known that were just kind of dropping dead, were getting infected. For me it was like trying to work out through fiction how that was happening. The heroin as well was just a manifestation of it, there were so many other things going on in people's lives and the saddest thing is, if you talk to a lot of people who are HIV, they've just been crushed by so many other things like poverty and unemployment that HIV on top of that is just another thing to deal with.[3]

So although the work of heroin addict writers, such as the American William Burroughs or the Scot Alexander Trocchi, seem obvious precursors for *Trainspotting*, the use of the drug by a significant proportion of Edinburgh's marginalised working class necessitates a distinct shift in socio-cultural emphasis from the decadent, bohemian addict in the fiction of Burroughs and Trocchi. Welsh comments:

> The junkie in Trocchi and Burroughs's fiction was by and large a culturally middle-class figure – a member of the intelligentsia, a rebel who saw society as not having done anything for them, so they're into this drug that's their own, a symbol of their rebellion. There's always been that sort of bohemian type drug sub-culture. But in Edinburgh, in the eighties you're talking about people who wouldn't normally be involved in the heroin scene, people who didn't have that Trocchi-esque attitude of setting themselves up in opposition to society. It was just people who really didn't have a fucking clue as to what was going on.[4]

Trainspotting does not concern a déclassé aristocrat or intellectual who is still bounded by a restive bourgeois decadence but rather situates its consideration of heroin use specifically in the context of an unravelling working-class milieu. The novel is not merely about heroin as such but instead utilises the drug's social environment to meditate upon the paradigm shifts that ruptured traditional working-class identity and community in the late 1970s and 1980s. Welsh's effort to understand the material and symbolic import of heroin use in Edinburgh deals with social process not individual predilection. It also entails a more contextual reconsideration of the addict figure, which in the tradition of Scottish West Coast writing appears only as an isolated and disruptive bogeyman preying upon a settled working-class community:

> I've always found the treatment of someone who's got drug problems a bit offensive in Scottish literature. In classic Scottish fiction such as William McIlvanney and Alan Spence you see the junkie coming into their books as this sort of shadowy cardboard cut-out figure who's there to undermine or subvert decent Scottish working-class values – Alan Spence has this guy standing outside a playground trying to push drugs to kids! . . . I wanted to show a broader network. I wasn't really interested in telling the story of one or two people with drug problems so much as showing that such behaviour always takes place within a context. It's not isolated. Such behaviour has repercussions for the individual and for the people surrounding that individual. I didn't want to present the junkie as isolated and cut off. I wanted to focus on the relationships and cultural pressures surrounding these characters. Obviously there are extremes of behaviour people can get into, extremes of anti-social and fucked up behaviour and I didn't want to spare that.[5]

In dealing with its dark subject matter, the novel's title is deliberately understated and evocative. Welsh explains the parallel between heroin use and the eponymous obsessional hobby thus: 'Trainspotting is an activity which is completely pointless. I can't understand why someone would want to stand on a freezing platform trying to collect the number of every train in the country when it's both impossible and futile. I can't understand why someone would want to nullify their existence in this way'. Trainspotting and heroin, Welsh continues, 'both fill in time, but are otherwise completely futile. They are both a symptom of some sort of lack, of a deep spiritual crisis'.[6] In terms of the onset of modernity and contemporary capitalist society, railways are also highly charged artefacts as the train was one of the driving engines of the industrial revolution and its attendant social transformation. As a hobby, trainspotting tries to impose a pattern –

however arbitrary or finally meaningless – upon the confusions of modernity and latterly postmodernity through the collation of train numbers. The novel itself is cadenced by sequences of serially numbered sections that fall between its main chapters – entitled, by turns, 'Junk Dilemmas' and 'Straight Dilemmas' according to the character's state of heroin use or withdrawal at the time. These sequential and interspersed episodes in the novel compound the trainspotting metaphor by bespeaking heroin's reduction of contemporary life to a meaningless pattern of inexorable and unchanging seriality. Murray Smith asserts that both trainspotting and heroin addiction disclose the stasis and entrapment that characterise the lives of the novel's main characters: 'To be a trainspotter – in the literal sense – is to stand for hours, in the same place, watching trains go by. To board a train is to go somewhere, to move on. To move on is to open oneself up to change'.[7] Of the novels main characters – Mark Renton, Simon Williamson or Sick Boy, Spud or Danny Murphy, and Francis Begbie – it is only Renton who finally resolves to change and move on at the novel's close when he steals the money which the gang make from a drug deal in London and departs to begin a new life in Amsterdam away from the deadening entrapments which encircle life in Edinburgh.

So the guiding themes in this chapter's study of *Trainspotting*, which will remain apposite in considering Welsh's work as a whole, address themselves directly to a dialectic of social stagnation for the majority of the characters and limited opportunity for a few as individuals. One of this novel's many strengths resides in the fact that it grasps this apparently anomalous dialectic of entrenched poverty and social climbing as mutually comprising a shared and dependent economic process. *Trainspotting* refutes the dominant doctrines of contemporary consumer freedom by darkly tracing the increased disadvantage and disenfranchisement upon which that entrepreneurial ethos is based. In doing so, the novel also poses some difficult questions about contemporary working-class community and affiliation and demarcates a profound crisis in class identities which this chapter will evaluate. Moreover, the dissection of traditional social identities in the novel also entails a consideration of gender relations and the disruption of inherited paradigms of masculinity. Although the novel is driven by an indomitable rage and resistance to dominant accounts of social improvement and access for all, it also harbours a deeply pessimistic musing upon the internecine and regressive

violent identities that can be borne out of this disintegration of traditional class and masculine alignments. Given the novel's direct confrontation with the tenets of Thatcherism and its neo-liberal advocacy
of the individual over the social, this chapter will also discuss certain
ambivalences in the text concerning individualism, most especially in
relation to Renton's actions at the novel's close.

'The skag boys, Jean-Claude Van Damme and Mother Superior'

The first lines of *Trainspotting* embed the reader in the demotic that
forms much of the novel's narrative: 'The sweat wis lashing oafay Sick
Boy; he wis trembling. Ah wis just sitting thair, focusing on the telly,
tryin no tae notice the cunt. He wis bringing me doon. Ah tried tae
keep ma attention oan the Jean-Claude Van Damme video' (*T* 3).
Mark Renton's first person narrative introduces not only his own
voice and the character of Sick Boy but also some of the book's major
themes. Significantly, the novel begins with a male body in crisis – in
the figure of Sick Boy who is ravaged by heroin withdrawal symptoms. Peter Stallybrass and Allon White's maxim – 'thinking the body
is thinking social topography and vice versa'[8] – helps set this corporeal malfunction in a wider social context. The opening immediately
severs *Trainspotting* from a Scottish West Coast tradition of working-
class writing typified by William McIlvanney's 1975 novel *Docherty* –
an epic account of working-class struggle and solidarity through the
First World War, the General Strike and the Depression. In *Docherty*
the eponymous central character is a traditional male hard man from
a mining community and we are told that 'wherever he stood he established a territory'.[9] Thus, Docherty's physically expressive and working-class masculinity, which is grounded in industrial labour,
organically controls and regulates not only itself but also an entire
community of relations. In Stallybrass and White's terms, then, Sick
Boy's bodily disintegration mediates a more general social malaise
that demarcates the decimation of traditional forms of community
and collective life by de-industrialisation and unemployment.
Trainspotting, and much of Welsh's other works, emerge from a historical moment in which working-class communities are not working
– both in the sense of being characterised by mass unemployment
and of ceasing to function as networks of collective experience and
tradition.

Notably, Renton seeks to forestall his awareness of Sick Boy's foundering body and his own disintegration by concentrating upon the Jean-Claude Van Damme video. The historical emergence of the contemporary muscle-bound action hero – a trend in which Van Damme follows actors such as Sylvester Stallone (particularly his *Rocky* and *Rambo* films) and Arnold Schwarzenegger – significantly occurs amidst the de-industrialisation and decline of manual labour in Western societies from the late 1970s to the present. Such films offer a compensatory physically expressive masculinity and redisplay of the male body in an era where traditional forms of male action and identity based on physicality have been undermined by economic change.[10] Indeed, the term 'body building' which is so closely associated with the personae of Schwarzenegger and Van Damme itself strives to define this highly specialised hypermasculine body in an ethos of hard work and construction that hankers after industrial labour. Renton's psychic investment in the Van Damme film is also driven by the desire to witness the action hero's decimation of avowedly lesser embodiments of masculinity: 'Ah wanted tae see Jean-Claude smash up this arrogant fucker' (*T* 3). To this end, Hal Foster posits that the fantasy of a muscle-bound masculinity provides a kind of armouring that not only wills the obliteration of inferiorised bodies but also seeks in the process to repress 'the point where the masculine subject confronts its greatest fear: its own fragmentation, disintegration, and dissolution'.[11] The fact that the action hero on screen provides a fantasy corporeal identity for a male body in crisis is confirmed when Renton and Sick Boy leave their flat to procure heroin and almost become involved in a street fight on the way – Renton berates Sick Boy: 'Ye think ah'm Jean-Claude Van Fuckin Damme?' (*T* 5). Upon reaching the flat of the drug dealer, Johnny Swann, the abscission of the male body from its patriarchal ideal is further evidenced. When Swann's female friend, Ali, declares of heroin – 'That beats any meat injection . . . that beats any fuckin cock in the world' – Renton concedes: 'It unnerves us tae the extent that ah feel ma ain genitals through my troosers tae see if they're still thair. Touchin masel makes us feel queasy though' (*T* 9). Renton's alienation from his own male body adumbrates the novel's broader detailing of the abjection of traditional identities. The opening chapter also subverts the conventional working-class industrial community of the West of Scotland tradition that is regulated by a hard man such as McIlvanney's character Docherty by playing with the slang term for a drug dealer – 'the Man'. In this instance, 'the Man' in question who regulates the community of heroin users, Johnny Swann, is feminised by his appellation: 'We called Johnny "Mother Superior" because ay the length ay time he'd hud his habit' (*T* 6). In addition to 'the Man' presiding over a matriarchal community of drug addicts in an inversion the workerist patriarchy of the Glasgow novel, Swann's nickname also parodically highlights the decline of religion as a social nexus. The confusion of gender identities and the collapse of traditional community and belonging embodied by Mother Superior anticipate the book's guiding themes.

As Robert A. Morace observes, funerals constitute the only surviving traditional form of communal ritual and interaction in the novel – a fact whose ironic symbolism itself testifies to the death of an entire social way of life and belonging.[12] Tradition can now only congregate to mourn its own passing. One of *Trainspotting*'s strengths is to attach to heroin use an excoriating social symbolism that helps evidence the determinants of that communal decline. When Mother Superior slyly declares of the heroin subculture in which he trades – 'Nae friends in this game. Jist associates' (*T* 6) – Renton is impelled to muse later: 'We are all acquaintances now. It seems tae go beyond our personal circumstances; a brilliant metaphor for our times' (*T* 11).

Consuming heroin

Although Martin Brüggernmeier and Horst W. Drescher suggest that 'the subculture depicted in *Trainspotting* rejects the ideals of consumerism',[13] the consumption of heroin in the novel actually helps to foreground the dominant trends and assumptions of contemporary capitalism. Hence, the novel's political critique stems, in large part, not from the unfolding of oppositional vantage points but instead from the rendering of the deadening logic of mainstream society in its most illustrative and terminal extremes. Such was the encroachment of the Thatcherite, neo-liberal hostility to the very concept of society that the subcultural detritus of *Trainspotting* attests not only to the effects of such economics but also to their capacity to invade and deform all aspects of social life. The apotheosis of heroin addiction entails the enjoyment of a self that is not one's own and the simultaneous shackling of a self that is. Consuming heroin therefore provides a telling metaphor for the loss of identity in late capitalist consciousness and the putative pleasures and freedoms of consumer

society. It affirms that consumer pleasure is a deeply alienated enjoyment. When Sick Boy refuses to share needles with the other users,
Mother Superior retorts: 'Now that's no very social . . . nae sharin, nae
shootin' (*T* 9). But with the fear of contracting AIDS rife, it is significant that sharing became dangerous, even fatal. So the network of
heroin users is a community which paradoxically effaces community,
a community based upon the antithesis of communal values and
sharing. Indeed, the novel is filled with the inversion of the conventional resonances of words and social entities – for which David
Harold's cover image prepares us given that it appears as a kind of
photographic negative – and another notable transmutation of meaning specifically in relation to AIDS is that HIV positive as a negative
condition. So in the fragmentary and bewildering world confronting
the characters in the novel, positives become negatives, communities
become repositories of sequestered solitudes.

In terms of the wider social import of the heroin, William
Burroughs' account of the atomised destitution of heroin addiction is
imbued by a strong sense of individual helplessness that is also prescient in this context: 'basically no one can help anyone else . . . I have
learned the junk equation. Junk is not, like alcohol or weed, a means
to an increased enjoyment of life. Junk is not a kick. It is a way of
life'.[14] In addition to individual alienation, Burroughs also here
notably designates heroin not a constituent facet of existence but
rather an all-consuming way of life in itself. This peremptory and
totalising drive to consume existence in its entirety further extends
heroin's use as a metaphor in comprehending the mechanics of contemporary capitalism. As Jean Baudrillard avers:

> Consumption is not a passive mode of assimilation (*absorption*) and
> appropriation which we can oppose to an active mode of production . . .
> From the outset, we must clearly state that consumption is an active
> mode of relations (not only to objects, but to the collectivity and to the
> world), a systematic mode of activity and a global response on which our
> whole cultural system is founded.[15]

In consumption, Baudrillard argues, human relations are both 'ful-
filled' and 'annulled'. Baudrillard's analysis plays upon the double
meaning in French of the verb *consommer*, which means both to
consummate (hence the promise of complete fulfilment) and to consume in the sense of annulment or absolute depletion.[16] This totalising imperative of consumerism has enormous implications for

traditional working-class identities. Baudrillard's dialectic of fulfilment and annulment suggests that when working-class people buy
into the logic of consumerism, the individual pleasures attained come
at the cost of the destruction of the traditional identities, communities
and solidarities of collective life. Most working-class literature deals
with facets of working life and labour. There is therefore a profound
rupture in that social and cultural experience in an era of de-industrialisation and unemployment. None of the main characters in
Trainspotting work. Does that mean they are no longer working-class?
We supposedly now live in the West in a postmodern consumer society where one can pick and choose at will. Interestingly, then, the
heroin addicts are designated not by the work they undertake but
rather by what they consume. And their consumption subsumes all
other aspects of their identities and lives.

However, *Trainspotting* and Baudrillard's analysis help indicate that
not everyone has equal access to the benefits of that pervasive consumption. They provide a counterpoint to works such as Francis
Fukuyama's *The End of History and the Last Man* or Daniel Bell's *The
End of Ideology*, which proclaim a new and supposedly emancipated
era in the Western world in which older forms of political belief and
social affiliation are deemed unnecessary due to the personal freedoms of consumer capitalism.[17] Perhaps the most famous espousal of
this postmodern world is François Lyotard and his theory of a 'crisis
of narratives' that demarcates the postmodern: 'if a metanarrative
implying a philosophy of history is used to legitimate knowledge,
questions are raised concerning the validity of the institutions governing the social bond: these must be legitimated as well. Thus
justice is consigned to the grand narrative in the same way as truth
. . . I define *postmodern* as incredulity toward metanarratives'.[18] For
thinkers such as Lyotard or Fukuyama, we inhabit a new postmodern
present in which older forms of collective human emancipation or
means of explaining the world (grand narratives) are no longer tenable or even desirable – for Fukuyama history itself has ceased to
exist. Instead, according to such thought, we live in an epoch where
satisfaction is achieved at a micro-political and individual level. The
irony is that this postmodern narrative of the contemporary world –
for all its hostility to supposedly totalising or universalising forms of
thought and agency – is itself offered as the only means of explaining
ourselves and our societies; it has effectively become another grand
narrative. Notably, Lyotard's definition of the freedoms of post-

modernity is inflected by specific economic, consumerist determinants: 'one listens to reggae, watches a western, wears Paris perfume in Tokyo and "retro" clothes in Hong Kong'.[19] This celebratory affirmation of postmodern hybridity and flux elicits the following engaged riposte from Alex Callinicos: 'To whom then is this particular combination of experiences available? What particular political subject does the idea of a postmodern epoch help constitute?'[20] Callinicos' rebuttal indicts this sense of universal possibility by observing that it is essentially an economic and consumer driven experience to which many people do not have access. The fact that freedom is defined in economic terms – or those of consumer choice – rather than through meaningful political or ethical emancipation is articulated by Renton's now famous tirade against the dominant strands of his society:

> Choose us. Choose life. Chose mortgage payments; choose washing machines; choose cars; choose sitting oan a couch watching mind-numbing and spirit-crushing game shows, stuffing fuckin junk food intae yir mooth. Choose rotting away, pishing and shiteing yersel in a home, a total fuckin embarrassment tae the selfish, fucked-up brats ye've produced. Choose life. Well, ah choose no tae choose life. If the cunts cannae handle that, it's thair fuckin problem. (*T* 187–188)

As Naomi Klein demonstrates, the supposed plethora of contemporary consumer choice actually masks the solidification of power in the hands of the few:

> The branded multinationals may talk diversity, but the visible result of their actions is an army of teen clones marching – in 'uniform', as the marketers say – into the global mall . . . Dazzled by the array of consumer choices, we may at first fail to notice the tremendous consolidation taking place in the boardrooms of the entertainment, media and retail industries . . . the world goes monochromatic and doors slam shut from all sides: every other story – whether the announcements of a new buyout, an untimely bankruptcy, a colossal merger – points directly to a loss of meaningful choice.[21]

As Robert A. Morace asserts: 'the drug economy is capitalism in its purest and most lethal form'.[22] Notably, capitalism relies upon a fundamental division between production and consumption, between those who produce and distribute goods and those who consume them. The idea of a consumer society necessarily represses the fact of labour, the reality that workers must produce the consumer goods that are used, in effect, to sell people a sense of their own avowed freedom. In this context, heroin use is again a great metaphor because it is entirely centred on the act of consumption – Renton knows that for the addict 'nothing exists outside the moment' (*T* 17) – not production or distribution, for these are things that its economy must repress and secrete in order to avoid detection. Similarly, the hostility of Thatcherite economics to state regulation finds a correlative in the heroin users' networks which of necessity seek to circumvent police detection. Renton comments: 'On the issue of drugs, we wir classical liberals, vehemently opposed tae state intervention in any form' (*T* 53).

Trainspotting lays bare the economic logic of consumer freedom, and the void at the core of most of its characters' experience of consuming demonstrates that such pleasures and fulfilments are not universal – despite masquerading as such – but rather depend upon the destruction or annulment of the experiences and communities of others. As discussed in the introduction, the historical modification of class identities does not inevitably entail the disappearance of class. *Trainspotting* illustrates that the inequalities and disadvantages of social class are still operative despite postmodernism's effort to repress them. By way of illustration, perhaps the key symbolic scene in the novel occurs in the chapter, 'Trainspotting at Leith Central Station', which takes place in a long-defunct train station. There is an interesting juxtaposition of social experiences in this chapter. As the upper and middle classes stream out from the opera having watched Bizet's *Carmen*, Renton and Begbie stand in the hollowed out train station which gestures to the fragmentation of a former network of connection, community and indeed industrial labour. Begbie even fails to recognise or at least acknowledge his own drunken father, further signifying a total collapse of a sense of the past and tradition, a temporal entrapment in a meaningless and voided present that also precludes the envisaging of a future. By contrast, the opera-goers have indulged themselves in a work which celebrates living only for the moment by voyeuristically experiencing the passion projected on to a factory worker.[23] Whilst Renton and Begbie are entrapped in the present devoid of futurity or even a past to guide them – the scene symbolically finishes with 'neither ay us looking back once' (*T* 309) – the opera set return to the comfort of their lives and their futures as they head off to restaurants where, we are told, 'reservations have been made' (*T* 306). This scene evidences succinctly two fundamentally opposed readings of the postmodern condition. One account offers the postmodern as stylisation and cultural indulgence facilitated by one's economic status: a status which permits one to play at being reckless, to consume the passionate consumption of others. The other demarcates a profound political crisis that must of necessity be traduced if economic and social relations are to be altered. So the addicts of *Trainspotting*, in an indication of a social paradigm shift, are not identified as workers, they are consumers. But they are consumers who consume that which will destroy them, their former identities and attachments. Hence the characters have no *station* in another sense, they have no social station since the former working-class identity which structured Leith and north Edinburgh has collapsed. They are now merely an underclass, a subclass, unsure of their designation since their status as working class has been disrupted by economic change and unemployment whilst the lure of the benefits of being a consumer is an empty, false promise that actually destroys identity rather than fulfils it. So, in a further unfolding of the novel's inversions, this postmodern freedom is actually an enslavement, to be a consumer is in fact to be consumed.

The plight of the disused station, which is to be converted into leisure and service economy space, produces in Renton a moment of nostalgia even though he cannot himself remember a time when trains ran through Central Station: 'We go fir a pish in the auld Central Station at the Fit ay the Walk, now a barren, desolate hangar, which is soon tae be demolished and replaced by a supermarket and swimming centre. Somehow, that makes us sad, even though ah wis eywis too young tae mind ay trains ever being there' (*T* 308). Jean Baudrillard's theory, that 'when the real is no longer what it used to be, nostalgia assumes its full meaning',[24] helps explain Renton's sense of a loss not only of the past but also his waning grasp of the present. To this end, the term *nostalgia* does not merely convey a temporal loss but also a yearning for home (or *nostos*) or belonging in the present. In Baudrillard's terms, nostalgia indicates a crisis of our sense of our surrounding social reality. The train station as cultural icon has an enormous social and historical resonance given that the railway was one of the founding narrative engines and drives of the intellectual and practical narratives of modernity. The meaningless and empty present in Leith Central Station conveys symbolically that those modern narratives have broken down. The characters are entrapped in a present born out of modernity but which the narratives of modernity no longer seem to map or comprehend. When Begbie's father wryly asks Renton and Begbie if they are trainspotting in the derelict station, the futility of looking for trains in a place where they no longer run elaborates the broader untenability of seeking to understand the present in terms of the past, of trying to map the postmodern world in terms of a former modernity. When Begbie's father urges them to 'keep up the trainspottin mind' (*T* 309), his entreaty also contains an instructive pun. As Cairns Craig asserts: 'The "Trainspottin mind" is a mind that has lost its connection, one whose language is spoken to no one'.[25] Leith Central Station is a site of missed connections historically and socially, where the reality which engulfs the characters becomes increasingly difficult to map and understand. It is the task of this 'trainspottin mind' – and Welsh's subsequent work more broadly – to try to reconvene a sense of that social reality, to find new cognitive means by which an era of de-industrialisation and dislocation may be discerned and critiqued.

One of the most striking disruptions of social reality in the novel is found in the blurring of the boundaries between the living and the dead. As noted above, death and funerals pervade the novel. The funeral is conventionally an event whereby families and communities come to an acceptance of death that is restorative and ensures a continuation of memory, tradition and values in the consciousness and culture of the living but more often than not the characters are 'no wiser now than at the start' (*T* 299). *Trainspotting* is strewn with figures who dissolve clear cut distinctions between the living and the dead. Those suffering with AIDS, such as Tommy, Wee Goagsie or Davie Mitchell, experience a kind of death in life, whilst in the chapter, 'There Is a Light that Never Goes Out', Spud thinks of himself and his associates in terms of the undead:

> They emerge from the stairdoor into the darkness of the deserted street. Some of them move in a jerky, manic way; exuberant and noisy. Others cruise along silently, like ghosts; hurting inside, yet fearful of the imminence of even greater pain and discomfort . . . It has been, Spud reflects, a few days since he'd seen the light. They were like vampires, living a largely nocturnal existence, completely out of synchronisation with most of the other people who inhabited the tenements and lived by a rota of sleep and work. (*T* 262–263)

Correspondingly, there are the dead who refuse to die. In 'Growing Up in Public', it appears that Renton and Nina's Uncle Andy's corpse is sweating and still alive – though it transpires than an electric blanket was left on. Renton, during his hallucinatory withdrawal symptoms in 'House Arrest', is haunted by the ghost of Lesley's baby Dawn, who is also described in vampiric terms: 'The bairn has sharp, vampire teeth wi blood drippin fae them' (*T* 196). Indeed, when Dawn harangues Renton – 'litmefuckindie' (*T* 196) – this is perhaps as much an outright accusation ('you let me die') as it is a tortured plea ('please let me die'). The significance of these figures of death in life and of living death can be understood through the work of Slavoj Žižek. Žižek argues, in terms of collective social psychology, that funerals reassure a community of its own regeneration, the reconciliation of the death of individuals with the continued popular memory of the community. Whereas the living dead – who so often obsess popular culture and film – designate a profound crisis in the codes and value systems of a society or culture (what he terms the symbolic order):

> The return of the dead is a sign of a disturbance in the symbolic rite, in the process of symbolization; the dead return as collectors of some unpaid symbolic debt . . . the funeral rite exemplifies symbolization at its purest: through it, the dead are inscribed in the text of symbolic tradition, they are assured that, in spite of their death, they will 'continue to live' in the memory of the community. The 'return of the living dead' is, on the other hand, the reverse of the proper funeral rite. While the latter implies a certain reconciliation, an acceptance of loss, the return of the dead signifies that they cannot find their proper place in the text of tradition.[26]

In these terms, the many figures who stalk *Trainspotting* and confuse the boundaries between living and dead further evidence a crisis of community and tradition and an incapacity of the working-class constituencies of the novel to comprehend the social reality which overwhelms them. This highly unsettled sense of what is real and unreal is indicative of a fragmentation of historical, social and ethical perspectives as the reality of the present is subsumed by the unburied ghosts and injustices of a past that offers not tradition and continuity but rupture and disconnection. The fact that Lesley's baby who dies in her cot is called Dawn also intimates another false dawn or hope of regeneration in the novel, another liminal twilight unable to realise the reproduction of community or the family.

From thoughtless idiots to thoughtful idiolects

The social disjunction of the novel is embedded in its very language. Whilst Welsh's technique unleashes an Edinburgh demotic that gives voices to a social class that either had been completely silenced or appeared in caricature form without thought or emotional and inner complexity, the subtleties between the registers of the diverse range of protagonists serves to highlight the disruption of community between them. So although Welsh's vernacular monologues and epiphanies grant an interiority to a class of characters who would once have been represented as thoughtless idiots whose personalities are transcribed and explained to readers in Standard English, his range of distinctive demotic rhythms offers not *sociolect* (a communally shared social language) but *idiolect*. As Derek Paget outlines:

> The strength of idiolect in the novel is ultimately the element most 'transformable' in terms of acted performance on stage and screen. 'Idiolect' (a term from linguistics) conflates the prefix 'idio-', or personal and private, and the suffix '-lect', or language system. The word was coined to provide an individualized equivalent to the collective 'dialect' (or shared local/regional language system) . . . It is a kind of vocal fingerprinting.[27]

Hence, as Alan Freeman argues: 'With its serially published episodes and many voices, *Trainspotting* embodies in its form not just the local system of working-class Edinburgh dialect, without compromise to a supposed standard position in language; it also enacts the tension within this system, between different social registers, divergent discourses within which to interpret reality'.[28] One of the most obvious distinctions between competing idioms and discursive constructions of reality concerns the gender politics of the novel. Whilst the names of the female characters remain fixed – Diane, Kelly, Lesley and so on – the male figures are subject to continually shifting designations. Mark Renton is most often referred to as Rents and Rent Boy, whilst Simon David Williamson is termed Sick Boy – due to his offensive humour and actions rather than for health reasons – though he prefers Si and Simone, most notably when re-inventing himself as a parodic James Bond figure in an invented friendship with Edinburgh-born actor Sean Connery. Daniel Murphy is commonly Spud – so much so that he even confesses that 'ah sometimes forget ma name' (*T* 124) – whilst the psychotic Francis Begbie is also known as Franco, the General, the Beggar (though no one has the temerity to refer to him as this to his face). The various guises denote different positions with male subcultures and peer group hierarchies. For example, Rab McLaughlin is dubbed Second Prize due to his tendency to lose fights that he is involved in. Indeed, Renton complains that 'hardly anybody calls us Mark. It's usually Rents, or worse, the Rent Boy. That is fuckin awful getting called that' (*T* 11). He notably refers to himself as 'us', as a compendium of identities. All of his nicknames – whether Rents or Rent Boy – connote a lack of proper ownership of himself or his locale and a sense of commercial and sexual exploitation. The multifarious nature of the male nicknames at one level heightens the sense of masculinity in crisis, designated a fractured multiplicity of competing identities for each character. These plural identities indicate the differing and often contradictory peer groups and social circumstances in which the male characters function. At another level, however, it can also be suggested that the reason there are so many different male names, whilst the female characters' names remained fixed, resides in the fact that the male characters are dealt with in much more depth and sustained interest than the occasional interventions of female personae.

Often the male characters relate to women as objects upon which they project their various anxieties, hostilities, desires. Paradigmatic here is Tommy's desire to reduce his girlfriend Lizzy to a purely sexual object bounded by a domestic rather than public or social sphere: 'Ah know ah shouldnae be disclosing aboot our life, man, but the image of her in bed is so strong that even her social coarseness and permanent sense ay outrage fail to weaken it. Ah jist pure wish that Lizzy could always be like she is in bed' (*T* 72). Christopher Whyte suggests that: 'While the men in Irvine Welsh's *Trainspotting* are far from idealised, the book does not exactly apologise for the contempt they show their women'.[29] Nonetheless, there are moments in the novel in which the female characters are permitted a voice that radically redraws the male dominated narrative or when individual male characters themselves become detached from the homosocial bonds that so often define them. Diane's first person narration in the chapter 'Feeling Free' offers a notable site of a resistant female agency challenging the dominant male assumptions of the novel and the society it represents. Diane and Ali's confrontation with the overbearing sexism of a gang of men in the pub also produces an alliance with two New Zealand lesbians that marks a rare instance of female solidarity – from which Renton tactfully withdraws. This unmediated

female freedom is then followed by 'The Elusive Mr Hunt' in which
Sick Boy's prank phone call tricks the barmaid Kelly into asking the
punters if anyone has seen Mark Hunt ('my cunt'). But amidst the
raucous laughter of the men in the bar, the third person narrative
retreats from complicity with this very male and public humiliation of
Kelly into Renton's jarring awareness:

> Renton looks at her and sees her pain and anger. It cuts him up. It con-
> fuses him. Kelly has a great sense of humour. What's wrong with her?
> The knee-jerk thought: *Wrong time of the month* is forming in his head
> when he looks about and picks up the intonations of the laughter
> around the bar. It's not funny laughter . . . This is lynch mob laughter'.
> (*T* 279)

Self-reflexively, Welsh professes that as a writer he is engaged in
undercutting such male peer group behaviour rather than recapitu-
lating it:

> what is it about listening to horrible things that makes people feel good?
> It's a vicarious thing, it's a weird fucking *Schadenfreude*: it's like if some-
> thing's happening to someone else and it's not happening to me then
> therefore I should rejoice. But it's a horrible mirthless laughter. And
> when you tap into that level, then that's not really representing the cul-
> ture at all'.[30]

In terms of gender, then, the polyphony of voices which comprises
Trainspotting and which undermines the supremacy of any one voice
therein does permit an underscoring of the admittedly dominant
male viewpoints and peer groups. Kelly offers the following picture of
Renton: 'Mark can be affectionate, but he doesnae seem tae really
need people' (*T* 302). There is a parallel abnegation of responsibilities
towards women between Renton's vagueness about whether he was
the father of the child which Kelly had to have aborted and Sick Boy's
refusal to declare that he fathered Lesley's baby Dawn who dies in
infancy. But overall, in contrast to the unchecked and self-serving nar-
cissism of Sick Boy, chapters such as 'The Elusive Mr Hunt' suggest
that Renton sometimes displays empathy towards women and offers
glimpses of a more progressive model of masculinity to be wrought
out of the crisis of its traditional forms. Renton also admits having a
homosexual encounter in 'London Crawling' (*T* 233–234) and though
the incident is not represented in straightforwardly enlightened
terms Renton does allow that other experiences and fulfilments are
possible. If he is self-aware without always acting upon that aware-

ness morally, Renton is the novel's most shrewd reader of the inter-relations between language and power and his own capacity to code shift – to employ a term from linguistics, to navigate differing regis-ter of language according to specific circumstances – is at some level a model for *Trainspotting* itself and its modulation of discourses and tones. Renton's skill in negotiating a subversive path through the implications of power in language is demonstrated by 'Speedy Recruitment' and 'Courting Disaster'.

'Speedy Recruitment' recounts the strategies of Renton and Spud who have been sent for an amphetamine-fuelled interview by the dole office and who want to fail the interview but yet not appear to have deliberately done so or their unemployment benefit will be halted. Renton fears the interview is going too well and neatly shifts into an earnest, repenting Standard English through which to impart his guarantor of continuing unemployment: 'I've had a long-standing problem with heroin addiction. I've been trying to combat this, but it has curtailed my employment activities. I feel it's important to be honest and mention this to you, as a potential future employer. A stunning *coup de maître*. They shift nervously in their seats' (*T* 65). Spud, on the other hand, fears he will get the job when it is obvious both to the interview panel and to the reader that he stands no chance. When asked by the interviewers if he has any weaknesses, Spud responds: 'Ah suppose man, ah'm too much ay a perfectionist, ken? It's likesay, if things go a bit dodgy, ah jist cannae be bothered. Y'know? Ah git good vibes aboot this interview the day though man, ken?' (*T* 67). 'Courting Disaster' makes the differences between Renton and Spud more tragically apparent, as Spud is sent to prison for stealing books whilst Renton avoids incarceration due to his manipulation of the social and linguistic etiquettes of the courtroom. Renton shifts codes from his Leith vernacular to Standard English and when the disbelieving judge questions him about his claim that he stole the books to read rather than to sell, Renton offers an articu-late reading of Søren Kierkegaard's philosophy as evidence thereof. However, he also returns to his Leith demotic to display due 'defer-ence' so as not to antagonise the judge by appearing 'a smart cunt' (*T* 166). When he escapes a prison sentence, Renton duly returns solemnly to Standard English to profess to the judge: 'With god's help, I'll beat this disease. Thank you again . . . The magistrate looks closely at us tae see if thirs any sign ay mockery oan ma face. No chance it'll show' (*T* 167). So Renton is able to subvert the language of power, to expose it as merely one discourse amongst others, and he makes a mockery of its claims to truth, justice, objectivity. Renton turns the language of the court against itself, exploiting its codes and conventions. For the reader, the scene establishes Renton as a fundamentally unreliable narrator who can code shift and appropriate different registers of language for his own purposes. Renton is also therefore a figure of the novel itself and its formal techniques which strategically blend the vernacular and Standard English. By contrast, Spud's voice is struck by 'confusion' (T 166) and it is notable that whilst the judge affords Renton an understanding and takes his heroin addiction into account – due to his appeal to the judge in the language of power – he is incapable of granting Spud any sense of interiority and instead considers him a habitual thief without conscience or remorse who must be given a custodial ten month sentence. Standard English, therefore, is incapable of registering Spud's experience or feelings and, if you like, the sentences which it hands down are also an inaccessible form for him to try to convey that experience. The incapacity of the court and its language of power to understand Spud's predicament is symptomatic of a broader misapprehension of the experiences of the oppressed by those in power. The judge's inability to attribute feelings to Spud is directly related to the incapacity of the dominant discourse which the judge represents to permit an articulation of oppressed voices. Hence, the importance of the vernacular in *Trainspotting* is that it is offered as a mode that is capable of thought, feeling, intelligence, philosophy and so on. The polyphony of demotic voices provides a range of experiential discourses that articulate those oppressed groups without register in Standard English.

The chapter, 'The First Day of the Edinburgh Festival', details Renton's desperate attempts to score heroin from Mikey Forrester and juxtaposes a Bakhtinian carnivalesque culture with the official city arts festival. Having been fobbed off with opium suppositories rather than heroin which he can inject, Renton inserts them but then must suddenly rush to the only available toilet in a bookmaker's shop on his walk home:

> Ah empty ma guts, feeling as if everything; bowel, stomach, intestines, spleen, liver, kidneys, heart, lungs and fucking brains are aw falling through ma arsehole intae the bowl. As ah shit, flies batter oaf ma face, sending shivers through ma body. Ah grab at one, and tae ma surprise and elation, feel it buzzing in ma hand. Ah squeeze tightly enough tae

immobilise it. Ah open ma mitt tae see a huge, filthy bluebottle, a big, furry currant ay a bastard.

Ah smear it against the wall opposite; tracing out an 'H' then an 'I' then a 'B' wi ma index finger, using its guts, tissue and blood as ink. Ah start oan the 'S' but ma supply grows thin. Nae problem. Ah borrow fae the 'H', which has a thick surplus, and complete the 'S'. Ah sit back as far as ah can, withoot sliding intae the shit-pit below ays, and admire ma handiwork. The vile bluebottle, which caused me a great deal of distress, has been transformed intae a work of art which gives me much pleasure tae look at (*T* 26).

Nicholas M. Williams avers that:

> Welsh's Scots resists the transparency of much novelistic discourse to draw attention to itself as a writing from the body . . . The meaning of the suppository, and perhaps the meaning of heroin generally throughout the book, is to reveal the material basis of all 'elevated' notions, the lowness hidden beneath all highs, whether they be art, middle-class respectability, English superiority, or the English language itself.[31]

Part of the transgressive, carnivalesque force of this passage – given its juxtaposition with the Edinburgh Festival – resides in its consideration of cultural production and its collapsing of the boundaries between high and low culture. Renton's work of art is tellingly produced in a bookmakers – so that this production of art is housed by a space of financial speculation and a keeping of a very different kind of books. It serves to meld artistic production – and *Trainspotting* itself – to the imperatives of the market. In addition to commenting upon the contemporary interrelations of art and commerce, the scene also serves to reclaim art as popular cultural practice and to displace it from a high-minded bourgeois plateau. Susan Buck-Morss notes that the word aesthetics derives its etymology from the Greek term *Aisthitkos*, or, that which is perceptive by feeling. So aesthetics in the original import of the term foregrounds physicality and the body rather than the now established bourgeois codes of Truth, Art, Beauty.[32] Buck-Morss asserts that *an*aesthetics is a more apt term for bourgeois aesthetics which signal a shift from aesthetics being a cognitive mode of being in touch with reality to serving as a means of blocking out reality. For Buck-Morss, this bourgeois *an*aesthetics thus destroys the capacity to react politically, to map and rewrite the material reality or our selves and societies.[33] Similarly, Terry Eagleton argues that 'aesthetics is born as a discourse of the body',[34] which for-

merly encompassed the whole range of human feeling and perception rather than its contemporary attenuation as a privileged and rar-
efied domain of conceptual thought and appreciation. Eagleton
comments: 'The ultimate binding force of the bourgeois social order,
in contrast to the coercive apparatus of absolutism, will be habits,
pieties, sentiments and affections. And this is equivalent to saying
that power in such an order has become *aestheticized*'.[35] So the importance of the political reclamation of aesthetics in *Trainspotting* and
throughout Welsh's subsequent work resides in its enabling of a writing that repossesses social experience and challenges the delimitative
parameters of bourgeois discourse. In other words, such writing is
not simply an excremental exhibitionism but instead a directly political intervention that returns art to a material reality. Other key
moments in the novel of a carnivalesque transgression of established
pieties include the chapter, 'Traditional Sunday Breakfast', wherein
Davie Mitchell covers the family of his girlfriend in the excrement
which he had been attempting to smuggle out of the house in bed
linen which he had despoiled the previous evening. Most particularly,
'Eating Out' details the revenge taken by Kelly when working as a
waitress in a restaurant upon an obnoxious group of male customers.
Kelly corrupts the food of the offensive diners with bodily emissions
such as her period discharge, excrement and urine, which she adds to
their wine as the 'pish de resistance' (*T* 304). This pun notably
debases the term *pièce de la résistance* and demonstrates that the very
language and form of Welsh's writing provides a site of highly
charged resistance to the normative codes of bourgeois values.
Trainspotting began with a self-referential consideration of cultural
forms, as Renton discerns the formula of the Jean-Claude Van
Damme film which he and Sick Boy are watching: 'As happened in
such movies, they started oaf wi an obligatory dramatic opening' (*T* 3).
Trainspotting itself defeats conventional ideas of form, it is non-linear,
episodic and the politics of the body in the novel also finds a correlative in its form which flows through various openings, emissions,
transgressive fluidities.

The other character who possesses a comparable and manipulative
capacity to code shift through differing linguistic registers is Sick
Boy. After the novel's first three chapters powered by Renton's voice,
'In Overdrive' introduces Sick Boy's first person narration with the
following words: 'I do wish that ma semen-rectumed chum, the
Rent Boy, would stop slavering in ma fucking ear' (*T* 27). On a self-

referential level, this is exactly what has so far comprised the novel itself, through the intimate enveloping of the reader in Renton's voice and thoughts. A dramatic change of perspective is instigated that typifies the whole novel's shifting, cinematic montage of viewpoints and voices. Aptly, therefore, Renton and Sick Boy are asked by a group of female Chinese tourists if they know the venue of a performance of Bertolt Brecht's work during the festival. Sick Boy – adopting his satiric Sean Connery/James Bond persona – comments: 'Now Rents is gibbering oan aboot *Galileo* and *Mother Courage* and *Baal* and aw that shite. The bitches seem quite impressed n aw. Why fuck me insensible! This doss cunt actually does have his uses. It's an amazing world. *Yesh Shimon, the more I shee, the less I believe.* You and me boash, Sean' (*T* 29–30). Brecht is an apposite cultural allusion in comprehending the narrative technique of the novel since he developed a theory termed the *Verfremdungseffekt* or *alienation effect*. Writing specifically about the theatre, Brecht outlines the alienation effect thus: 'The efforts in question were directed to playing in such a way that the audience was hindered from simply identifying itself with the characters in the play. Acceptance or rejection of their actions and utterances was meant to take place on a conscious plane, instead of, as hitherto, in the audience's subconscious'.[36] *Mutatis mutandis*, the narrative of *Trainspotting* continually immerses us in the thoughts of individual characters, then alienates and distances us from them through radical shifts of voice or through a withdrawal into a dissecting third person overview in a process which continually repositions the reader critically. The direct political purpose, for Brecht, in this effect was an 'alienating of the familiar' in order 'to free socially-conditioned phenomena from that stamp of familiarity which protects them against grasp today'.[37] The polyphonic narrative method deployed by *Trainspotting* similarly refuses the reader's desire to establish supposedly intuitive empathy or affinity with each character by drawing us into their monologues but then distancing us from them, so that each character and the political and social features that they represent are engaged with critically and starkly.

The contradictions of Sick Boy's persona and politics are foregrounded in this chapter with cutting clarity. When accused by Renton of being sexist, Sick Boy retorts: 'The fact that you use the term "cunt" in the same breath as "sexist" shows that ye display the same muddled, fucked-up thinking oan this issue as you do oan everything else' (*T* 27). However, it is Sick Boy's reasoning which is

uncovered as confused and self-defeating. To an extent, he and
Renton are adversarial alter-egos, parallel maverick individuals, but
Sick Boy lacks – and tends to highlight – Renton's redeeming self-
awareness and openness to change. Despite haranguing contemporary capitalism for 'throwing people into poverty and despair' (*T* 27),
Sick Boy is entirely self-possessed, as confirmed by the emulous Sean
Connery persona which he cultivates: 'One area in which wi differ is
looks. Sean is completely out-Sean in that department by Simone' (*T*
27). In addition to the homophobia that imbues his dismissals of his
friend Rent Boy, he regards the Chinese students with racist disdain
and labels them 'chinky chickies' and 'oriental manto'(*T* 30) – man-
tovani being rhyming slang for 'fanny' (*T* 30). More than Renton, he
is a user not just of drugs but of people too and his entrepreneurial
instincts find an outlet in his preying upon and pimping numerous
women. Where Renton offers a kind of dissenting or anarchic and
punk-influenced individualism, Sick Boy's character offers a direct
critique of the dominant market culture of the 1980s. He describes
himself as 'an extremely limited company' and declares:

> I am a dynamic young man, upwardly mobile and thrusting, thrusting,
> thrusting . . . the socialists go on about your comrades, your class, your
> union, and society. Fuck all that shite. The Tories go on about your
> employer, your country, your family. Fuck that even mair. It's me, me,
> fucking ME, Simon David Williamson, NUMERO FUCKING UNO,
> versus the world, and it's a one-sided swedge. (*T* 30)

In the context of the 1980s, Sick Boy's analysis is in fact somewhat
outmoded. As discussed in the introduction, the neo-liberal economics of Thatcherism dispensed with the older One Nation form of
Toryism and pursued a ruthlessly market-driven individualism. So
although Sick Boy believes he is engaged in oppositional thinking, he
actually voices the dominant ideology of the time and its entrepreneurial anomy: 'The score is ah'm looking eftir numero uno' (*T* 174).
If anything, Sick Boy here illustrates the contradictions of bourgeois
individualism. As Terry Eagleton explains: 'conscience, duty, legality
are essential foundations of the bourgeois social order; yet they also
serve to impede the unbridled self-development of the bourgeois subject'.[38] Although Sick Boy is keen to position himself as a dangerous
outsider who shuns the postwar social consensus, Margaret Thatcher
notably portrayed herself as a maverick figure regalvanising a sterile
mainstream:

in the eyes of the 'wet' Tory establishment I was not only a woman, but 'that woman', someone not just of a different sex, but of a different class, a person with an alarming conviction that the values and virtues of middle England should be brought to bear on the problems which the establishment consensus had created. I offended on many counts.[39]

So whilst the main characters in *Trainspotting* are often viewed as outsiders, Thatcher's sense of herself intimates that there is nothing inherently radical in such status. The meaning of the maverick outsider as a cultural figure is vastly overdetermined, as it has been historically appropriated by both left and right. In this instance, Sick Boy's seeming oppositional radicalism is nothing more than a reworking of the dominant strictures of the free-market policies pursued by the incumbent government in this decade. Hence, Murray Smith attests: 'far from railing against the conditions of their post-industrial environment, the characters in *Trainspotting* have adapted to it. Indeed in certain respects the group mirrors, rather than opposes, the strident individualism of Thatcherite neo-conservatism'.[40] And although the chapter focuses on Sick Boy's sense of himself as Numero Uno, it finishes with another number: 'as long as there's an opportunity tae get off wi a woman and her purse and that's it, that is it, ah've found fuck all else, ZERO, tae fill this big, BLACK HOLE like a clenched fist in the centre ay my fucking chest' (*T* 31). One–nil to society, one might say. For the malevolent void at the core of Sick Boy's individualism serves to indict the sustained assault upon working-class communal loyalties and belonging which the novel so darkly traces.

Against that individualism, it is Spud's character that grants the novel's most empathetic – if at times pathetic – consciousness. Most admirably, he stands up to the sectarianism and racism directed at his half-black Uncle Dode in 'Na Na and Other Nazis' whilst in 'Strolling Through the Meadows' he makes a stand for a squirrel which Renton and Sick Boy are intent upon killing: 'It's mibbe nae mair vermin thin you or me, likesay . . . whae's tae say what's vermin . . . they posh wifies think people like us ur vermin, likesay, does that make it right thit they should kill us . . .ah wis jist thinking ay innocent wee things, like Dawn the bairn, ken . . . ye shouldnae hurt things, likes' (*T* 160–161). The repeated phrases of his idiolect ('ken', 'likesay', 'likes', 'cat') provide a compassionate and recurrent rhythm for his thoughts. The only other alternative to individualism amongst the main characters is the highly forced and coercive community inculcated by

Begbie. This oppressive and ultimately destructive sense of belonging is first prefigured in 'Victory on New Year's Day', in which the narrative withdraws into a third person account of Stevie's experience of a party featuring the main characters. As they listen to the band the Wolftones singing songs of Irish rebellion, the narrative traces Stevie's distance from the others:

> Stevie worried about the singing. It had a desperate edge to it. It was as if by singing loudly enough, they would weld themselves into a powerful brotherhood. It was, as the song said, 'call to arms' music, and seemed to have little to do with Scotland and New Year. It was fighting music. Stevie didn't want to fight anyone. But it was also beautiful music. (T 46)

In this instance, a highly temporary and tenuous sense of community is attained and cemented through violence and hostility. The next day Stevie feels equally isolated from his mates at the Hibs versus Hearts Edinburgh derby football match. After the game he is attacked by Hearts fans who then turn their attentions to an Asian woman:

> What charming, sensitive young men, Stevie said to the woman, who looked at him like a rabbit looks at a weasel. She saw another white youth with slurred speech, bleeding and smelling of alcohol. Above all, she saw another football scar, like the one worn by the youths who abused her. There was no colour difference as far as she was concerned, and she was right, Stevie realised with a grim sadness. It was probably just as likely to be guys in green who hassled her. Every support had its arseholes. (T 50)

Community only congregates through a vicious victimisation of others and is forged though violence. Begbie embodies this coercive belonging more than any other character and spends much of the novel attempting to force his mates into having a good time – often at the expense of others. Significantly, Renton's parents perceive Begbie to be the paradigm of Scottish manhood and wish that Mark could be more like him. Begbie provides a dark satire on the West Coast tradition of the Scottish hardman, typified by William McIlvanney's eponymous hero *Docherty*, and the novel undercuts the mythic and idealised violence of such figures. This demystification of the Scottish hardman is most cogently outlined in Renton's account of the disjunction between the myths and realities of Begbie's persona and the social bonds that he seeks to forge:

Myth: Begbie's mates like him.
Reality: They fear him.
Myth: Begbie would never waste any ay his mates.
Reality: His mates are generally too cagey tae test oot this proposition, and
  oan the odd occasion they huv done so, huv succeeded in disproving it.
Myth: Begbie backs up his mates.
Reality: Begbie smashes fuck oot ay innocent wee daft cunts whae accidently
  spill your pint or bump intae ye. Psychopaths who terrorise Begbie's mates
  usually dae so wi impunity, as they tend tae be closer mates ay Begbie's
  than the punters he hings aboot wi. He kens thum aw through approved
  school, prison n the casuals' networks, the freemasonaries that bams share.
  (T 82–83)

In one scene, Begbie throws a pint glass from a balcony in a crowded
bar with the express intent of injuring a member of a gang of men in
order to then forge an alliance with them and beat up everyone else in
the bar. This event symbolically demonstrates that the community
which Begbie represents is coerced, internecine and ultimately false.
It also impels one of the most famous or notorious – depending on
one's point of view – passages in the novel as Renton launches into a
tirade against not only Begbie but the Scotland that he perceives him
as embodying.

Scotland and postcolonialism

Renton's outburst occurs in a chapter entitled 'The Glass', which
obviously refers to the pint glass that Begbie hurls across the crowded
bar, but the chapter also divulges the distorted reflection that an inferiorised culture produces in what James Joyce once termed 'the
cracked looking-glass of a servant'.[41] The sequence indicates the distorted image produced by mirroring oneself in one's master's terms.
Not only does Renton denigrate his own Scottishness but he also – in
supposedly finding affinity with other oppressed groups – employs
the language of power and domination in his references to 'pakis' and
'poofs':

Ah hate cunts like that. Cunts like Begbie. Cunts that are intae baseball-
batting every fucker that's different; pakis, poofs, n what huv ye. Fuckin
failures in a country ay failures. It's nae good blamin it oan the English
fir colonising us. Ah don't hate the English. They're just wankers. We
are colonised by wankers. We can't even pick a decent, vibrant, healthy
culture to be colonised by. No. We're ruled by effete arseholes. What

does that make us? The lowest of the fuckin low, the scum of the earth.
The most wretched, servile, miserable, pathetic trash that was ever shat
intae creation. Ah don't hate the English. They just git oan wi the shite
thuv goat. Ah hate the Scots. (*T* 78)[42]

Brüggernmeier and Drescher posit that 'Renton's statement is . . . a
call for a new cultural independence for Scotland which could raise
the country's prestige'.[43] However, even as Renton castigates the English, he also denigrates the Scottish and others and the entire tirade is
conducted through the oppressive terms and discourses of empire –
racism, sexism, homophobia. If the issue of heroin in *Trainspotting*
were to be read in terms of national allegory, it is noteworthy that the
main characters are dependent upon something, that is, they lack
independence. Moreover, they are dependent upon something which
destroys them, erases their identity. It is possible to interpret such a
plight as a symptom of the condition of a non-independent Scotland
whose incorporation within British historical paradigms extirpated its
own identity. Renton's loathing of Scotland and its baseness notably
echoes the title of one of postcolonial literature's foundational texts –
Frantz Fanon's *The Wretched of the Earth*.[44] Fanon maintains that in
the power dynamics of the colonial relationship: 'Every effort is made
to bring the colonised person to admit the inferiority of his culture
which has been transformed into instinctive patterns of behaviour, to
recognise the unreality of his "nation."'[45] Renton's outburst is entirely
in keeping with Fanon's diagnosis since it not only locates the
Scottish as inferior but also castigates Scotland's failure to be a coherent nation. However, Renton's claim that Scotland was colonised by
England – and this evocation of Fanon in relation to Scotland – are
contentious. In another key postcolonial text, *The Empire Writes Back*,
Bill Ashcroft, Gareth Griffiths and Helen Tiffin argue with regard to
Ireland, Scotland and Wales that: 'While it is possible to argue that
these societies were the first victims of English expansion, their subsequent complicity in the British imperial enterprise makes it difficult for colonized peoples outside Britain to accept their identity as
post-colonial'.[46] They perceive Ireland, Scotland and Wales as white,
European and metropolitan spaces that cannot be deemed postcolonial but may only be interpreted 'in relation to the English "mainstream"'.[47] In terms of *Trainspotting* itself, whilst Renton claims
colonial status for Scotland, his brother Billy represents a pro-British
and loyalist side not only of their family but also Scotland and he is
eventually killed serving in the British army in Northern Ireland. So

can Scotland be designated as coloniser or colonised? Or can it conceivably be both?

Two significant books that seek to justify the relevance of Fanon's work to Scotland's position in relation to England and Britishness are Craig Beveridge and Ronald Turnbull's *The Eclipse of Scottish Culture* and Cairns Craig's *Out of History*. In seeking to adapt Fanon's analysis to Scotland, Cairns Craig asserts:

> It is not by our colour, of course, that we have stood to be recognised as incomplete within the British context, it is by the colour of our vowels: the rigidity of class speech in Britain, the development of Received Pronunciation as a means of class identity, is the direct response of a dominant cultural group faced by a society in which the outsiders are indistinguishable by colour.[48]

This analysis, however, elides a class issue (the subordination of working-class language) with a national one (Scotland's marginalisation as a nation). Most problematically, there is also a danger in collapsing racisms based upon colour and ethnicity with inequalities derived from class or national distinctions ('the colour of our vowels'). Nevertheless, these very interstices of nation, ethnicity and class complicate one another in a productive way. Rather than trying to situate Scotland as a homogenous entity in one of two equally monolithic outcomes (coloniser or colonised), Scotland actually facilitates a consideration of the complexities of how colonialism functions. Michael Gardiner is keen to deny Scotland postcolonial status by stressing its links with imperialism but he is also aware of a certain doubleness of ambiguity through which aspects of Scottish society have been subordinated:

> Scotland's national growth has been projected through the same enlightenment colonial moment, yet has been ambivalently controlled in economic and cultural terms by another nation, in whose own colonial adventures Scotland is implicated. Scotland is not in any sense postcolonial, but suffers from economic and cultural inequalities which can in part be articulated as part of a historical process on a national level.[49]

Gardiner continues that 'attempts to locate Scottish culture either wholly inside or outside the metropolis, as in the question "Is Scottish literature a post-colonial literature?" will always be undermined by other types of subjective structuring such as class, ethnicity, sexual difference'.[50] However, issues such as class, race and gender do not preclude a postcolonial analysis but rather demand that it refines and defines its terms according to specific social and historical conditions. To this end, Welsh's work helps dissolve a mechanistic binary between coloniser and colonised, in this case a division of the British metropole and Scotland as already agreed and monolithic entities. Colin Graham saliently notes that the 'national' does not have to be the primary level at which postcolonial criticism can operate.[51] Graham comments:

> An essential component of postcolonial criticism has been its evolution as an ethical criticism. In that it is diagnostic of a political and historical situation, postcolonialism makes the crucial identification of who is the colonizer and who is the colonized – it also morally evaluates this colonial relationship as one of fundamental inequality . . . But to allow the nation to monopolise the postcolonial field is to withhold . . . a more radical interrogation by the difficult ethics of the colonial encounter.[52]

Graham specifically invokes the Subaltern Studies aspect of postcolonial criticism, which emanated primarily through the Subaltern Studies Group in India under Ranajit Guha and which derives its name from the Italian Marxist Antonio Gramsci's designation of oppressed groups of people as subalterns. The term subaltern incorporates class analysis but also expands upon it to investigate how class intersects with other disempowerments related to gender, sexuality, race, colonialism and so on. Subaltern Studies professedly:

> aligns itself with social groups which it sees as excluded, dominated, elided and oppressed by the state . . . and as something of a necessary by-product of this mission, Subaltern Studies allows for an understanding of the postcolonial nation in a new way – no longer need the nation be regarded as the glorious achievement and fruition of the labours of an oppressed people.[53]

Hence, the nation does not have to be the ethical *telos* or ultimate aim of decolonisation, nor should an analysis of colonialism as process be necessarily conducted in national terms. Consequently, the reconstitution of a devolved Scottish parliament in 1999 does not rid Scotland of poverty, racism, patriarchy, sexism and so on: rather it merely offers a national forum in which these issues may be tackled or for that matter a national framework wherein they may be perpetuated. And by extension, the new Scottish parliament does not suddenly make redundant the work of writers such as Welsh or his predecessors such as James Kelman, Tom Leonard or Lewis Grassic Gibbon as such writing was always concerned with more than a purely 'national' problematic of identity and, in many cases, was actually directly hostile to the hegemonic nation. The Subaltern Studies method therefore permits an understanding of how large sections of Scottish society benefited from British imperialism whilst others were subject to its destructive force. A subaltern methodology ruptures the idea that the nation proffers an identity of interest supposedly shared by all Scottish people equally. Moreover, it illustrates that the colonial binary – whether Britain/empire or England/Scotland – misleadingly implies that each homogeneous term contains a society comprised entirely of oppressors or victims respectively. Subaltern analysis demonstrates that colonialism also aims to hold in place specific sets of iniquitous social relations in the colonial nation or metropole – and its immediate peripheries – informed by class, gender and so on. Indeed, Gramsci's definition of subalternity facilitates an understanding of the very form of *Trainspotting* and much of Welsh's other disjointed fictions: 'The history of subaltern social groups is necessarily fragmented and episodic' and is 'continually interrupted by the activity of the ruling groups'.[54] Just as Renton's diatribe against the wretchedness of the Scots attests to the existence of a Scottish subaltern class, so too his brother Billy's military service in the British Army in Northern Ireland exposes other forms of Scottish identity that are complicit in the maintenance of Britishness and the residues of imperialism. So one of the novel's subtleties with regard to post-colonialism resides in its figuration of conflictual Scotlands at once willing participants and disenfranchised resistors in the cementing of the British nation state and empire.

Another instance of Scotland's impacted status as the collision of competing narratives of empire and decolonisation is granted by Sick Boy's mimicry of Sean Connery and James Bond. At one level, this parody forms part of Welsh's hostility to the conventional bourgeois hero in the novel. Welsh castigates bourgeois writing in which:

> every fucking male character is a derivation of the same white, male, aspirational, Cambridge-educated fucking James Bond – from even the good writing, like Martin Amis, to the worst, is [sic] all fucking just a derivation of that. I mean, one of the best writers in the world, in terms of writing technique, is Martin Amis – and even he just sets himself up, it's all just a derivation of that type.[55]

However, Bond as a figure is also often taken as the paradigm of a particularly British – even English – imperial hero. The author of the

Bond novels was the Scot, Ian Fleming, whilst Bond as a character is part Scottish.[56] Both Fleming and Bond as a character position Scotland in an assertion of British identity, empire and world dominance. Yet Sick Boy's parody also undermines that status in terms of social class and the disruptive voice of the subaltern. Homi Bhabha's theory of 'colonial mimicry' examines how the discourse of power is mimicked to subversive effect by 'a subject of a difference that is almost the same, but not quite'.[57] Rather than merely affirming Scotland's unitary relationship to empire, Sick Boy's mimicry problematises the capacity of this dominant Scotland and its attachment to the imperial voice of power, disrupts its capacity to incorporate, to universalise itself: 'mimicry is at once resemblance and menace . . . what emerges between mimesis and mimicry is a *writing*, a mode of representation, that marginalizes the monumentality of history, quite simply mocks its power to be a model, that power which supposedly makes it imitable'.[58]

The end of the line

Renton's decision at the end of the novel to violate the Leith code – never rip off your mates – and take the proceeds from the drug deal in London to embark on a new life in Amsterdam presents the reader with some interesting questions. Do we sympathise with his need to escape finally the deathly constriction of Leith? Or should we condemn his character in this clinching act of cynical opportunism? Is this the defiant act of a dissenting anti-hero? Or does Renton merely replicate the dominant, self-serving materialistic ethos of his age? Notably, Renton strives to justify his decision by divesting himself of the social attachment which the other characters represent. He feels that Sick Boy would do the same thing if given the opportunity, whilst Spud again functions as a conscience in the novel – this time encouraging a compassion in Renton that ensures he sends Spud his share of the money. It is Begbie, however, who embodies everything from which Renton seeks to escape and grants him his main reason for his action:

> Renton had used Begbie, used him to burn his boats completely and utterly. It was Begbie who ensured he could never return. He had done what he wanted to do. He could now never go back to Leith, to Edinburgh, even to Scotland, ever again. There, he could not be anything other than he was. Now, free from them all, for good, he could be what

he wanted to be. He'd stand or fall alone. This thought both terrified and excited him as he contemplated life in Amsterdam. (*T* 344)

It is highly germane that Renton should have been asked to explain the philosophy of Søren Kierkegaard during the courtroom scene. Kierkegaard (1813–55), who is generally considered one of the first existentialists, wanted his own epitaph to be 'That Individual'. The dialectic between terror and excitement which Renton experiences in the final lines of *Trainspotting* chimes with Kierkegaard's call for the assertion of the individual through true and meaningful personal choice characterised by a dread or *angst* that is really 'the dizziness of freedom, which occurs when freedom looks down into its own possibility'.[59] Kierkegaard argues that to avoid ultimate despair the individual must make a leap of faith and suspend ethical, universal or objective standards. Hence, the individual is not a product of its age but rather a product of its own choices. It is only in these moments of painful personal decision that we grasp the reality of our existences. Kierkegaard maintains: 'In making a choice, it is not so much a question of choosing the right as of the energy, the earnestness, the pathos with which one chooses. Thereby the personality announces its inner infinity, and thereby, in turn, the personality is consolidated'.[60] Kierkegaard's philosophy offers a supreme assertion of the individual and an attendant diminution of social codes. In the context of the Thatcherite 1980s, is Renton's final choice an antidote to the vacuous freedom that is defined solely in economic and consumer rather than ethical terms in his 'Choose Life' tirade? Or is it highly problematic – a recapitulation of that individual opportunism? The final chapter is significantly narrated in the third person, the conventional novelistic framework of the bourgeois individual and its milieu. In terms of the politics of literary register, the Standard English of this passage and its omniscient narration suggest that Renton's newly made selfhood is an assent to the bourgeois subject. Thus, Alan Sinfield avers: 'Like the standard hero(ine) of the bourgeois novel, he becomes wiser during the action of the book, reaches an accommodation with the world, and is ready, on the last page, to restart life from a new perspective'.[61] Ultimately it is money and a jettisoning of social belonging that facilitates Renton's freedom but this can be read as much as an indictment of his times as a capitulation to them. But Renton's decision to ditch the past and reinvent himself anew also adumbrates the Britain in which the novel was adapted for the cinema

screen and the *Trainspotting* product became a part of what was to
become Cool Britannia.

Trendspotting: screening *Trainspotting*

To screen is not only to display but also to vet and to conceal. Much as
Danny Boyle's 1995 film version of *Trainspotting* makes visually stunning use of Welsh's grotesque realism, it in many ways jettisons
important aspects of the novel's political force. John Hodge's screenplay occludes issues of de-industrialisation, class tensions, racism,
sectarianism, domestic violence, sexism or homophobia, precisely
due to the film's need to reach an international youth culture market.
If in the novel *Trainspotting* life is effaced by a pervasive atmosphere
of death, then in the film life is displaced by lifestyle. In fact, the
tensions between the novel and the film version of *Trainspotting* –
given that the latter completely eviscerates the powerful class content
of the former into a youth culture of styles and poses – serve to evidence further the novel's own points about the erasure of class
dynamics within the dominant intellectual strands of contemporary
society. It is tempting to regard the opening sequence of the film, in
which the screenwriter John Hodge cameos as one of the security
guards chasing Renton from Edinburgh city centre, as a striking
visual symbol of the banishing of the class content of the novel by the
screenplay. There is also a profound irony in the fact that the film was
mainly shot on location in Glasgow, given that the novel sought to
redress the Scottish West Coast domination of depictions of working-
class life. Moreover, the main film sets were constructed in the old
Wills' cigarette factory in Glasgow – which is now redeveloped as
office space – so that where the novel elegises the replacement of
Leith Central Station by commercial space, the film's production
materially makes entrepreneurial use of exactly that process of de-
industrialisation.[62]

In terms of the filmic representation of working-class life, the
1960s and 1970s witnessed a growth in social realist cinema which
sought to depict the realities and depredations of poverty. As John
Hill summarises: 'traditionally social realism within Britain has been
associated with the *making visible* of the working class'.[63] By contrast,
the film version of *Trainspotting* eschews social realism and if anything makes class *invisible*, overwritten by style and commodified
identities. Writing in the sleeve notes to *Trainspotting: The Definitive*

Edition DVD box set, Welsh expresses satisfaction with the film's adaptation and the politics of its stylistic technique:

> Almost everyone I spoke to about the sale of the film rights wanted to make a po-faced piece of social realism like *Christiane F.* or *The Basketball Diaries*; in other words, a piece of mind-numbing tedium which nobody outside of a few broadsheet bores wanted to watch. Refreshingly, Andrew Macdonald, Danny Boyle, and John Hodge shared my vision of *Trainspotting*. As Renton says in the film, 'Times were changing, drugs were changing, people were changing.' Nowadays, younger working-class people grow up in a society in which the main institutions of socialisation, where kids learn morality – the family, the community, the trade unions and the churches – have been emasculated by the promotion of consumerism and the market economy. They grow up exploring a psychoactive terrain, stimulated by computer technology and advertising. For the rampant consumerism of the Eighties had other outcomes: certain drugs, once the preserve of a bohemian elite, found their way into mass culture . . . Danny, Andrew, John, and myself were all determined that the characters in *Trainspotting* were not victims, but ordinary punters functioning within this social reality. To portray them as victims, à la Sixties and Seventies 'political art', may have been useful in a welfarist society, such as the postwar set-up in Britain. Here the (usually middle- or upper-class) artist could wallow in showing clichéd representations of misery and the adverse conditions of working-class life, in order to try to shame the powers-that-be into dedicating resources to make things better. Now all this approach provides is a smug affirmation for the bourgeoisie that it's better to be on the monied [sic] side. So tell us something we didn't know.

Whilst the desire to avoid cliché or a condescending portrayal of the characters as merely passive victims is salutary, there is nonetheless a dangerous insinuation that being underclass is nothing more than a lifestyle option if the socio-economic conditions facing working-class people are erased. Furthermore, although Welsh castigates middle-class writers and producers within social realist cinema for producing images of working-class life that ultimately affirm their own bourgeois values, surely the ultimate triumph of such a bourgeois value system would be to eradicate working-class culture altogether by rewriting it in the dominant bourgeois terms of society. So despite the accusation that social realism offers a stylised, middle-class view of working-class poverty, the film version of *Trainspotting* offers underclass existence not as the result of a complex set of socio-economic realities and conflicts but rather as a commodity to be consumed. Given that the decade in which the novel and film are set witnessed a full-scale assault upon working-class resistance to the policies of the free market and commodity culture, then such a Thatcherite project surely finds affinity with a film that arrogates the living culture of the working class and then seeks to remarket it back to them as a commodity. In terms of Thatcherism, the film also elides difference between Sick Boy and Renton in the novel, as Renton in the film version extols the virtues of London and its economic opportunities by choosing almost exactly Margaret Thatcher's pronouncement on the redundancy of the reality and concept of society: 'There was no such thing as society, and even if there was I most certainly had nothing to do with it. For the first time in my adult life, I was almost content'.[64] As Alan Sinfield comments: 'there is no equivalent to any of this in the novel . . . By destroying the distinction between them, the film cancels Renton's leftish rebellion, making Thatcherite selfishness the "natural" way, on or off heroin, to live'.[65]

One of the most stringent critiques of the film and the figure of Renton came from the novelist Will Self who maintains that the whole project panders to the whims of a somewhat professional class disenchantment and ennui: 'I very much doubt that anyone who comes out of *Trainspotting* will spend the next few hours earnestly debating the whys and wherefores of the human tragedy it profits from'. Instead, Self argues, the film is 'evocative of a more generalised nihilism that infests twenty-somethings at the moment'.[66] Self – a former heroin addict himself – accuses Welsh of being a 'drug voyeur' who is able to write convincingly about travails of drug addiction without being an addict and Self goes further in reading the visual symbolism of Renton's figure at the film's closure: 'I can't help feeling that the closing sequence of the film, in which Mark Renton 'free of junk' heads for the open road with a flight bag full of cash, having ripped off his mates, isn't in some way an ironic reflection of Irvine Welsh, breaking for the border with his profits from this meretricious adaptation of an important book'.[67] On that note, it is telling that the marketing of the film in various forms – as video, as DVD, spin-off compilations of music, and reprints of the novel – employs Renton's 'Choose Life' monologue which was originally designed to vitiate the vacuity of consumer culture. A *Trainspotting 2* CD was released in 1997 to coincide with the first screening of the film on British television on 26 November 1997, whilst in 2003 on the tenth anniversary of the publication of the novel a DVD re-issue of the film was marketed in the following way on its cover and publicity advertisements: 'Choose the 2 disc Definitive Edition, pumped full of extras; Choose the best British film of the decade. Choose *Trainspotting*'. With these successive *Trainspotting* releases, *Trainspotting* as product has been reduced to the meaningless and seemingly unending seriality of late capitalism which the trainspotting metaphor of the novel itself first identifies.

Given that the novel gave voice to an unrepresented and marginalised substrata of Edinburgh who were excluded from the mainstream narratives of society, it is also heavily ironic that the film and the *Trainspotting* commodity became a constituent parts of a dominant reassertion of Britishness from the mid-1990s to the present that was typified in 1997 by the victorious New Labour government's sponsoring of 'Cool Britannia'.[68] Cool Britannia – which has served as the title of a Bonzo Dog Do Dah Band song in 1967 and a flavour of Ben & Jerry's ice cream in the 1990s – obviously puns upon Rule Britannia and the term was utilised as part of a concerted and government co-ordinated effort to replace Britain's Victorian, imperial and industrial history with a newly marketable image of hipness and diversity. The New Labour Culture Secretary Chris Smith pronounced in 1997 that 'Cool Britannia is here to stay'.[69] Before that, the then Conservative Culture Secretary Virginia Bottomley attended a screening of *Trainspotting* at Cannes Film Festival in May 1996 and offered the following explanation for doing so despite the drugs content of the movie: 'I think I should see a film that's been so successful'.[70] One key source of this global rebranding of Britain as seductive commodity was the political Think Tank, Demos, who published a book by Mark Leonard in 1997 entitled *BritainTM: Renewing Our Identity*.[71] Leonard argues:

> where Britain is recognised, it is seen as a country whose time has come and gone – bogged down by tradition, riven by class and threatened by industrial disputes, the IRA and poverty-stricken inner cities [. . .] There has been a renaissance of the British film industry, with the success of such films as *Four Weddings and a Funeral* (the most successful British film ever, grossing more than £160 million world-wide), *Trainspotting* and *The English Patient* . . . Britain is a hybrid nation – always mixing diverse elements together into something new. Not a melting pot that moulds disparate ethnicities into a conformist whole, but a country that thrives on diversity and uses it to constantly renew and re-energise itself [. . .] But it is not just ethnicities that are mixed – Britain is also the

world's capital of ways of living, the home of happily co-existing subcultures—from punks and ravers to freemasons and gentlemen's clubs.
Britain is the least pure of European countries, more mongrel and better
prepared for a world that is continually generating new hybrid forms.[72]

Notably, *Trainspotting* is here included in an assertion of a healthy cultural diversity and plurality not as a document of social exclusion or
inequality. The erasure of the novel's class dynamics results in a shift
from recognising social difference as constituted by inequality and
disadvantage to the depoliticised celebration of social difference as
cultural diversity. Under such terms, the de-industrialisation and the
destruction of traditional working-class communities and alliances
that are so darkly traced by the novel in fact become positively valued
attributes of a vibrantly rebranded Britishness. Similarly, Martin
Wroe distinguishes between 'Jane Spotters' and 'Trainspotters' as two
distinct sociological groups – those consumers who flock to watch
Sense and Sensibility and those who viewed *Trainspotting*: 'two films
that define the sensibilities of the nation'.[73] Again *Trainspotting* is
enlisted to make a point about cultural and consumer diversity of the
nation rather than its inequalities. Furthermore, the nation in question is Britain. This reassertion of Britishness as Cool Britannia coin-
cides exactly with the establishment of newly devolved parliaments
and assemblies in Scotland, Wales and Northern Ireland. As Murray
Pittock asserts: 'it is no coincidence that the Demos-led rebranding of
Britain, whether as "Cool Britannia" or otherwise, has accompanied
the first major redefinitions of Britishness in three-quarters of a century'.[74] Pittock continues:

> the extent to which English identity has found its recent historic expres-
> sion only through notions of Britishness emphasizes the degree to
> which the Celtic margins are organically important in confirming,
> through their own marginality, the English possession of that British-
> ness: it is no coincidence that English *qua* English identity is now being
> more closely examined in the aftermath of Scotland's (more especially
> than Wales's) 1997 referendum. The knee-jerk hostility often visible to
> what some see as Scotland's special pleading for a difference greater
> than Yorkshire is often, on close examination, seen to be an anger at per-
> ceived theft. Scotland has made claims for its own territoriality: and as
> Britons, many English believe that Scotland belongs to them.[75]

The rebranded Britain became a new means through which to
reassert a territorial claim over newly regalvanised constituent parts

which in turn renewed the whole. The film version of *Trainspotting* helped to provide a shot in the arm for British film production and cinema, as well as popular music such as the Britpop trend. Notable Britpop artists such Damon Albarn and Sleeper recorded songs for the soundtrack album and, in doing so, threw the timeframe and the musical references off kilter by replacing 1980s songs, such as The Smiths' 'There Is a Light that Never Goes Out', that are alluded to in the novel. Welsh had attributed some of his own success to a by-product of the 'colonial guilt-trip, a sense that the mainstream of writers has run out of ideas, that they're just the same middle-class Oxbridge voices writing about the same stuff, the same concerns, that may be relevant to a small culture but not to a big society. Literary culture exists for its own references and just goes up its own arse'.[76] The Cool Britannia project deliberately sought to incorporate the Celtic and provincial fringes as a means of re-invigorating a culturally deadened British and metropolitan centre. Welsh is forthright in his unease with the appropriation of *Trainspotting* in the New Labour cultural agenda:

> the major problem was the dishonesty. If Tony Blair or Chris Smith had've come up to me and said, 'We want to suck your cock' . . . but they actually sucked it without me noticing . . . It was fucking terrible, man. Naw, but that's how I feel. Also, the whole [*effects Standard English accent*] 'Britain's very hip and very cool, look at *Trainspotting*' but then at the same time, 'But, *Trainspotting*, ooh, drugs – bad, bad'. They basked in the whole afterglow of the film, isn't this cool, isn't this hip and that, without having the bollocks to admit that it was a massive contributory factor to the whole process.[77]

So despite Welsh's obvious distaste at the reappropriation by others of his prize possession – *Trainspotting*, that is – the film version has imprinted upon not only its own content and reworking of the novel but also its institutional and distributional realities the economic creeds that were the original focus of the author's contempt. The contradictions of the mainstream annexation of *Trainspotting* as both novel and film are exemplified by the reworking of its drug content. So-called 'Heroin Chic' became the fashion look of the mid-1990s, as exemplified by Kate Moss's modelling for Calvin Klein.[78] Kevin Williamson notes dryly:

> When the film *Trainspotting* hit the cinema screens in February '96, despite the intentions of all concerned with its production, the anti-hero

Renton played by Ewan McGregor – a good-looking, glamorous and hardly the archetypal junkie – became a national icon. In the wake of the movie, style magazines like *The Face, iD*, and *Blah Blah Blah* ran fashion shoots featuring gaunt skinny models in deliberately scruffy clothing which were obviously based on the idea of so-called 'heroin chic'. It was said that people who should have known better were inadvertently creating positive images of the drug that could only add to its mystique and allure. And it didn't take long for fingers to point at the movie for being responsible for an increase in the popularity of heroin. Even Presidential candidate Bob Dole jumped on the bandwagon and slammed *Trainspotting* in the 1996 US election campaign.[79]

Ewan McGregor lost two stone to play the part of Renton, though this was apparently achieved by cutting out beer, butter and milk. The novel conveys – and the film version serves as material proof – that all things may be commodified, stylised and voided of their original meanings and social referents by the economic logic of the society in which *Trainspotting* is set. The final moment in which Renton rips off his mates, as Claire Monk points out, 'addresses a generation of "Thatcher's Children" for whom the conflation of subcultural dissent and entrepreneurial capitalism holds no contradictions'.[80] The contradiction between the content of the novel's critique of consumer capitalism and the implication of *Trainspotting* as product in precisely those economic imperatives is an issue that impinges upon all of Welsh's subsequent work and impels a consideration, as 'The First Day of the Edinburgh Festival' had done, of the deep interrelations of cultural production and commerce.

Notes

1 I am grateful to Duncan McLean for discussing the matter with me in an interview on the 20 March 2003.
2 Duncan McLean, 'Introduction', *Ahead of Its Time: A Clocktower Press Anthology* (London: Jonathan Cape, 1997), xiv.
3 *In Your Face. Irvine Welsh: Condemn More, Understand Less*. BBC2. Broadcast 27 Nov 1995.
4 Elizabeth Young, 'Blood on the tracks', *Guardian* (14 Aug 1993), 33.
5 Young, 'Blood on the tracks', 33.
6 Iain Grant, 'Dealing out the capital punishment', *Sunday Times* (5 Sep 1993), 14.
7 Murray Smith, *Trainspotting* (London: BFI Publishing, 2002), 17.
8 Peter Stallybrass and Allon White, *The Politics and Poetics of Transgression* (London: Methuen, 1986), 192.

9 William McIlvanney, *Docherty* (London: Allen and Unwin, 1975), 5.

10 The most obvious example in contemporary British culture of this masculine problematic is Peter Cattaneo's 1997 film *The Full Monty*. Therein a group of steel workers in Sheffield who have been made redundant decide to become male strippers. As the title suggests, the film moves inexorably towards its final uncovering of these ex-labourers' naked bodies. Hence, the ravages of de-industrialisation are compensated in the film by a redisplay of the male body as part of a new service-based economy. Additionally, in terms of the disempowerment of traditional masculinity, one of the film's working titles was *No Man's Land*.

11 Hal Foster, 'Armor fou', *October* 57 (1991), 94.

12 Robert A. Morace, *Trainspotting: A Reader's Guide* (London: Continuum, 2001), 66.

13 Martin Brüggernmeier and Horst W. Drescher, 'A subculture and its characterization in Irvine Welsh's *Trainspotting*', *Anglistik & Englischunttericht* 63 (Winter 2000), 137.

14 William S. Burroughs, *Junky* (London: Penguin, 1977), xvi.

15 Jean Baudrillard, *Selected Writings* (Cambridge: Polity Press, 2001), 24.

16 Baudrillard, *Selected Writings*, 25.

17 See Francis Fukuyama, *The End of History and the Last Man* (London: Penguin, 1992); Daniel Bell, *The End of Ideology* (Cambridge, Mass: Harvard University Press, 1988).

18 Jean-François Lyotard, *The Postmodern Condition: A Report on Knowledge*. Trans. Geoff Bennington and Brian Massumi. Foreword by Fredric Jameson (Manchester: Manchester University Press, 1996), xxii, xxiv.

19 Lyotard, *The Postmodern Condition*, 76.

20 Alex Callinicos, *Against Postmodernism: A Marxist Critique* (Oxford: Polity Press, 1992), 162.

21 Naomi Klein, *No Logo: No Space, No Choice, No Jobs* (London: Flamingo, 2001), 129.

22 Morace, *Trainspotting*, 65.

23 Indeed, the scene, in which the middle classes patronise a work which was scandalous when first performed due to its supposed gritty realism and ground-breaking use of spoken dialogue, may be a self-referential consideration of his own middle-class readership by Welsh. Additionally, Bizet's work formed part of a long-standing tradition of French culture which exoticised and romanticised Spain and Spanish people, so that Welsh may also be flagging up his awareness of producing a touristic view of Edinburgh that panders to metropolitan stereotypes.

24 Baudrillard, *Selected Writings*, 171.

25 Cairns Craig, *The Modern Scottish Novel: Narrative and the National Imagination* (Edinburgh: Edinburgh University Press, 1999), 98.

26 Slavoj Žižek, *Looking Awry: An Introduction to Jacques Lacan through Popular Culture* (London: MIT Press, 1991), 23.

27 Derek Paget, 'Speaking out: the transformations of *Trainspotting*' in Deborah Cartmell and Imelda Whelehan, eds, *Adaptations: From Text to Screen, Screen to Text* (London: Routledge, 2002), 132–133.

28 Alan Freeman, 'Ghosts in sunny Leith: Irvine Welsh's *Trainspotting*' in Susanne Hagemann, ed., *Studies in Scottish Fiction: 1945 to the Present* (Frankfurt am Main: Peter Lang, 1996), 254.

29 Christopher Whyte, ed., *Gendering the Nation: Studies in Modern Scottish Literature* (Edinburgh: Edinburgh University Press, 1995), xv.

30 Cited in Aaron Kelly, 'Irvine Welsh in conversation with Aaron Kelly', *Edinburgh Review* 113 (2004), 10.

31 Nicholas M. Williams, 'The dialect of authenticity: the case of Irvine Welsh's *Trainspotting*' in T. Hoenselaars and Maruis Buning, eds, *English Literature and the Other Languages* (Amsterdam: Rodopi, 1999), 227.

32 Susan Buck-Morss, 'Aesthetics and anaesthetics: Walter Benjamin's artwork essay reconsidered', *October* 62 (Fall 1992), 6.

33 Buck-Morss, 'Aesthetics and anaesthetics', 18.

34 Terry Eagleton, *The Ideology of the Aesthetic* (Oxford: Basil Blackwell, 1990), 13.

35 Eagleton, *The Ideology of the Aesthetic*, 20.

36 John Willet, ed. and trans. *Brecht on Theatre* (London: Methuen, 2001), 91.

37 Willet, *Brecht on Theatre*, 192.

38 Eagleton, *The Ideology of the Aesthetic*, 242.

39 Margaret Thatcher, *The Downing Street Years* (London: Harper Collins, 1995), 129–130.

40 Smith, *Trainspotting*, 29.

41 James Joyce, *Ulysses* [1922] (London: Penguin, 1992), 6.

42 As Drew Milne notes, this passage was used in a Scottish National Party recruitment form in 1996, see 'The fiction of James Kelman and Irvine Welsh: accents, speech and writing' in Richard J. Lane et al., eds, *Contemporary British Fiction* (Oxford: Polity Press, 2003), 163.

43 Brüggernmeier and Drescher, 'A subculture and its characterization in Irvine Welsh's *Trainspotting*', 139.

44 Frantz Fanon, *The Wretched of the Earth*. Trans. Constance Farrington (Harmondsworth: Penguin, 1967).

45 Fanon, *The Wretched of the Earth*, 190.

46 Bill Ashcroft, Gareth Griffiths and Helen Tiffin, *The Empire Writes Back: Theory and Practice in Post-Colonial Literatures* (London: Routledge, 2002), 31–32.

47 Ashcroft, Griffiths and Tiffin, *The Empire Writes Back*, 31.

48 Cairns Craig, *Out of History: Narrative Paradigms in Scottish and British Culture* (Edinburgh: Polygon, 1996), 12.
49 Michael Gardiner, 'Democracy and Scotland's postcoloniality', *Scotlands* 3: 2 (1996), 36.
50 Gardiner, 'Democracy and Scotland's postcoloniality', 39.
51 Colin Graham, *Deconstructing Ireland* (Edinburgh: Edinburgh University Press, 2001), 81.
52 Graham, *Deconstructing Ireland*, 82.
53 Graham, *Deconstructing Ireland*, 83.
54 Antonio Gramsci, *Selections from the Prison Notebooks*. Ed. and trans. Quintin Hoare and Geoffrey Nowell Smith (London: Lawrence and Wishart, 1996), 54–55.
55 Cited in Kelly, 'Irvine Welsh in conversation with Aaron Kelly', 16–17.
56 Despite his worldwide association with Englishness, Bond has more often than not been played on screen by actors from the so-called Celtic fringes of the Commonwealth: Sean Connery, George Lazenby, Timothy Dalton, Pierce Brosnan.
57 Homi K. Bhabha, *The Location of Culture* (London: Routledge, 1994), 86.
58 Bhabha, *The Location of Culture*, 86–87.
59 Søren Kierkegaard, *The Concept of Dread* (1844). Trans. Walter Lowrie (Princeton: Princeton University Press, 1944), 55.
60 Søren Kierkegaard, *Either/Or: A Fragment of Life Vol. 2*. Trans. Walter Lowrie (Princeton: Princeton University Press, 1944), 141.
61 Alan Sinfield, *Literature, Politics and Culture in Postwar Britain* (London: Athlone Press, 1997), xiii–xiv.
62 The use of the site of the defunct Wills' cigarette factory also somewhat ironically invokes Bizet's *Carmen* once more.
63 John Hill, *British Cinema in the 1980s* (Oxford: Oxford University Press, 1999), 13.
64 John Hodge, *Trainspotting and Shallow Grave: The Screenplays* (London: Faber, 1996), 78.
65 Sinfield, *Literature, Politics and Culture in Postwar Britain*, xxvii.
66 Will Self, 'Carry on up the hypodermic', *Observer*, Review (11 Feb 1996), 6.
67 Self, 'Carry on up the hypodermic', 6.
68 Really informative and lively cultural histories of the term Cool Britannia are offered by Andy Beckett, 'The myth of the cool', *Guardian*, G2 (5 May 1998), 2–3, and Michael Gardiner, 'British territory: Irvine Welsh in English and Japanese', *Textual Practice* 17: 1 (2003), 101–117.
69 Beckett, 'The myth of the cool', 3.
70 Beckett, 'The myth of the cool', 3.
71 Mark Leonard, *BritainTM: Renewing Our Identity* (London: Demos, 1997). A brilliant reading of the film *Trainspotting* in the context of the

Demos agenda is provided by Claire Monk, 'Underbelly UK: the 1990s underclass film, masculinity, and the ideologies of "New Britannia"' in Justine Ashby and Andrew Higson, eds, *British Cinema: Past and Present* (London: Routledge, 2000), 274–287.

72 Leonard, *BritainTM*, 16, 54, 56.

73 Martin Wroe, 'Hard drugs and heroine addiction', *Observer* (10 Mar 1996), 13.

74 Murray Pittock, *Celtic Identity and the British Image* (Manchester: Manchester University Press, 1999), 144.

75 Pittock, *Celtic Identity and the British Image*, 142.

76 John Walsh, 'The not-so-shady past of Irvine Welsh', *Independent Weekend Section* (15 Apr 1995), 25.

77 Cited in Kelly, 'Irvine Welsh in conversation with Aaron Kelly', 15.

78 On heroin chic see Henry A. Giroux, *Stealing Innocence: Youth, Corporate Power, and the Politics of Culture* (New Yew York: St Martin's Press, 2000).

79 Kevin Williamson, *Drugs and the Party Line* (Edinburgh: Rebel Inc, 1997), 94.

80 Monk 'Underbelly UK', 285.

2

The Acid House (1994)

Welsh's second major publication, *The Acid House*, comprises a collection of short stories and a novella, which had, in large part, been written coterminously with much of the *Trainspotting* materials. As Welsh explains: 'I had this other stuff that I'd done, these stories, I put these stories in with the novella. They came out six months later which was very quick in publishing terms after the first one. It was actually, originally, *The Acid House* which was the one to do it, because of the title, the packaging. It started to sell. It outsold *Trainspotting* in the first period'.[1] In the rush to get this work out on to the market, Elizabeth Young finds the collection 'patchy', but the opinion of Helen Birch represented many reviewers by insisting that the collection 'demonstrates that there is much more to Irvine Welsh than the semi-autobiographical voice of an ethnographer. It shows him pushing the limits of his versatility, experimenting with form, style and structure, with typographic innovation, surrealism and fantasy, and always finding something new to say'.[2]

As the title of the collection itself suggests, Welsh's perspective is sharpened by the spirit of acid house music, which he differentiates markedly from what he perceives to be the fundamental complicity of the punk scene of his own youth with the social mainstream:

> Whereas punk was saying: 'You're all crap, we can do better' what acid house is saying is very different it's saying 'we don't want anything to do with this, we want to stay as far away from the mainstream as possible ... By the time you get K-Tel's Greatest Jungle Hits it's insipid and bland. No one's interested in it when it hits the shops. The whole point of the house thing is to be as apart from mainstream society as possible, not to be a part of it.[3]

Accordingly, as with his debut novel, the collection is peopled by marginalised and disaffected voices stalking the peripheries of various social milieus. Again such dissonance is embedded in the very form of the book, its diffuse arsenal of representational modes which harness elements of social realism, surrealism, satire, fantasy and gothic, and its bold experimentation with multiform typographies and languages.

The short story as form

For Willy Maley, the short story form is an apposite mode for Welsh's focus on peripheral figures and evolves from the ethos of his early publication in the pamphlet culture of Rebel Inc and the Clocktower Press:

> These fringe ventures afforded Welsh the freedom to explore the fanzine format at which he now excels, characterised by cartoon violence, endlessly inventive sloganeering, and increasingly intricate typographical experimentation. If the 'bittiness' of Welsh's writing, its episodic quality, is due in part to its origins in the pamphlet culture of small presses, it can also be seen to reflect the actual fragmentation of the culture at large. Where an earlier literature might have perceived its aim as inventing or proclaiming 'Scotland' in the singular, and a more recent writing may have regarded its mission as debunking the myths of an idealised Scotland, the new fiction is concerned with the proliferation of 'Scotlands', plural and diverse.[4]

Maley grasps the socio-political appropriateness of the form in relation to Mary Louise Pratt's theory of 'the short story being used to introduce new regions or groups into an established national literature, or into an emerging national literature in the process of decolonisation'.[5] Hence, Maley maintains:

> There is an argument for seeing in the short story a literary form that offers an insight into post-colonial resistance. The civic and social specificity of Welsh's shorter fiction undermines the claims to inclusiveness of larger narratives of nation and empire, and sets up counter-narratives of regional dissent. Welsh's style – sampling, streetwise, synthesising – is implicitly anti-colonial. Welsh is more inclined than his predecessors to shift through the junk and pulp of Scottish culture, hence his cult status.[6]

Consequently, it is important not to cede analysis of the short story to narratives of historical development wherein only supposedly mature

and stable societies are capable of producing the novel in its canonical form. In other words, the short story mode of *The Acid House*,
which is also a favoured form of James Kelman's fiction, should not
be read as a confirmation of Scotland's anomaly in contradistinction
to the allegedly ordered society of England and its normative cultural
documents. As noted in the introduction, the bourgeois ideology of
the novel sought to construct an imaginary harmony that sought to
submerge the very pressing social conflicts of class, gender and place
through the construction of a monologic national language of power.
As Cairns Craig cogently puts it: 'powerful cultures make themselves
coherent – and ensure their sense of their own superiority by insisting that coherence and continuity are the definitions of successful
culture'.[7] The short story form attests not to the fractious peculiarity
of Scotland as a nation but to the untenability of the conventional
novel's effort to construct the nation as a unitary entity. Thus, when
Declan Kiberd argues – 'without the concept of a normal society, the
novel is impossible; but the short story is particularly appropriate to a
society in which revolutionary upheavals have shattered the very idea
of normality'[8] – such insight should be brought to bear on an awareness that the discourse of normativity is itself an ideological code. So
the short story can be politically deployed not as an inferior version of
the novel's national narrative but rather as a means of representing
precisely the substrata of people and places which the imagined unity
of that dominant form seeks to repress. In this light, Willy Maley
regards *The Acid House* thus:

> The short story is a form that lends itself perfectly to the view of theory
> as a local activity, and literature as a local intervention. Where the novel
> has as one of its central aims the narration of the nation, the short story
> unfolds somewhere in the region of marginality, inarticulacy, eccentric-
> ity . . . In its twenty-one short stories and closing novella Welsh can be
> seen to be mapping a linguistic and geographical domain hitherto dis-
> regarded or disenfranchised.[9]

For Maley, the story 'Eurortash' is paradigmatic of this trajectory. It
concerns Euan's life in Amsterdam which is blighted by a wearied
nihilism towards all forms of belief and belonging: 'I was anti-every-
thing and everyone' (A 10). Euan's own disaffected attitude also finds
an outward correlative in the interchangeable and crushing unifor-
mity of his environment: 'It could've been anywhere. You need a city
centre to give you a sense of place. I could've been back in one of those

places I came here to get away from. Only I hadn't got away. One dustbin for the poor outside of *action strasser* is much the same as any other, regardless of the city it serves' (*A* 11). Indeed, Euan's cynicism extends to a hostility towards national attachment when he is asked where he is from: 'All over really, I replied. Bland and blasé. Did it really matter which indistinct shite-arsed towns and schemes I was dragged through, growing up in that dull and dire little country?' (*A* 13). And when he is later referred to as British, Euan's irritation readily collapses into a condemnation of national identity as a redundant and stifling entrapment:

> I felt a surge of anger rise in me. I was almost tempted to go into a spiel about how I was Scottish, not British, and that the Scots were the last oppressed colony of the British Empire. I don't really believe it though; the Scots oppress themselves by their obsession with the English which breeds the negatives of hatred, fear, servility, contempt and dependency. (*A* 17)

It is not only national identity that is a casualty of Euan's cynicism however. He decides to befriend Chrissie in a bar with the sole intention of manipulating her and driving a wedge between her and her boyfriend Richard: 'I read her as a grubby map of all the places you didn't want to go: addiction, mental breakdown, drug psychosis, sexual exploitation' (*A* 13). After Chrissie's suicide a guilt-ridden Euan resolves to attend her funeral whereupon he discovers she was actually once male and called Christopher whose entire life had been a difficult struggle to come to terms with his sexuality. Finally capable of some compassion, Euan understands Richard and Chrissie as like himself and everyone else in Amsterdam: 'Not Eurotrash, just people trying to get by' (*A* 31). For a story so driven by a brutal cynicism and which, according to Willy Maley, traces the lives of the disenfranchised, this ending is perhaps a somewhat timid capitulation to a vague and apolitical humanism upon which the dominant order of society's maintenance of its status quo depends.

The acid test of politics

The powerfully written first person narrative of the novella, *A Smart Cunt*, which ends the collection, equivalently broaches issues of politics, disenchantment and marginality. Brian works for the Edinburgh council's Parks Department and also lives and sleeps in his small office to avoid having to pay rent for a flat of his own – a succinct example of the reciprocal impingement of work on leisure and leisure on work in Welsh's fiction. Once more, Brian's outlook is governed by a consummate pessimism: 'I was surrounded by demons and monsters. We're all bad people. There's no hope for the world. I left and walked along the disused railway line and cried my eyes out at the futility of it all' (A 232). Brian had participated in the mugging of a blind man, who dies of his injuries, but insisted that his part was only to kick snow in the victim's face until his narrative eventually concedes that he actually booted him in the head in what was probably the death blow. Maley registers that there is an ethical purpose to the dynamic yet unsettling first person narrative: 'The reader is carried along with the perpetrators, until the lines blur, and slowly it dawns that behind every perpetrator is a victim. It's a strong moral stance that seeks to understand rather than condemn, and to comprehend first and foremost by entering the worlds and words of the individual and their community'.[10] In the marginalised constituency represented by Brian it is the putative counter-culture of acid house music and clubbing that provides respite from the grinding persistence of the capitalist system and not mainstream political organisation, as demonstrated in Brian's argument with Donny:

> what can I do, really do for the emancipation of working people in this country, shat on by the rich, tied into political inaction by servile reliance on a reactionary, moribund and yet still unelectable Labour Party? The answer is a resounding fuck all. Getting up early to sell a couple of papers in a shopping centre is not my idea of the best way to chill out after raving . . . I'll stick to drugs to get me through the long, dark night of late capitalism. (A 240)

It should nevertheless be noted that Brian does not completely dismiss the merits of Donny's political activism regardless of his ambivalence about its potential success: 'He does look healthy and happier than me though; he has a glow to him. The involvement in the process of political struggle may indeed be quite liberating in itself, irrespective of the results it yields, or rather doesnae yield' (A 240). However, Willy Maley argues that Welsh's narrative focalisation on Brian, who is ostensibly a murderer, resists facile orthodoxies and is deeply permeated by a sense of the wider social context of disintegration and corruption that it ultimately castigates:

Welsh champions not only the socially excluded but the politically inarticulate and even the morally reprehensible. Which is not to say that he is amoral, merely that his subjects are not the deliberately dissenting individuals that a certain radical criticism finds it all too easy to counte- nance and indeed support, but a less palatable rabble whose unspeak- able hatred and violence is shown to have a source and a referent, an objective correlative, in the shape of a complacent political culture.[11]

In designating those people, like Brian, who are neglected both by the dominant order of society and by the traditional mainstream reformist challenge to that system, Maley invokes the idea of the 'sub- altern' – which has already been discussed in the previous chapter in relation to *Trainspotting* – though specifically Gayatri Spivak's defini- tion of the term: 'Subalternity is the name I borrow for the space out of any serious touch with the logic of capitalism or socialism . . . Please do not confuse it with unorganised labour, women as such, the proletarian, the colonized, the object of ethnography, migrant labour, political refuges, etc. Nothing useful comes out of this confusion'.[12]

What is significant about Spivak's rendering of the term subaltern is its rebuttal of class terminology and other given forms of collective identity. Resultantly, Maley concludes that 'the space of subalternity is the natural habitat of Welsh's spivs – who are clearly "out of any serious touch with the logic of capitalism or socialism" . . . Welsh attacks both Romantic Scotland and Radical Scotland, Kailyard and Clydeside'.[13] Certainly *The Acid House* and the subalternity or sub- strata of disenchanted voices that it depicts are deeply circumspect about mainstream socialism or trade unionism. 'A Blockage in the System' deals not only with a blocked sewer but also with the sewer- age workers' efforts to obstruct the smooth running of their council department as they eventually spite their bosses not by going on strike but by heading off for a pint. As Helen Birch posits, in the story 'old working-class orthodoxies about the dignity of labour are satirised. With its petty hierarchies work, Welsh suggests, is for many people – especially those whom we patronisingly deem to be lucky to have a job – is a necessary bore, to be tolerated between footie and the pub' (1994, 29). Welsh himself has been keen to distinguish his work from the West Coast workerist tradition of working-class writing:

Growing up through the punk era made a great impression on a lot of people. A lot of the Glasgow writers are concerned with work and the alienation from work and now you've got a generation who've grown up with the dole queue and YTS schemes – there is no work. The rave kids coming up now – they know that work's a pile of shit. Because of the industry in Glasgow there's a kind of machismo about work – that dignity of labour thing. Many of the older Glasgow writers are aligned to industrial socialism. I think work is a horrible thing. People should avoid it at all costs.[14]

And it is not only mainstream political allegiances and solidarities that are dismissed as defeated and decayed reformism. Equally, inter-personal friendships, familial bonds and codes of sociality seem irreparably sundered by the enveloping late capitalist economic system. In the first person narrative of 'Stoke Newington Blues', Euan is locked up by racist, corrupt cops and decides to help fit up his black friend in exchange for his release and a bag of heroin. Similarly, 'The House of John Deaf' is characterised by internecine tension and alien-ation, whilst family, community and belonging are interrogated in 'Granny's Old Junk'. The only 'home' in the story is the artificially constructed old people's residence where the heroin addict Graham travels to steal from his grandmother: 'Very few families are close nowadays. People move around, live in different parts of the country, lead different lives. It's pointless lamenting something as inevitable as the decline of the extended family network' (*A* 94). Codes such as family loyalty are clearly decimated: 'Her life savings. Savings for what? Savings for us, that's what, the daft auld cunt: too feeble, too inadequate to enjoy or even use her wealth. Well I shall just have my share now' (*A* 94). It ensues that Graham's grandmother is not only a heroin user but also survives financially by being a dealer too. In the surreal satire, 'Snowman Building Parts for Rico the Squirrel', the eponymous animal brings love back to a dysfunctional all-American home, whilst the television programme, *The Skatch Femilee Rabirtson*, which features a Scottish housing scheme family, is turned off because it is too disgusting for wholesome family viewing. Again Willy Maley's summations are highly pertinent:

> Scottish subalterns cannot be represented by the magic eye in the corner of the room, only distracted by it. Culture and technology have failed them. This world of failures and consumers is marked by pessimism, but also, paradoxically, by a realism that is much more acute and accu-rate than the old stereotypes of masculine workerism and principled opposition that we find in the fiction of William McIlvanney. Welsh's characters seldom have recourse to officially sanctioned forms of politi-cal resistance, or even wildcat actions such as strikes or sit-ins. Instead,

they practice a subtle and pervasive guerrilla warfare, blocking rather
than tackling its moral agents and servants of power.[15]

However, whilst Maley is undeniably correct in demonstrating the
breakdown of mainstream trade unionism and parliamentary socialism, both he, and by extension Spivak, are on dangerous ground
when implying that their definition of the subaltern occupies a space
not only beyond the traditional left but also 'the logic of capitalism'.
'The Granton Star Cause' illustrates that it is perhaps unwise for any
properly oppositional criticism to harbour the illusion of both conceptual and concretely social resistances and posturings outwith the
peremptory and logic of capitalism in this era of its global colonisa-
tion. The third person narrative follows the disastrous turn in the life
of the social 'leper' (A 121) Boab Coyle, culminating in his being
turned into a fly by God. Initially, Boab not only loses his place in the
Granton Star football team, but is told to leave home by his parents to
allow them more intimate time together: 'He saw them for what they
were: sleazy, lecherous bastards' (A 122). Boab is also dumped by his
girlfriend, who it transpires is seeing Tambo, the very same guy who
replaced him in the football team. Upon smashing up a phone box in
frustration, he is arrested by passing police car officers, who admin-
ister an especially severe beating in the cells due to the officer concerned having shares in the privatised British Telecom: 'ah feel like
ah've goat mair ay a stake now, son. So ah don't want any lumpen-pro-
letarian malcontents threatening ma investment' (A 126). Upon his
release Boab eats an egg roll in a café before remembering that he
does not have enough money to pay for it and is further assaulted by
the irate café owner. He then loses his removals firm job due to cut-
backs caused by 'market positioning' (A 127) and finally makes the
mistake of cursing God for his predicament. God then harangues
Boab in a bar and tells him: 'That cunt Nietzsche wis wide ay the mark
whin he sais ah wis deid. Ah'm no deid; ah jist dinnae gie a fuck. It's
no fir me tae sort every cunt's problems oot. Nae other cunt gies a
fuck so how should ah? Eh?' (A 129). Part of the horror resides in
God's apathy: had this been a Nietzschean universe in which God is
dead then that at least would have offered some certitude in the sense
that it would have precipitated the absolute negation of Christianity as
a system. Instead, God's self-serving indifference has simply internalised the *laissez-faire* economics already presaged by the story's
references to privatisation, monetarism and downsizing. The fact
that God is also subject to that economic imperative intimates that

neo-liberal economics is no longer merely a creed advocated by a few thinkers but has become a pervasive and superintending reality governing society. Hence, Fredric Jameson argues that in late capitalism market ideology has come to replace other governing systems such as religion or nationality and has become for its apologists a 'consoling replacement for the divinity':

> Market ideology assures us that human beings make a mess of it when they try to control their destinies ('socialism is impossible') and that we are fortunate in possessing an interpersonal mechanism – the market – which can substitute for human hubris and planning and replace human decisions altogether.[16]

God's spitefully arbitrary decision to transform Boab into a fly itself provides an allegory of the estrangements of human identity under late capitalism and our seeming incapacity to comprehend the profound and bewildering systemic changes taking place under globalisation even as, paradoxically, capitalism's routine seems more dully repetitive and constant than ever. For although Boab's environment remains the same immutable blankness of the housing scheme, he himself has undergone a metamorphosis to which he must struggle unsuccessfully to adapt.[17] Having stayed at his mate Kev's house, alerting Kev to his presence by writing his name on the wall in tomato ketchup, Boab gains some revenge by using his new form to chew excrement and vomit it upon his ex-girlfriend and her new lover's food, and administers rat poison to his former boss. But Boab is eventually killed when swotted by his mother – though not before he has witnessed his mother and father engaged in some very sordid sexual activity. The empty, reiterative nature of this environment is emphasised in the story's close when Kev starts to undergo the same throes as Boab, losing his girlfriend, his job and possibly even his place in the Granton Star team. For Marie-Odile Pittin-Hédon the nihilistic circularity and stasis which marks the story even structures the meaningless repetition of Boab's name:

> 'Boab Coyle' is both his and his father's name, thereby foregrounding repetition; the surname is a homophone of 'coil', which gives the repetition its spiral effect . . . the Christian name 'Bob' – preferred to 'Rob' or even 'Rab' – being a palindrome . . . indicates the hesitancy, the reversibility of worlds, while the added 'a' stresses localism, giving a definitely Scottish background to the stagnation of both worlds.[18]

One other specifically Scottish inflection imbuing the story is the 'dreadful' (A 127) confrontation with God, which, as discussed in relation to the fearful hold that Begbie's character exerts in *Trainspotting*, discloses the saturating influence of Calvinism on Scottish culture. Calvinism also has broader implications for the status of fiction itself in Scottish society. Cairns Craig discusses how John Knox's 'Appellation' announces the supremacy of the Bible over all other books as part of his injunction against idolatry. Humanity, Knox avers, 'should ratify and confirm whatsoever was written in the book of God'.[19] The writing of fiction, the use of the human imagination to ratify a language other than the true Word of God, is for Knox fundamentally deceitful or even evil:

> In Knox's terms . . . the dialogue between man and his creator can only take place in and through 'whatever was written in the book of God', not in and through the constructions of the human imagination. Imagination, when not engaged with the Word of God, acts at the behest of the 'yester hara', and is necessarily in league with the devil. For generations of Scottish writers the created word has been caught in an inevitable conflict with the Word of creation, and this profound awareness of the necessary evil of the work of art is one of the determining elements of the tradition of the Scottish novel: it is not a matter of whether the writer belongs or does not belong to a Calvinist tradition, but to the fact that the Calvinist distrust of imagination, building on a powerful interpretative tradition in Judeo-Christian theology, has become part of the very fabric of the traditions of Scottish writing and Scottish thought.[20]

This dominant Calvinist doctrine helps explain why so many of Welsh's narrators in *The Acid House* and throughout his *oeuvre* are unreliable and engaged, whether playfully, guiltily or nefariously, in the construction of artifices that perpetually accentuate their own fictitiousness and thwart the assemblage of language, truth and authority in the Knoxian doctrine of the one True Word.

Fantasy

Modes such as the gothic and the fantastic are also readily turned to political purposes given that both forms predominantly concern experiences denied or invalidated by the dominant construction of what is real and what is possible. Such modes challenge the supposedly common, sensibly true and consensual version of social reality produced by both the political and literary representational systems of power. Rosemary Jackson, for instance, posits that:

> fantastic literature points to or suggests the basis upon which cultural order rests, for it opens up for a brief moment, on to disorder, on to illegality, on to that which lies outside the law, that which is outside dominant value systems. The fantastic traces the unsaid and the unseen of culture: that which has been silenced, made invisible, covered over and made 'absent'.[21]

The story, 'The Acid House', from which the collection gleans its title, intertwines the lives of the Hibs Casual, Coco Bryce, who is tripping on LSD, and the bourgeois couple, Rory Watson and Jenny Moore. Coco is struck by lightening at the same moment that it strikes the ambulance in which Jenny Moore is giving birth to her and Rory's son. Miraculously, Coco and the baby switch bodies in this instant. The transformation indicates Welsh's inventive writerly skills as it is rendered through the fragmentation of the text into a series of flashbacks from Coco's life that appear in the form of dispersed boxes over the repeated word LIGHT which functions as a visual backdrop. It is at the end of this light that Coco re-enters the world in the form of Jenny's baby and the baby's soul emerges in the frame of Coco's comatose and drug-addled person in hospital. Whilst Coco's girlfriend and mates by his bedside plausibly assume that his infantile state is due to too much LSD, Jenny and Rory take home a baby who gets sexually aroused when being breast-fed, steals alcohol from the fridge and eagerly stands up in his cot watching his parents have sex – which eventually makes Rory unable to perform, much to Jenny's frustration.

Indeed, the story provides a satire on contemporary masculinity, particularly the idea of the caring, sharing New Man in touch with his feminine side. Rory believes that his resentment towards the baby and his new found impotence are exemplary New Man traits that he can share with the men's group which he attends: 'He'd have to see about this terrible jealousy, talk it through with the other men who were in touch with their feelings' (*A* 165). While when Jenny discovers that her baby can talk (she decides that his curiously working-class accent has been gleaned from listening to the workmen in their house), she finds in him a possible replacement New Man for her sexually and socially 'inadequate' (*A* 168) partner: 'With her guiding his development he would grow up non-sexist and sensitive, but strong and genuinely expressive, rather than an insipid clown who clings to a type of behaviour for limp ideological reasons. He'd be the perfect new man' (*A* 170). In terms of the intersection of gender and class stereotyping, there is something troubling about this construction of an ideal man as the compendium of supposedly developed middle-class refinement and natural working-class rawness. Consequently, the underlying structure of the story highlights the strategy of the new breed of men's magazines, such as *Loaded*, for which Welsh regularly wrote. Such publications seek to construct a comforting, fantasy masculinity for their largely middle-class readers by allowing a stylised bourgeois male sensibility to annex its own highly stereotyped perception of 'authentic' working-class masculinity and attitudes to sex and sexuality. It is a compensatory fantasy that reassures young middle-class males that they can be successful, professional and sophisticated but still be men through recourse to this elemental masculinity that is seen simultaneously as both the natural Ur-state of working-class men and conveniently open to universal appropriation.[22]

Nonetheless, the story's broader transplantation of souls does unhinge the normative and immutable selves of conventional fiction. As Rosemary Jackson imparts: 'The many partial, dual, multiple and dismembered selves scattered throughout literary fantasies violate the most cherished of all human unities: the unity of "character"'.[23] Jackson continues that such doubling and splintering of selfhood sabotages what Hélène Cixous deems the bourgeois obsession with hermetically self-contained individual character: 'The ideology underlying this fetishization of "character" is that of an "I" who is a *whole* subject, conscious, knowable; and the enunciatory "I" *expresses himself* in the text, just as the world is *represented* complimentarily in the text in a form equivalent to pictorial representation, as a simulacrum'.[24] Moreover, the typographic experimentalism, most evident in the textual mosaic of 'The Acid House', not only visually undermines the sanctity and unity of the printed text on the page but also further dismantles the capacity of conventional characterisation to formulate identity through the construction of stable social 'types' and 'typical' personalities. Hence, Welsh's scrambling of types subverts not only on the level of characterisation but also on the level of the very mechanics of language in which that ideology of unitary, single character is assembled. It then follows, according to the implications of Cixous' argument, that Welsh also scrutinises the conflictual way that reality itself is constituted ideologically through differing literary and cultural modes. The unitary notion of a singular, shared worldview (which itself excludes many of the people Welsh chooses to focus upon in his writing) is exposed not as universal truth but as a particular and partial construction of reality in a hegemonic form. As Marie-Odile Pittin-Hédon remarks, *The Acid House* is engaged in 'interchanging the status of respectively "real life" and obviously fantastic imaginings, thereby challenging not only our notions of the place occupied by fiction in postmodern fantasy, but also the reality status of our very conception of "the real"'.[25] In the story 'The Acid House' the sanctity of both the bourgeois subject and the bourgeois domestic interior in which that individual is encased are violated, the universality of a bourgeois value system undermined by confronting it with the other experiences and peoples which it designedly represses. So, leaving aside its denotation of a particular style of dance music, the term 'acid house' is entirely appropriate for the story's caustic use of working-class rave culture to corrupt the hallowed interior terrain of bourgeois belonging.

Undesirable types

Welsh's typographic experimentation is also used to comic effect in the story 'Sport for All', featuring a football casual accosting a middle-class Scottish rugby fan at a bar, wherein the text is split on either side of the page between what he says to the rugby supporter and then to his mates. Although a comic vignette, its structure does also convey the lack of a common, overarching language in which to construct a homogenous Scottish nationalist identity, in keeping with the subversive potential of the short story outlined above. Perhaps most effectively, 'Across the Hall', concerning the lives of two lonely people who live opposite one another and fantasise about being together, employs two simultaneous narratives bifurcated down the page under headings of their flat numbers, 15/2 Collingwood and 15/8 Gillespie. The parallel narratives, when read across the page as a single chain, do occasionally conjoin but only to produce sentences voided of meaning or connection. Hence, the typographic form itself discloses the abject alienation of both people. Significantly, when they do meet actually in the hallway they are 'both lost for words' (*A* 105), as, not for the first time in Welsh's work, language effaces its own positive capacity as a form of communication and becomes instead an imprisoning barrier to expression. In this story and in the collection as a whole, there is

something of both the atmosphere and form of James Joyce's *Dubliners* and its 'unfinished sentences', its catalogue of beleaguered, alienated selves and linguistic and social breakdown.[26]

There are undeniably comic moments, as best illustrated by the
'Sexual Disaster Quartet' comprising four brief set-pieces, the first of
which, 'A Good Son', satirically rewrites Freud as an exasperated
father tells his son: 'Aye, Oedipus, yir a complex fucker right enough'
(*A* 61). The second part, 'The Cruel Bastard and the Selfish Fucker
Get It On', contains a great scene in which the eponymous couple
confront one another naked:

> Who dae ye expect tae satisfy wi that? She asked.
> –, Masel, he said. (*A* 62)

This tale of vitriol and mutual loathing ends: 'Within a few weeks they
were living together. People say it seems to be working out' (*A* 62).
'Lots of Laughter and Sex' involves a man responding to his partner's
dictum that laughter and sex are central to any relationship: 'Don't get
me wrong. I couldn't agree more. But no at the same time, ya fuckin
cow' (*A* 63), and the quartet concludes with the brief 'Robert K. Laird:
A Sexual History': 'Rab's nivir hud a ride in ehs puff; perr wee cunt.
Disnae seem too bothered, mind you' (*A* 64). Even so, as Jonathan
Coe observes: 'There's an undertow of real pain behind even the
lightest of the stories'.[27] Though deeply amusing, the 'Sexual Disaster
Quartet' does have an undercurrent of masculine disempowerment,
of the existential emptiness of human relationships, of the deadening, cyclical incarceration of contemporary living. To that end, 'Wayne
Foster' depicts a classically educated barman named Craig who
refuses to serve two 'Sparryheids' discussing Wayne Foster's footballing abilities. Craig's main problem though is two women –
referred to as *She* and *Her* – drinking in the bar who are making den-
igrating remarks about his sexual performance. This story offers a
neat illustration of a traditionally male environment and empowerment being encroached upon and undermined by women. 'A Soft
Touch' is written in the first person narrative of John and recounts
how his wife, Katriona Doyle, left him with their baby for Larry, the
psychotic guy in the flat upstairs. As John is afraid of both Larry and
Katriona's brothers, he lets the couple walk all over him. This tale of
ritualised humiliation entails John allowing them to take his television and video and pass an extension cable down to his flat to use his
electricity, whilst Larry offers to let him have sex with Katriona again

at £10 per time. Having met Katriona again in a pub, she tells John that Larry left her when she fell pregnant. Having spent the entire story demonstrating his anger and frustration, when Katriona asks him if he wants to go out with her again, Larry replies 'Ah suppose so' (*A* 53).

The dramatic propulsion of the first person narration of 'The Shooter' ends with Gary, who feels 'invisible' (*A* 1) in his own home, turning his shotgun on the narrator and pulling the trigger. 'The Last Resort on the Adriatic', in which Welsh attempts a standard, middle-class voice, relates the last futile hours in the life of Jim Banks who throws himself overboard a cruise ship in an exact replication of his wife's suicide on the same cruise a decade previously. Most pessimistic of all the stories is the starkly existential 'Snuff', which traces the 'self-contained' (*A* 66) life of Ian Smith from his boring office job during the day to the emptiness of his evenings which he spends watching and filling in comments on all the films in *Halliwell's Film Guide*. Neither the death of his mother nor his wife leaving him manage to inspire any emotion in Smith. The third person narrative is especially fitting as its forensic precision brilliantly embodies the cold, distanced alienation that it depicts. Having finished reviewing all the films listed in *Halliwell's*, Smith buys a video recorder and films his own hanging, watching himself on the screen. The story attests to what J. G. Ballard terms 'the most terrifying casualty of the century: the death of affect'.[28] As with the metaphor of trainspotting in Welsh's debut novel, Smith's desire for a meaning to existence within the drudgery of late capitalism only finds release in the ultimately mindless seriality of the lists of films in his guide, an engagement not with life but with its reification and second order mediation. Before his suicide, Smith has sex with a prostitute in an effort to experience some kind of feeling or connection but finds: 'Her expression was frozen; her eyes clouded by opiates or apathy. Smith saw his own countenance reflected in hers' (*A* 73). As during sex with his former wife, the prostitute reaches orgasm but Smith is unable to climax, leading her to dismiss him as nothing more than a 'prick. Fuckin prick' (*A* 73).

If masculinity is emotionally and psychically destroyed by the *reductio ad absurdum* of its biological condition in 'Snuff' then a contrasting yet reciprocal problematic occurs in 'Vat '96'. Therein the upper-middle-class couple, Crawford and Valerie, visit the home of friends Fiona and Keith and discover that after a car accident Keith is merely a disembodied head in a tank kept alive by pioneering new

technology: 'His body has been smashed to pieces. Most of his major
organs are useless. However, his head and brain are still intact' (*A*
44). Keith's head now functions as an ornament in the living room
where Fiona has sex with her new lover before his helpless gaze. In
this instance, masculinity is detached from its physical and sexual
identity and becomes merely a display of its own impotence. Both
cases demonstrate a profound dislocation and malfunctioning of
masculine sexuality and identity, an incapacity to make its contradictory components and aims cohere ideologically. Therefore, when
dominant models undergo historical shifts they lose their ability to
naturalise themselves, to cover over their social contradictions
through the transparency and normalcy that sheer power affords:
'There is the daily antagonistic clashing between diverse masculine
identities – like child-carer, authoritarian father, loving, supportive
friend, single parent father, "macho" manager, depressed unemployed worker, strong leader – struggling for overall supremacy'.[29]

'Where the Debris Meets the Sea' is possibly Welsh's most brilliant
vignette and also advances an understanding of contemporary paradigm shifts in gender relations. In their Santa Monica beach mansion
Madonna, Kylie Minogue, Kim Basinger and Victoria Principal
peruse glossy soft porn magazines such as Wide-o, Scheme Scene
and Bevvy Merchants. Madonna, gazing at Deek Prentice in his shell-
suit Radge, utters the first words: 'Phoah! Ah'd shag the erse oafay
that anywey' (*A* 88). The story is one of the few instances where Welsh
uses quotation marks around the spoken word, highlighting further
the defamiliarisation taking place as working-class Edinburgh vernacular is transposed on to the speech of Hollywood celebrities. In
this regard, the story is perhaps most indebted to Tom Leonard's
poetry, especially 'Unrelated Incidents 3' wherein a BBC newsreader
speaks in Glaswegian demotic in an inversion which radically subverts the putatively universal and objective truth of the standardised
voice of power.[30] Welsh explains his intentions thus: 'What I'm trying
to do is to undermine prejudices by shaking things up, by putting
people into different situations that they would not usually be in. With
that kind of vignette you can say all kinds of things about the star
system, about sexism, about class'.[31] The reversal not only of language
but also of gender positioning in which it is women who gaze at men
does denaturalise the pervasive sexism of patriarchal society and renders its structural dynamics explicit. The story also satirically
acknowledges a shift in gender relations within consumer capitalism,

whereby men are no longer secure as merely the dominant subjects who affirm their power through the scopic regulation of women as objects, and are becoming the object of various social, commercial and cultural gazes themselves. As Frank Mort argues, young men are increasingly being sold images which undermine traditional models of masculinity in that they are stimulated to look at themselves and other men as objects of consumer desire, to indulge in pleasures previously branded as feminine.[32] However, although women are now also permitted access to varying kinds of consumer subjectivity, Laura Mulvey's account of the 'masculinisation' of the viewing subject by patriarchy is germane.[33] It instructs that there is still a pervasive masculine hegemony, that women are only able to look through the terms of a dominant patriarchy as masquerading or temporary 'men'. And less subversively perhaps, the fact that the story features a group of women behaving like men reading soft porn can also be interpreted self-referentially as a commentary on much of Welsh's own fiction, which can be said to privilege a particular kind of optimal male reader in whose terms all readers are encouraged by the text to respond. In terms of class, Kim Basinger's dismissal of the dreams of the others that they may meet these men one day – 'We'll nivir go tae fuckin Leith! . . . Yous are fuckin dreamin . . . in their heart of hearts, they knew that Kim was right' (*A* 92) – is of course loaded with irony in that the reader too is well aware of this fact precisely because of the chasm between their celebrity lifestyle and the peripheral housing schemes in which the male models reside.

Language and power

Another story, 'The Two Philosophers', comparably demystifies the supposedly neutral voice of power. Two philosophers, the middle-class Scottish Tory, Gus McGlone, and the working-class Chicago Jew, Lou Ornstein, have a long-standing argument concerning Ornstein's materialist view of magic as 'unknown science', that so-called unexplained phenomena are just scientific blindspots and that the ruling class seeks to repress ideas that run counter to the prevailing paradigms until pressure for change becomes unbearable. They decide to settle the argument by going outside the academy to get a layperson's perspective in a working-class Glaswegian pub in Govan on the day of an Old Firm game between Celtic and Rangers. They are eventually encouraged by the drinkers in the bar to step outside and fight it out themselves and Ornstein administers a beating to McGlone before both are apprehended by the police. In a commentary on British class relations, Ornstein is released without charge due to his accent, whilst McGlone, because he is Scottish and was caught fighting in Govan, is treated as a drunken lunatic when he tries to claim he is a university professor and he is subsequently roughed up by the police and detained for a breach of the peace. At a comic level, the entire story is merely the build-up to the final punch line. On the Glasgow underground a youth who witnessed the fight tells Ornstein – 'Ye were magic, so ye wir' – to which Ornstein replies 'No . . . I was unknown science' (A 117). More seriously though, it also demystifies the avowedly reasonable and humane nature of bourgeois society and foregrounds the constitutive violence of the class system that supports it. As Willy Maley elaborates:

> It makes manifest the latent violence and hierarchical structure of academic debate and exposes what was carefully hidden in the academic institution, namely aggression and exclusivity. The entrenched resistance to Irvine Welsh within the Scottish education establishment, especially in departments of English and Scottish literature, can be read in terms of the kind of macho posturing that 'The Two Philosophers' locates within an apparently civil discourse.[34]

In its own throwaway fashion, 'Lisa's Mum Meets the Queen Mother' also unmasks the limitations and contradictions of our society's governing discourse of truth and righteousness. Having always been instructed to tell the truth, young Lisa does exactly that upon meeting the Queen Mother: 'That old lady's got bad breath and smells of wee' (A 107). Without wanting to over-interpret, here power rests on the suppression of various truths and not their articulation. Welsh's fondness for a Bakhtinian *grammatica jocosa* is subversively evident in 'Disnae Matter', wherein an unemployed worker takes his daughter to Disneyland with his redundancy payoff. Although he assaults an employee in a bear costume who frightens his daughter, when management step in he refuses to have the man sacked – a rare moment of solidarity between workers in the collection. And although the speaker is not just materially but also linguistically disenfranchised – he renders the American accents in the story in his own voice with the dispensation – 'this is aw American, likesay, ye ken how aw they doss cunts talk, oan the telly n that' (A 119) – the pun of the story's title sabotages the corporate power of the Disney brand.

Overall, the stories that comprise *The Acid House* crystallise Welsh's careful attention to the deep relationship of language and power and also serve to illustrate his capacity to subvert that power through a range of marginalised and suppressed demotic voices. The fragmentary form of the collection, as with the episodic cadences of his first novel, itself offers a commentary upon the disintegrating nature of working-class life and milieu in late capitalism. Whilst it mines these dark themes, however, the collection's title also chimed with the emergence of acid house music and helped to popularise further Welsh's work amongst new readerships, in particular his first novel – which is now the book for which Welsh is most famous but whose initial surge in sales was driven by the success of his short story collection. Ironically, then, given that the film adaptation of *Trainspotting* directly sought a mass market, the screen version of *The Acid House* – the book which initially established Welsh's commercial clout – designedly eschewed mainstream acceptance.

The film adaptation of *The Acid House* comprises reworkings of three stories: 'A Soft Touch', 'The Granton Star Cause' and 'The Acid House'. Welsh avowedly intended his screenplay to resist the Cool Britannia appropriation undergone by *Trainspotting* and its substantial implication in the institutions of mainstream cinema:

> When I did *The Acid House* film I liked the idea that I could do something in my own way and make it hardcore . . . Things become appropriated so quickly now. You can become quite a radical force and a reactionary force at the same time just depending on where you're sitting, your glass being half empty or half full sort of thing. I wanted to get rid of all the 'Britpop' style wankers, I wanted to get back to doing something that was nasty again, that was edgy and pushing things further.[35]

Consequently, Murray Smith finds the film version a radical and confrontational departure from the adaptation of Welsh's first novel: '*The Acid House* invests its humour with a confrontational rawness largely absent from *Trainspotting* . . . While *The Acid House* revels in this abrasive comedy and unremitting interpersonal brutality, *Trainspotting* contains its black humour for the sake of a broader range of emotional tones'.[36] The three reworkings feature British acting luminaries such as Jemma Redgrave and Martin Clunes, as well as another strong performance from Ewan Bremner. Additionally, there is a Britpop and British dance music soundtrack. But the fact that Welsh's deliberately non-commercial abrasiveness was carried through in the filming is illustrated by Geoff Brown's reaction:

> The tales . . . come with accents and slang impenetrable enough to make the film as easy on the ears to any audience south of the border as Romanian folk drama . . . This is subjective criticism, of course. I am English and middle-class, and have as much personal experience of chemical substances and the culture around them as I have of the surface of the moon.[37]

Notably Brown first seeks to exoticise the film through analogy with a (both spatially and temporally) peripheral cultural form and then utterly erases the material conditions of the film's production by insinuating that its aesthetic is so otherworldly that it is not even of this earth. In contrast to the refined accents and stylised unity of *Trainspotting*, then, the film versions of these three stories make little concession to mainstream cinema or acceptance and galvanise the unsettling vigour of the book itself. In terms of the development of Welsh's fiction, his next book, *Marabou Stork Nightmares*, intensified even more starkly the dark and uncompromising currents found in the detailing of contemporary society in both *Trainspotting* and *The Acid House*.

Notes

1 Cited in Steve Redhead, *Repetitive Beat Generation* (Edinburgh: Rebel Inc, 2000), 140.
2 Elizabeth Young, 'Grubby faces', *Guardian*, G2T (8 Mar 1994), 14; Helen Birch, 'Meeting God down the pub: *The Acid House*', *Independent*, Weekend Supplement (16 Apr 1994), 29.
3 Cited in John Mulholland, 'Acid wit', *Guardian*, G2T (30 Mar 1995), 8.
4 Willy Maley, 'Subversion and squirrility in Irvine Welsh's shorter fiction' in Dermot Cavanagh and Tim Kirk, eds, *Subversion and Scurrility: Popular Discourse in Europe from 1500 to the Present* (Aldershot: Ashgate, 2000), 192.
5 See Mary Louise Pratt, 'The short story: the long and the short of it' in Charles E. May, ed., *New Short Story Theories* (Athens: Ohio University Press, 1994), 104.
6 Maley, 'Subversion and squirrility in Irvine Welsh's shorter fiction', 192.
7 Cairns Craig, *Out of History: Narrative Paradigms in Scottish and British Culture* (Edinburgh: Polygon, 1996), 19–20.
8 Declan Kiberd, 'Story-telling: the Gaelic tradition' in Patrick Rafroidi and Terence Brown, eds, *The Irish Short Story* (Lille: University of Lille, 1979), 15.

9 Maley, 'Subversion and squirrility in Irvine Welsh's shorter fiction', 191.

10 Maley, 'Subversion and squirrility in Irvine Welsh's shorter fiction', 195.

11 Maley, 'Subversion and squirrility in Irvine Welsh's shorter fiction', 195.

12 See Gayatri Spivak, 'Supplementing Marxism' in Bernd Magnus and Stephen Cullenberg, eds, *Whither Marxism? Global Crises in International Perspective* (London: Routledge, 1995), 115.

13 Maley, 'Subversion and squirrility in Irvine Welsh's shorter fiction', 194.

14 Elizabeth Young, 'Blood on the tracks', *Guardian* (14 Aug 1993), 33.

15 Maley, 'Subversion and squirrility in Irvine Welsh's shorter fiction', 201.

16 Fredric Jameson, *Postmodernism, or, the Cultural Logic of Late Capitalism* (London: Verso, 1991), 273.

17 One obvious influence of the story, then, is Franz Kafka's *Metamorphosis*. See *Metamorphosis and Other Stories*. Trans. Willa and Edwin Muir (London: Minerva, 1992), 9–63. The 1958 film *The Fly* and its 1986 remake starring Jeff Goldblum are also evident precursors.

18 Marie-Odile Pittin-Hédon, 'Postmodern fantasy: the supernatural in Gray's *Comedy of the White Dog* and Welsh's *Granton Star Cause*', *Etudes Ecossaises* 7 (2001), 70.

19 John Knox, 'Appellation' in Roger Mason, ed., *John Knox: On Rebellion* (Cambridge: Cambridge University Press, 1994), 90.

20 Cairns Craig, *The Modern Scottish Novel: Narrative and the National Imagination* (Edinburgh: Edinburgh University Press, 1999), 200–201.

21 Rosemary Jackson, *Fantasy: The Literature of Subversion* (London: Routledge, 1988), 4.

22 In our interview during the writing of this book Welsh admitted of *Loaded* that 'it's based on a restrictive view of working-class life'. See Aaron Kelly, 'Irvine Welsh in conversation with Aaron Kelly', *Edinburgh Review* 113 (2004), 17.

23 Jackson, *Fantasy*, 82.

24 Hélène Cixous, 'The character of "character"'. Trans. Keith Cohen. *New Literary History* 5: 2 (Winter 1974), 305, cited in Jackson, *Fantasy*, 84.

25 Pittin-Hédon, 'Postmodern fantasy', 67.

26 James Joyce, *Dubliners* [1914] (London: Granada, 1982), 8.

27 Jonathan Coe, 'Where authors fear to tread', *Sunday Times* (13 Mar 1994), 7.

28 J. G. Ballard. 'Introduction to the French edition of *Crash*' [1974]. *Crash* (London: Paladin, 1990), 5.

29 Men, Masculinities and Socialism Group, 'Changing men, changing politics', *Achilles Heel* 10 (1990), 18.

30 See Tom Leonard, *Intimate Voices: Selected Work 1965–1983* (Newcastle: Galloping Dog Press, 1984), 88.

31 Cited in Mulholland, 'Acid wit', 8.

32 See Frank Mort, 'Boy's own? Masculinity, style and popular culture' in Rowena Chapman and Jonathan Rutherford, eds, *Male Order: Unwrapping Masculinity* (London: Lawrence and Wishart, 1988), 193–224.

33 Laura Mulvey, *Visual and Other Pleasures* (London: Macmillan, 1989), 37.

34 Maley, 'Subversion and squirrility in Irvine Welsh's shorter fiction', 197.

35 Cited in Redhead, *Repetitive Beat Generation*, 143–144.

36 Murray Smith, *Trainspotting* (London: BFI Publishing, 2002), 78.

37 Geoff Brown, 'Set your phrases to mildly stun', *The Times* (31 Dec 1998), 37.

3

Marabou Stork Nightmares (1995)

Marabou Stork Nightmares charts the retrospective memories and fantasises of Roy Strang as he lies comatose in a hospital bed having attempted to commit suicide after finally being overwhelmed by guilt about his part in the brutal gang-rape of a young woman, Kirsty Chalmers. The novel is divided into four sections: 'Lost Empires', 'The City of Gold', 'On the Trail of the Stork' and 'The Paths of Self-Deliverance'. The narrative is multi-layered and interweaves Roy's reminiscences about his childhood on the Muirhouse housing scheme and his family's brief time in South Africa, his fantasy construction of a quest to kill the notorious Marabou Stork that is decimating flamingo communities in Africa, which is assembled from the materials of adventure fiction for boys and adolescents. Additionally, the interruptions in present time of hospital staff and his family trouble Roy's submerged and comatose consciousness and, despite his efforts at evasion, an account of the rape itself slowly emerges. One source of these interruptions comes from a visitor who is at first unnamed but eventually revealed to be Kirsty, who finally takes her revenge. The novel is one of Welsh's most formally experimental and continually mutates and merges differing typefaces and registers. As Welsh explains: 'The text moves all over the place, in and out of different realities, like Roy does in order to suspend the truth. The text is a dislocator, so he can escape the real world of the rape and his confusion. Like the storks are doppelgangers for his fears'.[1] For Welsh the novel is 'my favourite of all my books though in sales terms it's the runt of the litter' (4P, 4).[2] It was also written in just five weeks: '*Marabou* was a book I just wanted to get out of as soon as possible. Like method acting, it was method writing, and Roy's not a frame of mind that I particularly liked being in. The anger, his hatred'.[3] Roy's own endeavour to construct an imaginary masculinity in Africa yet deal with the reality of his life in Scotland saliently broaches a range of issues concerning imperialism (and Scotland's relationship to it) and the cultural and social production of masculinity itself – its prevailing myths and contradictions.

Although Welsh has used characters such as Begbie in *Trainspotting* and Brian in 'A Smart Cunt' from *The Acid House* to dissect destructive male behaviour these mediations were considered in relation to a series of other less oppressive models. *Marabou Stork Nightmares* marks Welsh's most unremitting portrayal so far in his fiction of a dominant and aggressive paradigm of masculinity in its terminal exegesis. Roy's imaginary pursuit of the Marabou Stork is ultimately a confrontation with the core of this damaged and damaging masculinity. Notably, another twentieth-century popular cultural novel that deploys the pursuit of a bird as a quest for masculinity, Dashiell Hammett's *The Maltese Falcon* (1930), finds not authenticity or an essential model but a fake, a cultural reproduction. Similarly, *Marabou Stork Nightmares* juxtaposes models of this dominant masculinity as an essential, biological disposition with an array of cultural and social constructions thereof – whether adventure books and Roy's own reworking of them, imperialist discourse, football, his father, uncle, brothers and peers – all of which prove inadequate and inauthentic and fail to instruct Roy how to behave, act or be like a 'man'. The novel darkly affirms Graham Dawson's postulation that 'masculinities are lived out in the flesh, but fashioned in the imagination'.[4] The effects of de-industrialisation upon traditional forms of masculinity are disclosed by Roy's comatose inaction, where the adventure literature that he reads lauds heroic action, a dominant but for him now impossible form of masculinity that emphasises *doing*. In a way, then, *Marabou Stork Nightmares* helps explain the strategic function of traditional masculinity's emphasis on doing and active assertion as a means of diverting critical attention and engagement with itself. Once the grounds of that active masculinity are undermined it must increasingly chart the 'hostile terrain' (*M* 12) of its own burgeoning self-awareness and self-reflection.

However, as Michael Roper and John Tosh point out, an illustration of the fragility of masculinity should not preclude an awareness of masculinity's formative role in the operation of men's power and patriarchy.[5] Indeed, Meb Kenyon and Phyllis Nagy attack the misogyny of contemporary male culture and its response to the contemporary flux of gender identity: 'The post-feminist era is confusing and frustrating for everyone, but while women talk about the current crisis in male/female relationships openly and with a certain amount of humour and self-awareness, most of their male counterparts seem to have retreated into a world of adolescent fantasy and misogyny'.[6] Jenny Turner disparages the novel in exactly these terms: 'all that sophomoric male-violence-as-colonialism rot'.[7] Pat Kane also finds perturbing elements in a dominant masculinity's efforts to chart its own collapse. Kane argues that the New Lad culture, typified by magazines such as *Loaded*, which was discussed in the previous chapter, is a reactionary response to feminism and the mutability of gender relations which has degenerated into what he terms a New Bastard culture of ultra-violence and blank resignation:

> the foulness of the material the New Bastards deal with is still worrying. What can shift the modern male's psyche from self-loathing to self-love? In a frank interview I conducted with Welsh for BBC Radio Scotland's *The Usual Suspects*, he quoted a survey claiming that 65% of men on American student campuses admitted they would commit rape if they could get away with it. Referring to *Marabou Stork Nightmares*, Welsh said: 'I couldn't have written a book like that if I said I was one of the 35% – no way. Maybe underneath we are all crazy demented beasts. I don't know.' Welsh's frankness is refreshing – but scary.[8]

The novel maintains a tension throughout as to whether masculinity is a bestial and biological determinant or a social construction. Its epigraphs also embody conflicting desires to interpret masculinity in relation to a set of socio-cultural and imperial interstices and to position it as a congenital recidivism that nullifies any attempt at analysis. The first epigraph quotes Paul Reekie, an Edinburgh writer and friend of Welsh: 'Scepticism was formed in Edinburgh two hundred years ago by David Hume and Adam Smith. They said: "Let's take religion to the black man, but we won't really believe it." It's the cutting edge of trade'. The second cites the then British Prime Minister John Major in the wake of the murder in 1993 of the toddler, Jamie Bulger, by two ten-year-old boys in Liverpool: 'We should condemn more and understand less'. Chris Savage King posits that the novel is more engaged in understanding than condemnation: 'Nobody is let off the hook, yet nobody is denied their humanity either. Nobody's nothing. The novel opens with John Major's statement: "We should condemn more and understand less." Welsh embarks on the work of understanding'.[9] Nevertheless, John Major's government's stance of 'zero tolerance' towards crime also intersects with another of the book's concerns that is introduced in its acknowledgements – the Zero Tolerance campaign which opposed male violence against women and children and originated in Edinburgh in 1992. Zero Tolerance was a public awareness campaign which gained the support of Edinburgh City Council and used the mass media to convey its message through a series of posters that were displayed on advertising billboards in commercial areas such as Princes Street and in shops and public buildings, as well as traditionally male-dominated environments such as pubs and football grounds. One of those visually striking messages on display, which is used in the novel, was 'There is never an excuse'.[10] It can also be noted that although the cabbaged masculinity of *Marabou Stork Nightmares* may seem a long way from the cabbage-patch of the Kailyard literature of Scotland, its use of fantasy and the unconscious does have key Scottish determinants. Roy's continual urge to voyage deeper into his self does chime with Colin Manlove's argument that 'English fantasy more often deals with the quest outwards, where Scots fantasy deals with the inwards search'.[11] Thus, Cairns Craig's account of the Calvinist dialectic between the fearful and the fearless is germane for the novel's imaginative voyage: 'Fear continues to rule the human imagination and every journey into that imagination is a journey back into the terrors of the primitive past'.[12]

Adventure, imperialism and masculinity

Although Jenny Turner dismisses the novel as adolescent prurience with little political substance, part of its point, in negotiating the antinomy between condemnation and understanding, is to show how masculinity is constructed through the raw materials of adventure stories, comics and boyhood yarns in Roy's submerged male unconscious. Welsh describes a profound sense of disjunction when attempting to emulate the models of identity in adventure novels such as Enid Blyton's *Famous Five* series in the housing estate of his own childhood:

> I remember growing up in Muirhouse and there was always this thing about going camping but there was never anywhere to fuckin' go camping. You lived in this massive concrete scheme and you'd get a couple of bars of chocolate and go down to a desolate beach and try to build a tree-

house. We were trying to live out all these *Famous Five* fantasies but we
had no material to hand to actually operate in that environment – we
had no aunt in Cornwall or in Wales. Our aunts just stayed around the
corner in the next street so there was nothing you could fashion that
kind of material from. Plus, there was no alternative fiction available.
There was a massive gap between your own experience and the literature you read.[13]

This autobiographical experience suffuses the novel itself as when
Roy and his mates in Muirhouse

would think aboot running away and going camping, like in the Enid
Blyton books. We usually just got as far as the fuckin beach, before getting fed up and going hame. Occasionally we'd walk to snobby bits like
Barnton, Cramond or Blackhall. The polis would always come around
and make us go hame, though. People in the big hooses, hooses that
were the same size as our block, which sixty families lived in; they would
just go away and phone the polis. They must have thought we were
guanny chorie aypils or something. Aw I wanted tae dae was tae watch
birds. I got an interest in birds, used to get loads ay books on them fae
the library. I got this from my auld man, I suppose. He was really interested in birds as well. (*M* 26)

Indeed, a major element in the confusion of Roy's identity stems
from his inability to reconcile the masculine myths of empowerment
and conquest with the deprivations and entrapments of his social
environment. To this end, Manuel Castells considers the cosmopolitanism of the elite and the tribalism of the local community to be 'the
fundamental division of our time':

It opposes the cosmopolitanism of the elite, living on a daily connection
to the whole world (functionally, socially, culturally), to the tribalism of
local communities, retrenched in their spaces that they try to control as
their last stand against the macro-forces that shape their lives out of
their reach. The fundamental dividing line in our cities is the inclusion
of the cosmopolitans in the making of the new history while excluding
the locals from the control of the global city to which ultimately their
neighbourhoods belong.[14]

Roy's experience is therefore paradigmatic of a late capitalist imperative wherein the inhabitants of housing schemes such as Muirhouse
are increasingly stranded in sequestered peripherality whilst simultaneously being bombarded with images and ideals of mobility, power
and diversity in the mass media and wider culture. *Marabou Stork*

Nightmares makes explicit the overarching global changes that are reducing de-industrialised areas such as Muirhouse to ghettos in an exchange between Roy and his imagined rival hunter, Dawson Lockhart, who contends 'that sport, like everything else, has been replaced by business' (*M* 45). Roy's riposte undercuts the myth of market freedom and diversity through its sense of an underlying stagnation: 'the increasing experience of leisure and sport indirectly, has encouraged a decrease in real participation, which is direct communion. Therefore, you have the replacement of one or two really decent experiences with loads and loads of crap things' (*M* 45–46).

The impact of contemporary social change upon communal social life in Muirhouse is illustrated in the second chapter 'The Scheme'. Once again in Welsh's work the family is not a stable unit through which social continuity and belonging are inured and naturalised: 'I grew up in what was not so much a family as a genetic disaster. While people always seem under the impression that their household is normal I, from an early age, almost as soon as I was aware, was embarrassed and ashamed of my family' (*M* 19). This family breakdown is contextualised in terms of a wider social malaise which is attributed directly to the misguided planning of schemes such as Muirhouse that actually produces the dehumanised antithesis of community:

> I suppose this awareness came from being huddled so close to other households in the ugly rabbit hutch we lived in. It was a systems built, 1960s maisonette block of flats, five storeys high, with long landings which were jokingly referred to as 'streets in the sky' but which had no shops or pubs or churches or post offices on them, nothing in fact, except more rabbit hutches. (*M* 19)

Roy's father, John, 'was a total basket case; completely away with it', whilst his mother, Verity or Vet, 'if anything, was worse' (*M* 19) and suffers repeated mental breakdowns. When his parents were engaged Verity eloped with an Italian nurse from the mental institution where she was staying to his native Italy. But she returns with two children – Roy's half-brothers Tony and Bernard who both have different fathers – and although John had subsequently got engaged to someone else, they decide to marry. A year later Roy is born and he is followed by a sister, Kim, and another brother Elgin who is named after the Highland town where he was supposedly conceived. The family name – Strang, meaning strong – is deeply ironic given the abject

poverty and powerlessness in which they live. The family name is further denigrated in an incident recalled by Roy: 'I remember once
watching my Ma, Vet, scrubbing the tartan nameplate on the door of
our maisonette flat. Somebody had added an "E" to our name' (*M* 23).
The 'strangeness' of this family and the incongruity of the mock
tartan on their flat in a housing scheme also neatly distil the dis-
placement and dislocation from social and national paradigms
endured by these and many of Welsh's other characters.[15]

When Roy is still a child he is savaged by his father's loyal Alsatian,
Winston – named in honour of Winston Churchill, to whose recorded
wartime speeches John also avidly listens – leaving Roy permanently
disfigured and with a limp. 'Remembering hurts' (*M* 21), Roy concedes in an admission that shed lights on the narrative strategy of the
novel as a whole. John, who works as a security guard having been in
prison, also beats Roy and hospitalises him on one occasion. John
decides further that Roy, due to his limp, and his brother Bernard,
who is viewed as effeminate by the rest of the family and later turns
out to be gay, should prove their questionable masculinity by boxing
each other in the living room. Masculinity in this environment is regulated through an economy of pain and Roy comes to envy his other
brother, Elgin, who is autistic and lives in an institution that is
euphemistically called the Gorgie Venture for Exceptional Young
Men: 'At such times I envied my younger brother Elgin, silently rock-
ing or gently humming, trapped in a world of his own, exempt from
this torture. Perhaps Elgin had the right idea; perhaps it was all just
psychic defence. At times I envied Elgin's autism. Now I have what he
has, his peace and detachment from it all' (*M* 30). So Roy's response
to his childhood experiences is to mirror Elgin's state in a broader
social strategy of what Roger Horrocks deems 'male autism',[16] which
characterises his subsequent life of steeled introversion and unfolds
its final logic in his coma. For although the text is polyphonic, all of
its voices occur in Roy's deeply withdrawn consciousness, his armour
against dialogue and contact with others.[17]

So both Roy's own masculinity and his social class are gyred in self-
imploding retrenchment. The novel's interlacing of Roy's interest in
adventure books (and the present imaginary safari of his coma) with
his family's decision to move to South Africa for an anticipated material advancement establishes a context in which to examine how
power and its contradictions structure a society, how its enticements
lure and assimilate the socially disadvantaged even as it continues to

oppress them. Roy's reading of adventure books and comics offer a dreamy tableau of active masculinity and adventure that inform his own efforts to assert himself in reality (*M* 35–36). The comic books proffer a compensatory masculinity structured by colonial adventure together with an attendant hierarchy of powerful and lesser models of maleness and the subjection of women. These power structures are played out exactly when in a later chapter – 'Trouble in the Hills' – Roy recalls stabbing another pupil at school and holding a female student at knife point whilst rubbing against her until he ejaculated (*M* 106) purely because she has teased him about his large ears – his nickname is 'Dumbo'. The reason Roy gives for why the police did not press charges in the stabbing incident – 'I was far too convincing in my mummy's boy role for them' (*M* 97) – also foregrounds his capacity to appropriate roles and personae. Roy's status as an unreliable narrator is evident from the outset – 'Did I really hear my parents or was it all my imagination? I know not and care less' (*M* 16); 'my memory is practically non-existent, this could have been a few days ago or since the beginning of time itself' (*M* 4) – and the reader's sense of this will become vital at the novel's close. In the present of the narrative, as Roy's consciousness adopts the euphuistic discourse of these adolescent adventure stories, the text also utilises more Standard English than Welsh's previous fiction. Welsh explains the politics of this choice of register in the following manner:

> I was looking at the way working-class people are taught to assimilate . . . Roy Strang's fantasized African adventures . . . he's creating this fantasy world out of the material you have growing up, James Bond and all that. The middle class character is an omnipotent, all-powerful character who nothing bad happens to, nothing goes wrong for. Roy's fashioning an escape world from these materials, and that was why the schemie voice, the working-class voice, was less ubiquitous in *Marabou*. This country is so class-based and linguistically imperialist, one of the only ways you can articulate your voice is by adopting or appropriating that BBC accent, the Standard English, all the middle class trappings.[18]

The novel's first line – 'It.was.me.and.Jamieson' (*M* 3) – captures the faltering commencement of Roy's narrative and his fragmentary consciousness, its stuttering entrance into a Standard English of supposed power and control. It is the fantasy hunt for the stork in Africa which gives his narrative periods of comparative fluency through its parody of adventure stories and Enid Blyton-esque exclamations of 'wizard' and 'positively yucky'. Sandy Jamieson, Roy's companion on this imaginary expedition, is a reworking of the footballer, Jimmy Sandison, who was playing for Airdrie against Dunfermline in the 1991 Scottish League Cup that Roy watched on television as he attempted to commit suicide through an overdose of painkillers and a plastic bag placed over his head. Sandison had been falsely adjudged to have handled the ball by the referee, an injustice upon which Roy's ailing consciousness fixates (*M* 255). However, Roy's efforts to assimilate himself into this language of power are continually impinged upon by the powerlessness of his present, as the voices of nurses, doctors and his family intrude from the margins of the page and disrupt his fantasy: 'But they were trying to disturb me, trying to wake me; the way they always did. They willnae let this sleeping dog lie. They always interfere. When the cunts start this shite it makes things get aw distorted and I have to try to go deeper' (*M* 3). Despite Roy's efforts at denial – a doctor shining a torch in Roy's eyes becomes the boiling African sun in his fantasy, whilst his injections are incorporated as attacks by the stork's beak – reality continually intervenes and Roy anticipates the ultimate confrontation with his true self: 'I have this persistent vision of one large blighter, a hideous and revolting specimen, which I know somehow must perish by my own hand' (*M* 4).

The novel significantly destabilises the escapist teleology of some readings of adventure fiction. According to John G. Cawelti, the adventure story offers 'an imaginary world in which the audience can encounter a maximum of excitement without being confronted with an overpowering sense of insecurity and danger that accompanies such forms of excitement in reality'.[19] However, Richard Phillips asserts that such adventure stories are not always escapist but actually contain a repressed meditation upon more immediate social concerns and relationships: 'Unknown, distant spaces of adventure are vehicles for reflecting upon and (re)defining domestic, "civilised" places'.[20] Roy's desperate endeavour to overcome his own subjugation to the fantasy world that he has constructed confirms Phillips' relay of the fundamental anxiety troubling adventure's effort to control its own cartography of power: 'Adventures, like other maps, create conceptual space in which to move, without completely determining where the reader or writer goes. As points of departure, adventures are ambivalent'.[21] In terms of the ambivalences that thwart adventure's task of constructing a fixed geography, Graham Dawson's definition of the form's ideological purpose is instructive:

the modern tradition of British adventure has furnished idealized, wish-fulfilling forms of masculinity to counter anxieties generated in a social world that is deeply divided along the fracture-lines of ethnicity and nation, gender and class . . . Identification with these heroes meets the wish to fix one's own place within the social world, to feel oneself to be coherent and powerful rather than fragmented and contradictory. It offers the assurance of a clearly recognizable gender identity and, through this, the security of belonging to a gendered national collectivity that imagines itself to be superior in strength and virtue to others.[22]

Marabou Stork Nightmares returns to the discourse of adventure, the social conflicts of class, gender and race that it traditionally seeks simultaneously to both order and repress. This disruption occurs not only in the form of the intrusions into Roy's consciousness of his past and the present activity of the hospital but also in Welsh's subversive mimicry of the imperial adventure genre that frustrates its desire for a unitary subject and cartography of power. In the land of the stork Jamieson plays football with the local native boys with a Coca Cola can as a ball and tells them – 'it's all about possession' (*M* 12) – a pun which succinctly encapsulates the novel's main themes of colonial appropriation and dominance together with an insinuation of newer multinational forms of economic imperialism. The casual racism of traditional British adventure is evident when Roy's and Sandy's native manservant Moses absconds with their money and goods: 'I find this attitude of "something for nothing" sadly prevalent amongst the non-white races' (*M* 5). However, Roy's superior tone is suspended by a creeping sexual content in the adventure's complacently ideal narrative: 'Sandy is masturbating in the back of the jeep and she is just laughing . . . eh . . . what the fuck's gaun oan here . . . what's *she* daein here . . . it's supposed tae be Sandy n me . . . I'm losing control' (*M* 5). This irruption of sexuality then precipitates the surfacing of submerged details about the gang-rape as the italicised text of the past cuts across the fantasy narrative:

> *Lexo said that it was important that we didnae lose our bottle. Nae cunt was tae shite oot; eftir aw, the fuckin hoor asked fir it . . . Aye, she goat slapped aroond a bit, but we wir fuckin vindicated, British justice n that. She wis jist in the wrong place at the wrong time n anywey, it was aw Lexo's fault . . .* change the subject . . . I don't want this. I want to keep hunting the Stork. The Stork's the personification of all this badness. If I kill the Stork I'll kill the badness in me. (*M* 9)

So where the ideology of adventure strives to fabricate a unitary subject out of the fracture of class, gender and race, here its hegemony falls apart as these conflictual components complicate one another and collapse the narrative upon itself, thereby returning Roy to the 'ugly world' (*M* 11) of his reality.

The novel also parodies the adventure story's revelling in homosociality in a manner that indicates further contradictions within dominant models of masculinity. There is a deep homoeroticism imbuing Roy's narratorial gaze upon his companion Sandy: 'It'll be great to stretch these damn pins! He smiled, extending his long, tanned muscular legs across the back seat' (*M* 4). Similarly, there are homoerotic undercurrents in Roy's appraisal of the local boys: 'For a while we had planned to engage the services of some young native boys, but the undernourished specimens we had encountered had proved to be unappetising prospects . . . that is, manifestly unfit for the physical demands adventures with Sandy and I would inevitably place upon them' (*M* 4–5). All of this insinuation is made explicit when Roy and Sandy embrace in an avowedly manly fashion and a native boy approaches and asks: 'Homosexual? . . . I suck you off for rand' (*M* 13). Such moments serve to demonstrate how traditional adventure constructs an almost exclusively male world based upon the strong bonds of empowered men yet also seeks to repress its own construction of a profoundly homosocial – and in its own fears homosexualised – world and to declare itself normatively and aggressively heterosexual. Accordingly, Jonathan Dollimore asks, in proposing homosexuality as not marginal but actually integral (though repressed) to society: 'Has the heterosexual reader been thrilled by the forbidden, in order to return safely back to the norm, or has s/he been reminded, once again, of the very precariousness of that norm?'[23] Roy's own hostility to his brother Bernard's homosexuality also attests to the contradictions of the patriarchal hypermasculinity that he wishes to embrace so thoroughly. Notably, when he forces a male pupil to masturbate him in the toilets at knife point, Roy foists the culpability on to his victim: 'while all my pals laughed at this, they looked at me sort of differently for a while, as if I was a poof like Bernard. I blamed the Dressed-By-His-Ma-Cunt, and nursed a violent wrath . . . I hated poofs. I hated the thought ay what those sick cunts did tae each other, pittin their cocks up each other's dirty arseholes' (*M* 109). The incident illustrates that Roy's aggressive assertion of dominant masculine identity is also the repression of large parts of his being.

Scotland, South Africa, empire

The fact that Roy's interest in adventure stories is not merely escapist fantasy but rather mirrors and is actually structured upon a larger imperial narrative of power and exploitation is conveyed by the family's move to South Africa. John explains to his family his reasoning for moving them to South Africa as they are 'meant fir better things . . . Ah ken thuv goat problems in Sooth Efrikay n aw, but at least thuv no goat this fuckin Labour Governmint . . . it's a white man's country . . . white is right oot thair' (*M* 24–25). The geographics of empowerment informing both Roy's fantasy and his family's actual move to South Africa confirms Martin Green's point that adventure is 'the generic counterpart in literature to empire in politics'.[24] The first chapter of the novel's section, 'Into the City of Gold', charts the Strangs' arrival in apartheid South Africa where they stay with Roy's Uncle Gordon in a large house in the north-eastern suburbs of Johannesburg. Gordon, whose wife has left him, is a rabidly racist white supremacist who runs a property management and development company and he informs Roy that the colonial legacy of apartheid has furnished him with a status missing in his former life in Scotland: 'There I was nothing, another skinny teddy boy. Here, I count. No fucking Kaffir is going to take this away from me' (*M* 84). Although the city's name ('John's Town') seems also to promise John the empowerment and belonging that his life in Muirhouse lacks, he ends up working as a security guard in a supermarket, whilst Gordon obtains a secretarial job for Vet. In emerges that John's and Gordon's father was imprisoned for paedophile offences against young boys. Gordon systematically sexually abuses Roy – though the extent of the abuse only becomes clear towards the end of the novel due to Roy's unreliable narration glossing over the issue. It is after a trip to a nature reserve that Roy has his first Marabou Stork nightmare after encountering the bird attacking flamingos. On another trip into the bush – where the express purpose is to provide Gordon with an opportunity to rape Roy – Gordon is killed by an ANC bomb.

The anti-apartheid struggle helps refine an understanding of Scotland's relationship to imperialism as the schemies from Muirhouse seek to improve themselves through embracing an oppressively racist system that disempowers black Africans. As Alan Freeman asserts: 'The family's sojourn to South Africa provides an interesting reminder of the ambivalent status of Scots, as colonisers and colonised, reflecting the relativism of power and powerlessness which is always present in Welsh's work'.[25] Indeed, Welsh's use of South Africa evokes the work of another Scottish writer and public figure, John Buchan, who is best known for his Richard Hannay spy and adventure novels. Buchan, who was born in Perth on the east coast of Scotland and educated in Glasgow and then at Brasenose College in Oxford, diverted from his chosen career at the London Bar to serve Lord Milner, the British statesman sent to reconstruct South Africa after the Boer War. Buchan also became a Conservative MP in 1911 and between 1917 and 1918 was involved in covert propaganda work as Director General of Information. Most notably, in terms of *Marabou Stork Nightmares*, Buchan was a committed imperialist on the grounds of what he perceived to be its civilising effect upon the wider world and its benefits for those incorporated into its 'British-ness' at home as well. Buchan reminisced in 1940 about the impor-tance of South Africa to his imperial utopia:

> a vision of what the empire might be dawned upon certain minds with almost the force of revelation . . . I dreamed of a worldwide brotherhood with the background of a common race and creed, consecrated in the service of peace; Britain enriching the rest out of her culture and tradi-tions, and spirit of the Dominions like a strong wind freshening the stiffness of the old lands. I saw in the Empire a means of giving the con-gested masses at home open country instead of a blind alley . . . Our creed was not based on antagonism to any other people. It was human-itarian and international; we believed that we were laying the basis of a federation of the world.[26]

Significantly, Roy finds apartheid South Africa 'a sort of paradise' (*M* 77) that is filled with 'possibilities' (*M* 77). Roy enjoys school and wants to channel his interest in ornithology and nature into becom-ing a zoologist. Roy comments:

> I wanted to stay in South Africa. What I gained there was a perverse sense of empowerment; an ego even. I knew I was fuckin special, what-ever any of them tried to tell me. I knew I wasn't going to be like the rest of them; my old man, my old lady, Bernard, Tony, Kim, the other kids back in the scheme. They were rubbish. They were nothing. I was Roy Strang. (*M* 88)

However, this seemingly idealistic effort to make something of him-self is effaced by its implication in power and oppression. Roy's zool-ogy offers a means of control in its desire to catalogue and chart artefacts and is reflected in his father's own efforts to aggrandise himself in Muirhouse by keeping computer files on each of their neighbours which neurotically assesses their security threat. This urge to inventorise is imbricated in an overarching imperial project (together with adventure literature) grounded in the symbiotic complicity between *power* and *knowledge*. As Michel Foucault expounds: 'We should admit that power produces knowledge ... that power and knowledge directly imply one another; that there is no power relation without the correlative constitution of a field of knowledge, nor any knowledge that does not presuppose and constitute ... power relations'.[27]

In the context of colonialism and its discourse the naming of Roy's brother, Elgin, and indeed his sister, Kim, is highly significant. As Berthold Schoene-Harwood notes, Elgin's name evokes the case of the Elgin Marbles – as well as a pun on mental illness and losing one's marbles.[28] The Elgin Marbles, which were ancient Greek sculptures that originally formed part of the Parthenon in Athens, are now so-called because they were pillaged in an act of colonial appropriation by the Scottish Earl of Elgin, Thomas Bruce, during his time as a diplomat in Constantinople (1799–1803). Despite repeated efforts by successive Greek governments to have the marbles returned they are still displayed in the British Museum as an archival remnant of a distinctly British imperial arrogance. The fate of the marbles attests to the acquisitional capacity of power and knowledge in an imperial system. Yet it is the same aristocratic Scottish clan and head of the Bruce family, the Elgins, who helped to raise finds in 1930 to purchase fifty-eight acres of land around the site of the battle of Bannockburn where in 1314 Robert the Bruce defeated Edward II's invading English army and became Robert I of Scotland. So the Elgin clan are at once implicated in acts of British colonial dominance and the commemoration of Scottish independence and difference. Such contradiction between assertions of Scottish independence and obsequious compliance with British empire building is evidenced in John's decision to vote for the Scottish Nationalist Party in the British general election purely in protest at the Conservative government's introduction of the poll tax: 'no thit ah believe in Scottish independence. The Scots built the empire n these daft English cunts couldnae run it withoot us' (*M* 125). Andrew O'Hagan comments caustically:

> Scotland still resents England, but it doesn't resent it enough to raise an effective opposition to its authority. It has always wanted a little bit of

what England has; its commercial and ideological roots go down quite far with England's; their entanglement is of a kind that might raise a laugh in the breast of those who know enough history to know that – unlike, say, Eire – Scotland, far from being a colonised country, has been a bitter harvester, in its own right, of other peoples' freedom.[29]

Kim's name also intimates the impacted space of Scotland's relationship to (post)colonialism, as it recalls the novel *Kim* (1901) by Rudyard Kipling, one of the founding fathers of British colonial adventure literature. Kim's ambivalent status as both British and Indian offers him as a mediating figure whose cross-cultural espionage traverses the anxious intrigue and subterfuge through which Kipling regulates the colonised otherness of India in the novel.[30] Although Kim's first language is Urdu and he has grown up as a native his ancestry lies in the British military presence – yet it is also an Irish ancestry, adding a further complication to an effort to construct a straightforward coloniser–colonised opposition. Hence, Kim in Kipling's novel is the site wherein incommensurate narratives of coloniality collide and this charged liminality informs the unravelling imperial fabric woven by Roy's visions in *Marabou Stork Nightmares*.

Roy's plans to become a zoologist are ruined by his father's arrest for viciously assaulting a taxi driver after a drinking session, for which he is imprisoned for six months and the family is sent home. But Roy's return to the housing schemes of Edinburgh fills him with a 'dread' that produces a sharp revision of his former paradisal account of South Africa:

> Edinburgh to me represented serfdom. I realised that it was exactly the same situation as Johannesburg; the only difference was that the Kaffirs were white and called schemies or draftpacks. Back in Edinburgh, we would be kaffirs; condemned to live out our lives in townships like Muirhouse or So-Wester-Hailes-To or Niddrie, self-contained camps with fuck all in them, miles fae the toon. Brought in tae dae the crap jobs that nae other cunt wanted tae dae, then hassled by the polis if we hung around at night in groups. Edinburgh had the same politics as Johannesburg: it had the same politics as any city. Only we were on the other side. I detested the thought of going back to all that shite. (*M* 80)

The novel's undertaking to comprehend the tribalised ghetto of Edinburgh's housing schemes as 'exactly the same' as the banished townships that suffered under the apartheid regime is magnified by the above blurring of Westerhailes and Soweto. This elision of difference between Scotland's housing schemes and the townships of apartheid, as Alan Freeman cogently indicates,[31] is highly problematic, especially given that the novel tasks itself with undermining the assumptions of colonialism. There is a marked danger here of a perverse residual imperialism whereby an oppressed group in the Western world – in a seeming moment of solidarity – actually colonises and appropriates the suffering of others in order to bolster its own subaltern credentials.

Nonetheless, Berthold Schoene-Harwood argues that Roy's realisation facilitates an illumination of the contradictions of colonial power in terms of both class and masculinity:

> Within the context of Welsh's novel, this historical circumstance appears to assume figurative significance. Serving and no doubt benefiting as indispensable helpmates in the construction and maintenance of the British Empire, Scottish men – and those of a lower social rank especially – have never won perfect equality with their allegedly superior English counterparts. Quasi-English colonisers abroad, their acculturation at home has remained spurious and incomplete, a circumstance perhaps most poignantly illustrated in Welsh's novel by the mistranslation of the Strangs' family name into 'strange' rather than 'strong'. While living under the South African apartheid regime Scottish 'schemies' may pass for legitimate members of the master race. In Britain, however, they represent a severely disadvantaged underclass, of which the men especially find themselves at risk of 'losing their marbles' to the constant taunts and provocations of systemic emasculation.[32]

So, for Schoene-Harwood, imperial adventure and racist discourse permits disempowered working-class men access to a fantasy colonial worldview of untrammelled power and superiority, whilst the 'strangeness' of the Strangs resides precisely in their effort to put that fictitious power to use at 'home'. But such systemic oppression also requires a complicity in power relationships in Britain as well – whether the target is women, homosexuals, ethnic others and members of the working class who refute the imperialist model.

Hence, Michael Gardiner asserts that the novel possesses 'an explicitly political content, connecting the Unionist-Protestant identity concretized in Britain, and the colonialism which gave it a worldwide expression'. Gardiner continues that the 'British equation of sectarianism, class and colonialism is central to *Marabou Stork Nightmares*. Working-class loyalist aspiration has been a pillar of Britishness since its early days, especially in its "margins", and this aspiration undergoes ridicule in *Marabou Stork Nightmares*, as dialects are piled up against one another'.[33] Consequently, in Roy's fantasy hunt, Dawson Lockhart is head of the Jambola Safari Park and the private company, Jambola Park PLC – linking his terrain and power to the Hearts football team ('The Jambos' or 'Jam Tarts') and thus to working-class Protestantism and Loyalism – in contrast to the Irish Catholic immigrant origins of Hibernian. Moreover, one of Lockhart's hunting lodges is numbered 1690, punning on Protestant Orange Lodges that commemorate the Battle of the Boyne in 1690 in which the Protestant William of Orange defeated the Catholic James II and secured the British throne, its constitution and its political union of England, Scotland, Ireland and Wales in Protestant hands.

As Gardiner suggests, *Marabou Stork Nightmares* ridicules the ultimately self-negating loyalist working class's imperial aspirations through the 'strangeness' of Roy's mimicry of the discourse of colonial adventure. John M. MacKenzie notes that in popular British imperial masculinity the 'confusion between hunting as the pioneering archetype of freedom and the role of the Hunt as an elite ritual with an elaborate code was never resolved'.[34] The novel compounds this disjunction as Roy's attempts to interpolate himself in this elite register of imperial superiority actually divulge social impediments of class, gender and race that strictly determine such British 'freedoms'. Homi K. Bhabha discerns that:

> Mimicry is also the sign of the inappropriate . . . a difference or recalcitrance which coheres the dominant strategic function of colonial power, intensifies surveillance, and poses an immanent threat to both 'normalized' knowledges and disciplinary powers . . . The effect of mimicry on the authority of colonial discourse is profound and disturbing. For in 'normalizing' the colonial state or subject, the dream of post-Enlightenment civility alienates its own language of liberty and produces another knowledge of its norms.[35]

Roy's strange mimicry of imperial adventure not only defamiliarises its 'normalized' oppression of other nations and peoples but also estranges its Britishness at home so that its unitary façade of freedom collapses along the very interstices of class, race and gender that it is designed to repress. Therefore, when Roy describes Muirhouse, having been arrested at the age of nine for playing football in the street, as 'a concentration camp for the poor' (*M* 22), two points can be made. Firstly, this undue equivalence, this 'same politics' between two vastly differing historical moments, seems to overwhelm the

desired effect of engendering sympathy. But secondly, and more opti-
mistically in anti-imperial terms, it should be remembered that concentration camps were constructed at the behest of General Lord
Kitchener in the British campaign against the white South Africa
guerrillas in the Boer War of 1899–1902. These concentration camps
forcibly housed mainly women and children – around 25,000 of
whom died – as part of the British scorched earth policy intended to
starve the guerrillas of support. So the novel here links British imperial policy and oppression abroad with that at home. To this end,
Fintan O'Toole locates the nineteenth-century rise of Scotland in 'the
supreme *British* century – in the era of Queen Victoria and David Liv-
ingstone, of industry and empire' and posits: 'it is impossible for Scotland to cast itself as an opposed and colonized nation and at the same
time to locate its golden age in a time when it was most profoundly
at one with the supposed aggressor. It needs a different story'.[36]
Marabou Stork Nightmares offers a different story by suggesting that
Scotland is itself not a homogeneous entity that can be positioned as
either coloniser or colonised. Rather, it is a collision of both that benefited large sections of Scotland's upper and middle classes in addition to aspirant working-class imperialists who gain provisional
access to its benefits. Yet simultaneously, it further oppressed the rest
its own working and subaltern classes. So colonialism does not
merely seek to dominate and control overseas, it also strives to maintain specific sets of unequal social relations relating to class, gender,
sexuality and place at home.

Casual violence?

When the family returns to Muirhouse Roy's life follows its familiar
pattern regulated by the novel's economy of pain and violence.
Although he eventually obtains a job after leaving school as a computer systems analyst, the only sense of identity he gains is through
his inauguration into the Capital City Service, a group of Hibernian
football casuals, wherein he meets Lexo and the other members of the
gang who all eventually rape Kirsty. The third section of the book
begins with the chapter 'Casuals' in which Roy engages in his first
fight with the casuals 'like a demented animal' (*M* 134). So although
South Africa broached the subject of political violence in the form of
the armed struggle against apartheid, the naturalised violence of the
law of the wild embodied in the Marabou Stork again appears to recur

in Roy's behaviour – and there is an unsettling and underlying strain in the novel that wills the reduction of all violence to this supposedly natural and primordial imperative. Indeed, it is in a chapter called 'The Flamingo Massacres', as a result of his battle with Glasgow Rangers' fans, that Roy regains the ego he experienced in the relative empowerment of white South Africa (*M* 172).

When Roy's insecurities decide that Kirsty does not take him seriously enough – and as in his school days, he claims, makes him insecure about his physical appearance and large ears – it is a similar assertion of his brutal self that rationalises the rape: 'All I'm looking for is a bit of respect. It's my fuckin entitlement' (*M* 179). He and the gang spike Kirsty's drink with drugs and then subject her to a prolonged and violent rape – though Roy is keen to emphasis in his own mind that Lexo was its ringleader and that he had a peripheral part to play in it. The subsequent trial – in which Roy and the gang are all acquitted – forms part of the strand in the novel that resists viewing violence as natural aberration and seeks instead to place it in a social context of power relations. This is made plain in the correlation of the violence visited upon Kirsty during the rape and her treatment in the courtroom. The gang's defence counsel, Conrad Donaldson, emphasises this point in his pre-trial pep talk: 'Put yourself in my hands and we'll give her a damn good shafting' (*M* 207). Donaldson's excruciating metaphor indicates that the rape is to be situated in an aggressively patriarchal society where power is gendered in oppressively male terms whilst those without access to that power are 'shafted'. Whilst the gang behave as if they were the aggrieved 'victim' (*M* 212), Roy describes how 'It became like she was the one on trial; her past, her sexuality, her behaviour' (*M* 208). Later, as she sits by his bedside, Kirsty confesses to Roy: 'I was a fool Roy. A fool to go through the process. It was worse than the rape itself . . . The whole thing was a theatre. A theatre to humiliate and brutalise me all over again' (*M* 223).

Despite the not guilty verdict, the chapter 'Zero Tolerance' relates Roy's first encounter when walking along Princes Street with the Zero Tolerance posters proclaiming: No Man Has the Right; Male Abuse of Power is a Crime; When She Says No She Means No. Roy retreats to a bar but there is a poster there too so he finds another pub where he meets his boss and has a moment of clarity that surmounts the *displaced abjection*, to return to Stallybrass and White's term, entrapping so many of Welsh's characters:

It all came tae ays wi clarity; these are the cunts we should be hurtin, no the boys wi knock fuck oot ay at the fitba, no the birds we fuck aboot, no oor ain Ma n Dad, oor ain brothers n sisters, oor ain neighboors, oor ain mates. These cunts. Bit naw; we screw each other's hooses when there's fuck all in them, we terrorise oor ain people. (*M* 200–201)

Roy flees to a job in Manchester to escape his guilt and the Zero Tolerance campaign. On a night out with his work colleague, Dorie, and her friend Paula, Roy takes Ecstasy and finds feelings within in himself that he had always repressed: 'Dorie and Paula I loved; I just loved them. I couldn't stop hugging them, like I'd always wanted to hug pals, but it was too sappy, too poofy. I knew that after I came down I'd still love them. Something fundamental happened that night; something opened up in me' (*M* 237). Although Roy embarks on a relationship with Dorie and they get engaged it soon falls apart when he reads an article in the *Manchester Evening News* about the Zero Tolerance campaign and suffers a breakdown. Upon his return to Edinburgh to watch a Hibernian match Roy goes clubbing and takes Ecstasy, whereupon he meets Bernard, the homosexual brother he so persecuted, and embraces him and apologises. Bernard discloses that he is HIV positive and Roy decides to go to a rave called Rezurrection. However, the illuminated Z in the Rezurrection sign reminds Roy and his newly awakened sensitivities of the huge Z on the Zero Tolerance posters and he is consumed by a guilt that then leads to his suicide attempt – the narrative itself breaks up into huge Z shapes of text at this point.

Representing rape

Evelyn Gillan, one of the co-ordinators of the actual of Zero Tolerance campaign, accredits Welsh with locating rape in a culture of patriarchal domination but also voices concerns about the graphic detail of the novel's rape scene:

He makes it clear that rape is about one thing and one thing only and that's power and abuse of power. But there is a problem with these very graphic descriptions of violence – if you look at the rampant misogyny that is illustrated throughout the book and then you combine that with these very graphic descriptions, you really get a sense for women reading the book, the experience is very disempowering, you read it and you feel, 'God, do men really hate us this much?', the whole way that they talk to women, the whole way that they relate to women or don't relate to women.[37]

Welsh defends the novel by averring that the rape scene is necessarily brutal in order to convey the horror of the act. What is much more offensive, according to Welsh, is the conventional literary depiction of rape and the sanitised almost romantic legitimacy that it confers upon it:

> The first thing is that you're reacting against things. It's like you read how other writers treat rape, I mean like Catherine Cookson, for example, the rapist always ends up marrying the rapee, the rape victim falls in love with the rapist and they end up marrying. So you're kinda reacting against that quite ugly, insidious and nasty portrayal of rape . . . You get a lot of middle-class cultural commentators that go on about how horrific rape is – of course it's horrific and it has to be seen and demonstrated to be that way. Then they say, 'Oh God, this is too much, you shouldn't be showing it that way'. How do you show rape? Do you make it into a happy party, or make it into a Catherine Cookson thing, or do you ignore it and pretend that there is no such thing.[38]

It is noteworthy that during the court case the defence makes its case in precisely the terms of what Welsh deems a Catherine Cookson-type approach, as one of Kirsty's former boyfriends is brought to the witness stand to testify falsely that she divulged her fantasies about being gang-raped to him. According to Welsh's own argument, however, there is a highly problematic turn in the narrative when Kirsty informs the comatose Roy that she did in fact find him attractive: 'The funny thing is Roy, Roy Strang, that I actually fancied you. Honest . . . I was scared to talk to you though. You didn't show any interest in me, no like the others . . . The only reason I hung around with these morons was to get closer to you. How crazy is that then, eh?' (*M* 228). This moment recapitulates exactly the Catherine Cookson narrative disparaged by Welsh, as it transpires that the rape victim secretly desired the rapist. Additionally, Elspeth Findlay criticises the implications of the socio-linguistic registers employed to depict the rape and its aftermath: 'At the moment of the rape, the narrator is, "ah", a speaker of dialect. As he reflects remorsefully he turns into, "I". During the rape he says, "ay them". Afterwards he says, "Of her". The evil side of the narrator speaks dialect, the conscience-stricken side speaks Standard English'.[39] Ironically, given the parody of adventure stories in the novel and Roy's effort to assimilate himself to Standard English as a language of power and oppression, here it is absolved of any culpability. It is working-class language and culture – and the people contained therein – that are barbaric whilst Standard

English offers more complex sensibilities and reflections. Consequently, Alan Freeman posits: 'the novel seems to confirm the prejudices of the kind of bourgeois perspective it is intended to
challenge'.[40]

Evelyn Gillan is also troubled by the narrative's ultimate focalisation or point of view and Welsh's relationship thereto:

> He writes about women in a very physical way, not in an emotional way
> at all. And whilst you could argue that he's just writing about it as it is,
> and however painful that might be for us to confront, nevertheless there
> is a sense that there's some collusion going on, there's a sense of the
> writer colluding with the male readers. There's no sense anywhere that
> he's taking the side of his women characters.[41]

Therefore, when Roy's consciousness admits that the rape took
Kirsty's 'self, or her sense of it' (*M* 190), the narrative is perhaps itself
culpable of this arrogation. And whilst part of the point of the novel
has been to demonstrate that Roy's inability to experience others as
experiencing, to grant others interiority and selfhood – at least until it
is too late – the final chapter intensifies the problematics of Kirsty's
representation, her status, in Ellen-Raïssa Jackson and Willy Maley's
terms, as merely 'the butchered flamingo, a bloody symbol of someone else's life'.[42]

Facing the stork

Kirsty returns to Roy's bedside for the final time in the concluding
chapter 'Facing the Stork'. Kirsty's first revelation is that Roy's
account of the rape – brutally horrific as it was – is a sanitised version
and that he was actually its main instigator rather than an unwilling
accomplice:

> remember when you put the mirror at the foot of the mattress to see my
> face as you forced yourself into my arse . . . remember what you said?
> Do you? You said you wanted me to look at you, and you wanted to see
> my face. You wanted me to see Roy Strang. You wanted me to feel what
> happens to any cunt who fucks about with Roy Strang. Now I want to see
> you, Roy. I want you to see what you've made me, because you've made
> me just like you. (*M* 259)

Indeed, Roy has a flashback to his exclamation – 'Ah'm running this
fucking gig! Ah say whin the slag's hud enough!' (*M* 262) – when the
other members of the gang attempt to put an end to the rape. But as

with the difficulties generated by the 'same politics' being used to por-
tray Edinburgh housing schemes and apartheid townships, Kirsty's
becoming 'just like' Roy erases both sexual difference and the specific
calibrations of suffering. Having disclosed earlier that she has already
killed one member of the gang Kirsty now removes Roy's eyelids with
a knife before cutting off his penis and putting it in his mouth: 'Might
is right. You *take* the right. I'm taking the right Roy, taking the right
to fuck you off, son' (*M* 260). The sameness of what they both have
become is conveyed by Kirsty's taunts which echo those of the rape:
'Do I hear sounds there, Roy . . . I can't hear you . . . what are you
trying to tell me . . . I know you want this, I know you're asking for it'
(263). Welsh's stated aim in writing the novel was to use Roy's hunting fantasy as a parody of contemporary fiction's literary heroes – 'a
lot of fiction is written in the spirit of wish-fulfilment' – and to coun-
teract that with an anti-heroic vision in keeping with working-class
experience: 'Lads very seldom come out on top'.[43] Yet male hegemony
does come out on top. In a sense, Kirsty's revenge is a distinctly and
symbolically patriarchal punishment for the distinctly patriarchal
crime of Roy not being able to deal with the consequences of his allot-
ted patriarchal role. Kirsty's revenge, like the rape itself, is mediated
through the privileged patriarchal signifier of the phallus which ultimately retains its status both to confer and to deny power. As Berthold
Schoene-Harwood cogently elaborates:

> the ending of *Marabou Stork Nightmares* fails to introduce a construc-
> tive, emancipatory vision of how the vicious circle of violence and viola-
> tion could be broken. Instead of challenging the phallocentric principle
> of exploitative domination, Welsh's novel confirms and consolidates its
> hegemonic power. The moment Kirsty takes her revenge on Roy and
> cuts off his penis is not a moment of feminist emancipation but a
> moment of acute patriarchal subjection. Stepping into the shadow of the
> phallus, the victim succumbs to the binarist logic of oppression and re-
> emerges as yet another victimiser.[44]

Roy's effort to begin critiquing the logic of patriarchy which has so
impelled his own masculinity is silenced by that very same and deadening logic.

The action of the final pages is interspersed with slogans from the
Zero Tolerance campaign but the dialectic between condemnation
and understanding introduced by the epigraph from John Major is
unresolved:

> I understand her hurt, her pain, how it all just has to come out. It just
> goes round and round, the hurt. It takes an exceptionally strong person
> to just say: no more. It takes a weak one to just keep it all to themselves,
> let it tear them apart without hurting anyone else.
>   I'm not an exceptionally strong person.
>   Nor is Kirsty.
>   We're just ordinary and this is shite.
>   We both understand everything. (*M* 264)

Yet this 'everything' is understandable only according to an economy
of pain that is all-encompassing and 'never really ends' (*M* 223). If
behind every victimiser there stands a victim and every victim in turn
becomes a victimiser, does the novel's close affirm understanding or
is the revenge the culmination of condemnation? Moreover, as
Major's anti-crime reading of the Zero Tolerance message elides into
the feminist awareness campaign's motto, does this undermine that
campaign by implying that it fails to understand male pain? In terms
of the tension between nature and nurture, there is also a sense in
which the brutal law of the wild represented by the stork – and Roy's
symbolic attachment to it – dangerously exculpates Roy and other
abusers by suggesting they are merely products of natural imperatives. Under such analysis masculinity itself becomes a nightmarish
primitivism, a repressed subconscious still prompting the actions of
men in today's society even as they vainly seek to disguise it with
veneers of civility. Just as a troubling sameness diffuses the difference
between Soweto and Edinburgh, between masculinity and femininity, there is in the primitivism of natural selection a dissolution of the
divide between humans and animals – for just as Roy dehumanises
himself in his violence so too he regards Kirsty as an 'animal' (*M* 183)
in the rape scene.

The unreliability of the narration is accentuated as Roy retreats into
a final reverie:

> The sun is rising behind me and my shadow spills out away from it, out
> in front of me. My spindly legs, my large overcoat, my massive beak . . .
> I have no visible ears, I never really had much in the way of ears, it was
> always my nose, Captain Beaky, they used to call me at the school . . . it
> wasn't the ears, my memory hasn't been so good, nor has my hearing
> but I can think more clearly now. (*M* 264)

Not only has Roy's narrative misrepresented the rape scene but here
a different self emerges – his tales of being taunted at school for

having large ears ('Dumbo Strang') are erased as he presents us with a revised picture of himself that completely undermines not merely our sense of his physical appearance but also the suffering he endured on account of it. If such important details are revealed to be unfounded can any of the narrative be trusted? By extension, can we fully understand – rather than condemn – Roy's life and actions if their narration is entirely fictitious? Is the narrative finally another trick from a character who in his school days and adult life evaded punishment for his violent actions by duping teachers, police officers and courts through his adoption of various personae – the 'mummy's boy', the sensitive adolescent, the hard-working professional. Has the revenge scene with Kirsty occurred or it is merely another layering in Roy's comatose consciousness? The reader will remember that Roy's account of events by his bedside are also at times suspect – whether it is Kirsty professing the desire she felt for him before he raped her, or the nurse Patricia Devine performing oral sex on him. The narrative ends with a huge letter Z and this is also a brilliantly ambiguous stroke. It recalls the Zero Tolerance posters and their message – which have at least put an end to something in the form of the novel itself – and the Rezurrection rave where seeing the letter leads to Roy's remorse and suicide attempt. Yet the letter Z is also the traditional typographic figuration of sleep: has the supposed ending only been another event in perpetually submerged male subconscious, the living out of its most primal fear and insecurity rather than an exacting of revenge? Notably, in the safari of Roy's mind it is not Kirsty but a man who kills him – Sandy turns and fires a shotgun at Roy the stork. If we accept that Roy does die then the ending is not a recognisably feminist justice. The previous chapter noted how in the story 'Where the Debris Meets the Sea' – admittedly in a more comic vein – women were seen to assume a relative power only when they accepted the terms of patriarchal hegemony and hence became masquerading male subjects. So too, in a more tragic way, Kirsty's seizing of the symbolic and actual power of the phallus in order to become 'just like' Roy offers a temporary agency that only serves to reinforce the power of patriarchy and its symbolic order and to deny women access to any radical alternatives.

Nevertheless, where the novel does offer something beyond a consummate economy of pain is in Roy's discovery of Ecstasy and dance culture which reawakens feelings that he had long repressed in himself – and thus, also more positively, suggests that nurture or social conditioning produces dominant masculinities rather than an immutable law of nature. In short, dominant forms of masculinity are not unalterable but can be challenged, resisted, reshaped. Welsh comments that it is possible for a rapist to rationalise his actions 'provided you've been brutalized completely by the world you live in. And to commit rape in the first place, you must have had to have been abused yourself. Rape isn't a big problem for the rapists, as it wasn't for Roy and his gang at the time. It only becomes a big problem when you become sensitized, when you open up your feelings'.[45] So there are feelings denied by both Roy and the dominant codes of his society which undercut the blanket pessimism that the novel also seems to offer. And Welsh's next work offers an extended elaboration of the awakenings that he perceives in Ecstasy culture.

Notes

1 Cited in Berman, Jennifer, 'An interview with Irvine Welsh', *Bomb Magazine* 56 (1996), 58.
2 Welsh continues: 'I'm also quite precious about it, having knocked back a couple of approaches to turn it into a film. I wasn't keen on what the people involved had in mind' (*4P*, 4).
3 Cited in Berman, 'An interview with Irvine Welsh', 58.
4 Graham Dawson, *Soldier Heroes: British Adventure, Empire and the Imagining of Masculinities* (London: Routledge, 1994), 1.
5 Michael Roper and John Tosh, *Manful Assertions: Masculinities in Britain Since 1991* (London: Routledge, 1991), 15.
6 Meb Kenyon and Phyllis Nagy, 'Season of lad tidings', *Guardian*, G2 (4 Dec 1995), 7.
7 Jenny Turner, 'Love's chemistry', *Guardian*, G2T (31 May 1996) 17.
8 Pat Kane, 'Fatal knowledge of an inescapable masculinity', *Scotland on Sunday* (16 July 1995), 12.
9 Chris Savage King, 'Voices from the edge', *Sunday Times* (16 Apr 1995), 12.
10 See Fiona Mackay, *The Case of Zero Tolerance: Women's Politics in Action?* (Edinburgh: Waverley Papers, 1995).
11 Colin Manlove, *Scottish Fantasy Literature: A Critical Survey* (Edinburgh: Canongate, 1994), 12.
12 Cairns Craig, *The Modern Scottish Novel: Narrative and the National Imagination* (Edinburgh: Edinburgh University Press, 1999), 42.
13 Cited in John Mulholland, 'Acid wit', *Guardian*, G2T (30 Mar 1995), 8. In terms of emulous models for young men, the 'Famous Five' also have a resonance with Hibernian Football Club, as it is the collective nickname

of the players, Gordon Smith, Bobby Johnstone, Lawrie Reilly, Eddie Turnbull and Willie Ormond, who helped the club win the Scottish league championship three times in what is considered its golden age of the late 1940s and early 1950s. There is now a Famous Five stand at the club's Easter Road ground, which, as with the use of adventure fiction in *Marabou Stork Nightmares*, harks back to a perceived period of glory and wonder in the face of contemporary pressures.

14 Manuel Castells, 'European cities, the information society, and the global economy', *New Left Review* 204 (Mar/Apr 1994), 30.

15 The defamiliarisation and alterity of life in Muirhouse is compounded by Roy's parody of the tag-line from Ridley Scott's science fiction film *Alien* – 'In Space No One Can Hear You Scream': 'In Muirhoose nae cunt can hear ye scream . . . well, they can hear ye, they just dinnae gie a fuck' (*M* 141).

16 Roger Horrocks, *Masculinity in Crisis: Myths, Fantasies, Realities* (Houndmills: Macmillan, 1994), 107.

17 One of Roy's key rules is: 'say nowt tae nae cunt aboot anything' (*M* 142).

18 Cited in Berman, 'An interview with Irvine Welsh', 57.

19 John G. Cawelti, *Adventure, Mystery, and Romance: Formula Stories as Art and Popular Culture* (London: University of Chicago Press, 1976), 16.

20 Richard Phillips, *Mapping Men and Empire: A Geography of Adventure* (London: Routledge, 1997), 13.

21 Phillips, *Mapping Men and Empire*, 164.

22 Dawson, *Soldier Heroes*, 282.

23 Jonathan Dollimore, *Sexual Dissidence: Augustine to Wilde, Freud to Foucault* (London: Clarendon Press, 1991), 57.

24 Martin Green, *Dreams of Adventure, Deeds of Empire* (London: Routledge, 1980), 37.

25 Alan Freeman, 'Ourselves as others: *Marabou Stork Nightmares*', *Edinburgh Review* 95 (1996), 137.

26 John Buchan, *Memory Hold the Door* (London: Hodder and Staughton, 1940), 124–125.

27 Michel Foucault, *Power/Knowledge: Selected Interviews and Other Writings, 1972–1977*. Ed. Colin Gordon. Trans. Colin Gordon et al. (Brighton: Harvester Wheatsheaf, 1980), 27. For an application of Foucault's method in terms of colonialism see Edward W. Said, *Orientalism* (London: Penguin, 1995).

28 Berthold Schoene-Harwood, *Writing Men: Literary Masculinities from Frankenstein to the New Man* (Edinburgh: Edinburgh University Press, 2000), 152.

29 Andrew O'Hagan, 'Scotland's fine mess', *Guardian*, Weekend Section (23 July 1994), 24.

30 See Edward W. Said, *Culture and Imperialism* (London: Chatto and

Windus, 1993) and Thomas Richards, *The Imperial Archive: Knowledge and the Fantasy of Empire* (London: Verso, 1993).

31 See Freeman, 'Ourselves as others'.

32 Schoene-Harwood, *Writing Men*, 152.

33 Michael Gardiner, 'British territory: Irvine Welsh in English and Japanese', *Textual Practice* 17: 1 (2003), 110, 114.

34 John M. MacKenzie, 'The imperial pioneer and hunter and the British masculine stereotype in late Victorian and Edwardian times' in J. A. Mangan and James Walvin, eds, *Manliness and Morality: Middle-Class Masculinity in Britain and America 1800–1940* (Manchester: Manchester University Press, 1987), 193.

35 Homi K. Bhabha, *The Location of Culture* (London: Routledge, 1994), 86.

36 Fintan O'Toole, 'Imagining Scotland', *Granta* 56 (Winter 1996), 70–71.

37 *In Your Face. Irvine Welsh: Condemn More, Understand Less*. BBC2. Broadcast 27 Nov 1995.

38 *In Your Face.*

39 Elspeth Findlay, 'The bourgeois values of Irvine Welsh', *Cencrastus* 71 (2002), 6.

40 Freeman, 'Ourselves as others', 141.

41 *In Your Face.*

42 Ellen-Raïssa Jackson and Willy Maley, 'Birds of a feather? A postcolonial reading of Irvine Welsh's *Marabou Stork Nightmares*', *Revista Canaria de Estudios Ingleses* 41 (2000), 194.

43 Chris Savage King, 'Voices from the edge', *Sunday Times* (16 Apr 1995), 12.

44 Schoene-Harwood, *Writing Men*, 155–156.

45 Cited in Berman, 'An interview with Irvine Welsh', 59.

4

Ecstasy: Three Chemical Romances (1996)

Shortly before its publication, Welsh anticipated the trilogy of novellas in *Ecstasy* with a bold and defiant pronouncement:

> I've another book out in two months time, *Ecstasy: Three Chemical Romances*, and it's either going to get good reviews or it's going to get bad reviews, but it doesn't matter because it's going to sell a shitload whatever happens. I've been fortunate enough to discover my readership in my lifetime and what that's done is completely negate any part of these liberal critics who only like things that will affirm their own values, but won't challenge them. People are going to buy it anyway, whatever they say, whether they rave about it, or they slag it off. It makes no difference at all. And that's a comfortable position for me to be in.[1]

And whilst Welsh has always remained justifiably antagonistic to the literary establishment and the views of metropolitan critics, the key terms here are perhaps 'comfortable' and 'no difference', as Welsh's claim seems to transmit a somewhat self-satisfied indifference in writing the book based solely on assured sales. It is always a dangerous complacency when a writer associates his or her work with a zone of comfort, particularly a writer distinguished by his edgy and unsettling polemics against mainstream social consensus. For the book was roundly panned, particularly amongst critics who had always harboured suspicions about his talents and motives. Jenny Turner adjudged *Ecstasy* 'the worst book yet from a writer who has been going from weakness to weakness ever since *Trainspotting*'.[2] Pat Kane implied that Welsh's work was subject to a law of diminishing returns: 'Welsh's literary rushes are beginning to wear off. If his implied readership is deriving more profundity from chemicals, pals and dance-floor motion than anything else (certainly Good Books) then his join-the-dots Ecstasy style can be excused. But it's thin stuff, if you're not inside the bliss-out'.[3] Nick Curtis averred: 'It is sad and ironic to say it, but in establishing himself as a frontline spokesman for the unrepresented Ecstasy generation, Welsh may have written himself into a rut'.[4] Tim Adams, though praising *Trainspotting*, contended that Welsh's 'writing since that bright beginning has been at best patchy in the clumsy comedy of the short stories in *The Acid House* and at worst numbingly repetitive in the rambling *Marabou Stork Nightmares*. The three gormless novellas that fill the pages of *Ecstasy* are a still cruder imitation of the original'. For Adams, Welsh's work had become nothing more than a 'marketing exercise'.[5]

Nonetheless, Welsh has subsequently and self-critically castigated the book's failings: 'I never sat down properly with it. I was doing *The Acid House* screenplay at the time. *Ecstasy* was like somebody writing an Irvine Welsh exploitation book'.[6] Whilst still hailing its commercial success, Welsh has also conceded its artistic failings and praised Keith Wyatt's stage adaptation, as well as looking forward to an improvement with its filming:

> The ideas were good, they were just badly written. I was trying out different voices and it didn't work out. The third one was okay, but it made a better play. That's why I really love Keith's version of it. It made the writing worthwhile. It being a number-one best-seller made it worthwhile as well, I suppose, but artistically, the play delivered the book for me . . . I don't like *Ecstasy* as a book, so my expectations of it as a play weren't high. I saw it at the Edinburgh Fringe and I thought it would be studenty shite; some Canadians doing *Ecstasy* as a play. I was wrong. It was about the best adaptation/interpretation of my stuff for stage I've seen, and I've seen productions all over the world. (4P, 7)
>
> It's amazing that two of the stories in *Ecstasy*, the worst two, the first two, have been optioned as well so there's a chance that they'll hit the screen. Possibly for the better.[7]

The three novellas forming Ecstasy are 'Lorraine Goes to Livingston: A Rave and Regency Romance', which follows the developing friendship between the upper-class romance writer Rebecca Navarro and the working-class nurse Lorraine; 'Fortune's Always Hiding: A Corporate Drug Romance' featuring the bond between a West Ham United football casual, Dave, and Samantha, a woman on a quest for revenge against the manufacturers of the drug tenazedrine which caused her to be born without arms; and 'The Undefeated: An Acid House Romance' depicting the emotional rebirth of the bored wife Heather and her eventual new love for Leith party animal Lloyd. Despite the reservations of both critics and Welsh alike, the book does represent his most considered appraisal of the politics of both the drug Ecstasy and the possible communities that crystallised around its use. Already Renton in Trainspotting and Brian in the novella 'A Smart Cunt' from *The Acid House* had, however briefly experienced, unearthed a form of sociality in rave culture which they found hitherto lacking in their personal lives and in a fractured society at large. Similarly, in *Marabou Stork Nightmares* Roy Strang accessed a positive interpersonal connection and affirmation from Ecstasy to set against the degradation and atomisation of his everyday life in Muirhouse:

> It was euphoria . . . it was something that everyone should experience before they die if they can have said not to have wasted their life on this planet. I saw them all in our offices, the poor sad fools, I saw them in their suburbs, their schemes, their dole queues and their careers, their bookies shops and their yacht clubs . . . it didn't matter a fuck. I saw their limitation, the sheer vacuity of what they had on offer against this alternative. There would, I knew, be risks. Nothing this good came without risk. I couldn't go back though. No way. There was nothing to go back to. (M 237)

This utopian dimension to the drug is what Jenny Turner castigates most about *Ecstasy*: 'The very worst thing about *Ecstasy*, however, is all the Ecstasy in it. Or rather, it is the way that all a character has to do is to drop one in a raverie, and hey presto, entire personalities suddenly change for evermore. Whole lifestyles follow immediately. And it only takes one E to make a person fall lastingly in love as well'.[8] But just as Roy Strang realises that Ecstasy is not wholly positive and contains an inherent 'risk', Welsh's thoughts are much more nuanced than Turner allows:

> The dilemma that I was trying to resolve, and I don't think I have – not successfully anyway – is, if you don't have these feelings and you get them induced chemically, do you have a right to them? . . . I think it's one of the great unsung dangers of Ecstasy, and it's something I'm very interested in – the psychic damage it can do to people by giving them feelings that might not necessarily be the right ones to have . . . I genuinely would like for there to be absolutely no drugs at all – tobacco, alcohol, Ecstasy, cannabis, whatever we need to get us into some kind of spiritual relationship. I really would like it if we could get there without needing any of that, but I think the kind of world we live in makes it very difficult for that to happen.[9]

Hence, in 'Lorraine Goes to Livingston', Lorraine stops taking Ecstasy for a long period due to what she discerns as the falsity of the feelings engendered by its highs and lows: 'I think I love everyone, then I think I'm incapable of loving anyone' (E 55). So it is not so much the case that Welsh naively proposes Ecstasy as a ready-made panacea for all of society's ills. In Welsh's work Ecstasy is never offered as a direct replacement for human emotion and relationships, social connection and a yearned for collective experience. Rather, Ecstasy is a culture as much as a drug and can sometimes help facilitate the cognitive and social conditions necessary for the regeneration of collective life in a society where such communal experience in its traditional forms has been under sustained attack. This chapter seeks to appraise the conflictual politics of Ecstasy and the rave scene and to trace the symbolic import of romance as a cultural form, specifically in terms of how Welsh utilises its class and gender politics – an appropriation which allows Welsh certain utopian fulfilments but which also sets particular limitations on the radical potential of *Ecstasy*. Nonetheless, in terms of the development of Welsh's work, his engagement with romance as a form once more illustrates his capacity to parody and subvert mainstream discourses, to construct his narratives and voices from the detritus of both high and low cultural forms.

Political parties?

Simon Reynolds locates in Ecstasy and rave culture an antidote to the rabid individualism that typified the neo-liberal economic ethos of Thatcherism in the 1980s:

> Ecstasy acts as both party-igniting fun-fuel *non pareil* and the catalyst for ego-melting mass communication. What all these different uses of MDMA have in common is *ekstasis*: the Greek etymological root of ecstasy, its literal meaning is 'standing outside oneself'. MDMA is the 'we' drug. It's no coincidence that Ecstasy escalated into a pop cultural phenomenon at the end of the go-for-it, go-it-alone eighties (the real Me decade). For Ecstasy is the remedy for the alienation caused by an atomized society.[10]

Even so, Reynolds pinpoints a debilitating downside too: 'Taking Ecstasy is like going on an emotional spree, spending your happiness in advance. With irregular use, such extravagance isn't a problem. But with sustained and excessive use, the brain's serotonin levels become seriously depleted'.[11] Furthermore, Reynolds' use of an economic metaphor hints at the 1980s influence on this hedonism by chiming with the boom and bust economics of the Thatcher years, its reckless speculation and wild spending on credit. Reynolds' idea of *ekstasis*, standing outside oneself, also contains negative undertones by insinuating that drug use can be an alienation of the self, a reification or distancing from one's self in a more debilitating way.

Unlike the habit-forming way of life associated with heroin use, as depicted in *Trainspotting*, Ecstasy users cover a wide range of people. Often Ecstasy users can take the drug at weekends and then return to work every Monday, whether they are exploited workers or lawyers, accountants, finance executives and tycoons. Welsh himself situates contemporary drug use within a context of wider consumer choice:

> We live in a drug society, a chemical society. This is not new, it's always been the case that throughout recorded history people have ingested substances in order to achieve either an altered state of consciousness or simply some form of arousal or relaxation. What has happened recently concerning drugs is much the same as has happened in all other walks of life within our consumer capitalist society; there has been an expansion in the number of products available to the consumer.[12]

Pat Kane is eager to position both Welsh and the culture he depicts not as deeply counter-cultural but as fashionably informative for the young acquisitional and image-conscious professional:

> OK: let's concede that a sudden release of serotonin and dopamine from the brain's neurotransmitters creates a kind of empathy and physical relaxation that you don't get from any other recreational drug. Let's also accept that such a generation-in-ecstasy might well smash social boundaries – of class, gender, knowledge, expertise, emotion – as a result of this specific hedonism, this swedge at the doors of perception. In this light, Welsh's world can be seen to be as traditional as *Jane Eyre*. It provides useful narratives of the self for a constituency that needs to be as informed about drug choices as career choices (both flexibly defined).[13]

So, for Kane, Welsh's *Ecstasy* is the apotheosis of a wider movement towards not merely mainstream acceptance but also complicity:

> Ultimately, I wonder whether the mainstream consumer capitalism Welsh kicks against may in fact be what incites the Buzz: the system that turns us into infernal desiring machines in the first place. On top of that contradiction sits this book, and the whole Welsh multi-media industry . . . Welsh is a business-school graduate, and we should take his recently

expressed disaffection with a literary career as the signal of a real change of direction. Anyone who makes that much legitimate money from drugs has a shining future on the capitalist heights. Irvine Welsh as the Richard Branson of the 21st century? Now that would be swedgin.[14]

Although Kane is keen to overplay what he perceives as the cynical media manipulation of the Irvine Welsh brand, it is significant that when the rave scene first emerged it was marked by the anonymity of its producers, DJs and organisers in a testament to its collective and shared resonance. But dance culture slowly developed figureheads or personalities, whether writers, media presenters, club owners, DJs or musicians. Both Welsh and Ecstasy culture at large perhaps demonstrate the conversion of what Sarah Thornton terms *subcultural capital* into straightforwardly economic capital.[15] Thornton defines subcultural capital as a form of material accrual based on dissident hipness which confers social status:

> While subcultural capital may not convert into economic capital with the same ease or financial reward as cultural capital, a variety of occupations and incomes can be gained as a result of 'hipness'. DJs, club organizers, clothes designers, music and style journalists and various record industry professionals all make a living from their subcultural capital.[16]

However, it is perverse to hold Welsh as personally culpable for this trend as it illustrates the broader capacity of mainstream society to annex apparently oppositional forces in renewing its own hegemony. Ecstasy culture and its mainstream incorporation helped to reshape and reinvigorate flagging British leisure and entertainment industries. Major record labels began to dominate the dance music scene, brewing giants introduced new ranges of 'alcopop' drinks and beverages specially designed for a new generation of young consumers schooled in the instant fixes of rave culture, whilst night club and bar owners also profited from a phenomenon that had once seemed to threaten their existence. Matthew Collin also points to perhaps the ultimate assimilation and dilution of rave culture in New Labour's election victory in May 1997:

> As his election campaign theme, Blair had chosen to replace the socialist standard *The Red Flag* with an Ecstasy anthem, *Things Can Only Get Better*, written by an Ecstasy user, Peter Cunnah of D:Ream. Blair's closest colleague, chief spin doctor Peter Mandelson, had been loaned a chauffeur-driven car for the campaign by James Palumbo of the Ministry of Sound.[17]

So in a sense, the positives and negatives of Ecstasy culture, its contradictory terrain wherein the mainstream and the utopian impact, demonstrate the fundamental political ambivalence of all youth cultures in relation to mainstream society. On one level, the desire for immediate gratification, market deregulation and freedom of choice seem to ape Thatcherite dogma, yet on another, there persists a deeply rooted yearning for collective experience and communal equality that runs strongly counter to monetarism.

Criminal justice? Rave culture and the state

Although rave culture was riven by contradictions and had no unified political message, this does not necessitate its dismissal as apolitical. Similarly, its incorporation into the hegemonic logic of society in a highly sanitised version does not disqualify the radicalism of its culture in its entirety. Hillegonda Rietveld, for example, tends to depoliticise the Ecstasy scene due to its incompatibility with traditional forms of political organisation and activism:

> the intensity of dance parties is related to an equal sense of political disappointment and resultant apathy. Having attended a huge variety of dancefloors, it seemed as if the celebration revolved around a great void: void in the direction of energy on the dancefloor, void in the mind, void in articulated politics, with E convincing all that this void made sense, that it was not scary or depressing but a thing to feel good about.[18]

It is highly significant that where previous youth culture movements produced consternation and disapproval from the state, it was dance culture which led directly to John Major's government's introduction of the Criminal Justice and Public Order Act in 1994 with its legislation targeting gatherings playing music with 'repetitive beats'. And whilst of course not everyone involved in the rave scene was a dissenting political animal, the state's own direct intervention indicates that it saw in Ecstasy culture something more threatening than the meaningless political void suggested by Rietveld. As Welsh affirms:

> The loud, druggy hedonism of dance music has always sat uneasily with politics, though the relationship is more complex than it might at first appear. After all, it was acid house, so often regarded as devoid of principle or commitment, not 'political' punk, that instigated the repressive Criminal Justice Act. In Blackburn, Lancashire, in the early 1990s, 'rave culture', rather than football thuggery or industrial action, precipitated

the most arrests at an event in mainland Britain since the Second World War.[19]

Notably, *Ecstasy* was also published in the wake of a sustained media and tabloid campaign to criminalise and demonise the drug, its scene and its users following the Ecstasy-related death of Leah Betts, an ex-policeman's daughter, on 16 November 1995. The fact that both the state and the media maintained such a concerted effort to criminalise this large movement within popular culture itself politicised Ecstasy culture in new and challenging ways. Welsh comments:

> A lot of people pulled me up after *Trainspotting* for its absence of politics, but the argument I make is that the absence of politics is political as well. So many people have become divorced from the system, criminalised by their lifestyle. Ecstasy has criminalised just about everybody under 30. It's a strange state of affairs where you've got all these people in opposition to the state. They don't see themselves as criminals, but they're viewed by the state as criminals. It's a complete disenchantment but because it's not an overt political opposition like the miners' strike, it produces a cynicism and a tremendous rootlessness.[20]

In Scotland, the publication of *Ecstasy* coincided with the Scotland Against Drugs campaign launched in January 1996 by Michael Forsyth MP, then the Conservative Secretary of State for Scotland. In response, Welsh was involved in Scotland Against Drugs Hypocrisy (SADH) – along with Kevin Williamson, the Scottish Socialist MSP Tommy Sheridan, Graeme Steel – the son of the former speaker of the Scottish parliament, David Steel – and Clare Wyburn the Dance Editor of *M8* magazine. So the Ecstasy scene was not political in the mainstream construction of the term but helped formulate a new form of politics that did address the repressive policies of the state on this and many other issues.

High society: romance and spiritual ascent

Just as rave culture was highly fractious and housed often uneasy alliances between popular radicalism and conformism, so too romance as a cultural form is riven by tensions between subversive and conservative aspects of the genre. Scott McCracken deems contemporary popular romance a utopian genre that assuages the social fracture and alienation of capitalism: 'Its primary function of wish-fulfilment is the characteristic element of narratives that propel the reader into a fantasy world where a full and complete identity can be imagined'.[21] One of the primary structural functions of romance from the medieval period to the present is to transport the reader to an epiphanic higher plane through its code of renewal and symbolic rebirth. It is therefore an eminently suitable form for symbolising, if you like, the high society attained by the community of Ecstasy culture in Welsh's work. In his monumental study of romance genre, Northrop Frye demonstrates that the form is structured around archetypes of loss and restoration, exile and return.[22] Conventionally this structure entails the descent of the hero into a nightmare world of suffering and confusion together with a concomitant and profound loss of identity, then a return to the world from which he or she has come but which has been transformed by the experience. This underlying dynamic informs each of the novellas in *Ecstasy* and underpins a sense that rave culture has a capacity to re-energise fractured and dispirited lives that have been alienated or deprived by contemporary society. Moreover, Frye asserts that romance, despite its often aristocratic codes and settings, must also give voice to an insistent popular and proletarian utopian drive which demands fulfilment and indicts the degradations of the present social reality:

> The romance is nearest of all literary forms to the wish-fulfilment dream, and for that reason it has socially a curiously paradoxical role. In every age the ruling social or intellectual class tends to project its ideals in some form of romance, where the virtuous heroes and beautiful heroines represent the ideals and the villains the threats to their ascendancy. This is the general character of chivalric romance in the Middle Ages, aristocratic romance in the Renaissance, bourgeois romance since the eighteenth century, and revolutionary romance in contemporary Russia. Yet there is a genuinely 'proletarian' element in romance too which is never satisfied with its various incarnations, and in fact the incarnations themselves indicate that no matter how great a change may take place in society, romance will turn up again, as hungry as ever, looking for new hopes and desires to feed on. The perennially child-like quality of romance is marked by its extraordinarily persistent nostalgia, its search for some kind of imaginative golden age in time or space.[23]

Hence, romance must continually adapt throughout history according to social change – a change that will never fully satisfy those who are oppressed by society's continued inequalities. Welsh appropriates this highly political proletarian and utopian impulse within romance, its willed insistence on something better than what exists, and its yearning for unified states and experiences. In such utopian terms, romance then offers a paradigmatic representational mode for Welsh's effort to shore alternatives and angry responses to the disunities, disparities and inequalities of late capitalism. Significantly all three stories reprove the established order. 'Lorraine Goes to Livingston' castigates the delimitations of patriarchy and the corruptions of the ruling strata of society; 'Fortune's Always Hiding' berates corporate power and social injustice; whilst 'The Undefeated' condemns the government and the spiritual vacuity of bourgeois materialism.

Scott McCracken also points to the perceived feminisation of the genre under mass-market production that ensures it is not usually taken seriously due to its implication in the putatively feminine thrills of consumer pleasure.[24] For McCracken, masculine strains of romance today survive in transposed form as adventure stories, spy novels or thrillers. Yet David Salter illustrates that the comparatively low cultural status of the genre determined by its perception as a feminine form is less a new development and has been more a constant from the medieval period to the present.[25] Salter continues that this apparent feminisation conceals the underlying gender logic of the form: 'But, if we accept that romance is indeed a feminine genre, we are nonetheless presented with something of a paradox, for what seems to confronts us when we examine romance is a feminine genre with virtually no female heroines'.[26] Though romance is peopled by female characters, their primary function is to operate in a secondary or supporting role as defined by a central male figure. Whether women appear as wife, mother or daughter, Salter stresses that 'even those very restricted roles and identities that are available to women tend to be governed by masculine codes and concerns'.[27] And whilst Janice Radaway argues that romance can be an empowering genre for women as active readers, she also corroborates that romance's utmost concern is with the nature of masculinity and its implications for women.[28] Consequently, although it may at first appear odd that a writer such as Welsh, who so obsessively dwells upon the problematic of contemporary masculinity, should choose to appropriate an avowedly feminine form, romance's intrinsic formal logic traditionally privileges male experience and the construction of masculinity. Nonetheless, *Ecstasy* can be read in part as a sustained effort to overturn the masculine hierarchy of romance and to assert models of femininity in solidarity with one another rather than mediated and positioned by the code of a central masculinity. Welsh's use of the romance form in *Ecstasy*, therefore, simultaneously strives to construct new social and gender identities which forge progressive collective alliances, in keeping with his own reading of the heady commonality of rave culture and its blurring of boundaries, yet is also troubled by the overarching gender politics of the romance genre and its more masculine codes.

'Lorraine Goes to Livingston: A Rave and Regency Romance'

Welsh's effort to subvert the standard gender politics of the romance is evident in *Ecstasy*'s first novella: 'Lorraine Goes to Livingston'. After suffering a stroke at her plush Kensington flat the popular romance novelist, Rebecca Navarro, is rushed to hospital where she eventually develops a mutually transformative friendship with the young nurse Lorraine. Rebecca's popular Miss May Regency Romances series feature titles such as *Yasmin Goes to Yeovil* and *Lucy Goes to Liverpool*. Indeed, the novella offers Welsh the opportunity to parody Rebecca's supposed books and style. Whilst Nick Curtis censures that the story contains 'the bizarrely unedifying spectacle of Welsh trying to write like Barbara Cartland',[29] it does resume the parodic popular cultural mimicry of James Bond in *Trainspotting* and male adventure in *Marabou Stork Nightmares*.

Despite her success as a novelist, Rebecca is consumed by 'self-loathing' (*E* 3), in no small measure due to her harsh treatment by her husband Perky, whose immediate thoughts upon her illness are entirely mercenary: 'The best scenario: she dies and I am minted in the will' (*E* 11). Perky is concerned that her stroke and her depression have hampered her efforts to finish her latest novel only because he is reliant upon its success to fund his expensive tastes in prostitutes, gambling, restaurants and hardcore pornography. Perky is thus delighted with the growing friendship between Rebecca and Lorraine as it encourages his wife to turn to writing once more. Rebecca initially tries to stereotype Lorraine, her 'nursey', and to impose the stereotypes of romance fiction upon the reality of the young woman's life:

> You look just like a young French countess . . . in fact, you know, I think you look just like a portrait I once saw of Lady Caroline Lamb. It was a flattering portrait as she was never as lovely as you, my darling, but she's my heroine: a wonderfully romantic figure not afraid to risk scandal for love, like all the best women throughout history. (*E* 20)

Inspired by Lorraine, Rebecca resolves to commence writing again with a new heroine based upon Lorraine in keeping with the standard formula of young female heroines who are nevertheless at the mercy and behest of heroic masculine codes and characters.

However, Rebecca discovers Perky's secret flat and finds not only his pornography collection but also financial statements attesting to his squandering her fortune on his vices. She realises that, in contrast to the noble fantasy world of her romance novels, her married life to Perky has all been a 'lie' (*E* 40). Lorraine is at first unsympathetic to her upper-class friend's plight: 'you've had your heid stuck up your fanny for too long in that never-never land of yours . . . I see people who come into the hospital who've got nothing. Then I go hame, back up the road tae Livi and they've goat nothing. And you, well, you've goat everything. And what dae ye dae wi it? Ye let some pig fuckin waste it aw away!' (*E* 41). But Lorraine also relates how she ran away from home to train to be a nurse to escape the advances of her mother's lecherous new husband. She was also teased at school and dismissed as a lesbian in school because she refused to have sex with every young man who asked. Tired of heterosexual relationships, Lorraine also makes a disastrous amorous advance towards her nursing colleague Yvonne. Lorraine tells Rebecca – 'I want to find me first' (*E* 42) – and a strong feminist bond is formed between the two women through their treatment at the hands of men. This idea of rediscovering the self obviously evokes the romance's code of symbolic rebirth, whilst the cross-class alliance between the two women also reworks Frye's formulation of the genre as an aristocratic superstructure which houses popular or proletarian desires. Rebecca and Lorraine get drunk, watch Perky's pornographic videos and then begin to write together a more radical romance with an assertive and independent female heroine who acts in defiance of a dominant masculine code which is shown to be corrupt and malicious. When Perky finds the manuscript his horrified summation of its contents – 'buggery and revolution' (*E* 51) – comically distils the transformation of Rebecca's formerly florid writing through her collaboration with the angry and emancipated Lorraine.

Whereas previously Rebecca had used romance as an escapist means of ignoring social issues such as poverty and homelessness –'you want to believe everything but the truth' (*E* 54) – both women wish to bring the utopian spirit of romance upon that social reality: 'Surely there had to be room for romance, for true romance?

Romance for everyone, and not just from the pages of a book' (*E* 54). In the final section, 'Lorraine Goes to Livingston', at a rave in Lorraine's home town, a renewed and transformed Rebecca is on Ecstasy blissfully unconcerned that her new novel will never be published and glad of the concrete changes that its writing has induced in her formerly broken soul. Meanwhile Lorraine also embraces the utopianism of Ecstasy: 'in the midst of the Livingston jungle, something happened to Lorraine. She found herself necking with somebody, snogging the lips on a face that had been close to hers all night. It felt good. It felt right. She was glad she had come back up to Livingston. Come home' (*E* 72). In terms of social class, Lorraine's re-education of her upper-class friend through rave culture allows the proletarian desire for change to overwhelm the aristocratic framework of the form identified by Frye rather than being merely contained by it.

The story also subverts the governing masculine code of romance in the sense that Lorraine and Rebecca's solidarity usurps the corrupt amoral centre provided by Perky. Indeed, a nefarious masculinity comes to embody a wider social corruption in the novella through Perky's friendship with the necrophiliac television presenter, Freddy Royle. Royle's fundraising indispensability for the cash-strapped hospital helps him to blackmail the hospital manager into allowing him to satiate his desires in the hospital morgue: 'There was nothing like the sight of a stiff to give Freddy Royle a stiffy' (*E* 8). The customary justice of the romance ending nonetheless ensures that when a forlorn and rejected Perky gets drunk and is run over by a car, as he dies he hears Freddy's eager voice talking with the ambulance crew that have arrived. However, more conventionally perhaps in regard to gender, it is notable that Lorraine does finally enter into another heterosexual relationship whilst Yvonne, the nurse she had made advances towards, falls in love with fellow hospital employee Gary. So despite the feminist affiliation between Lorraine and Rebecca, which helps the latter achieve a rounded, independent character, the narrative does also close with two heterosexual relationships in place and perhaps suggests an unconscious desire for conventionally gendered resolution.

'Fortune's Always Hiding: A Corporate Drug Romance'

A consonant tension is found in 'Fortune's Always Hiding', as once more there is a deep ambivalence in the story's gender politics. This novella traces Samantha's quest for revenge against United Pharmacology – a conglomerate marketing drugs, food and alcohol – the makers of the fictionalised drug tenazedrine. It helps illustrate Welsh's point about the hypocrisy of current drugs legislation and the harm that can be done by drugs manufactured by huge corporate pharmaceutical interests with the state's blessing. Tania Modleski posits that there is a submerged feminist politics in even the most formulaic of popular romances: 'the desire to be taken by force (manifest content) conceals anxiety about rape and longings for power and revenge (latent content)'.³⁰ In Modleski's terms, Samantha's desire for both justice and retribution against the manufacturers of the drug that caused her to be born without arms can therefore be construed as making explicit this suppressed feminist and ethical exigency.

The horrible consequences of the drug and the deprivations of Samantha's childhood are intimated through the interweaving of a series of retrospective sections with the present action, as in 'Wolverhampton 1961' in which Samantha's parents must confront her birth defects and 'Toronto 1967' wherein her father looks at his newborn son and it transpires that he has left her and her mother behind: 'For a second he thought about another country, another wife and another child . . . no' (E 99). These flashbacks are interspersed with a history of the development of the drug and the mercenary role the now knighted Bruce Sturgess played in getting tenazedrine on to the market in spite of the call for more precautionary tests from the scientist Gunther Emerlich. Samantha's first act of revenge together with Andreas, another tenazedrine victim, is to burn Barry Drysdale, a director of the drugs company, to death in his holiday cottage. They later kidnap Emerlich's son and cut off his arms and post them to his father and mother. Samantha later realises 'When she killed the baby, part of her died with it' (E 143).

The first person narrative of the chapter 'Aggravation' introduces the West Ham football casual Dave.³¹ In addition to hooliganism, Dave is involved in violent organised crime and is a Thatcherite Cockney hard man who feels his burglaries and robberies are patriotic: 'it's business, and what's good for business is good for Britain and I like to do my bit for the Union Jack' (E 89). He also despises his 'slag' (E 93) of an ex-partner and when he occasionally has sex with her when visiting his son he claims he wants to 'rip her fucking smelly cunt apart, to really fucking hurt that dirty bitch' (E 95). During a brutal armed robbery at the home of a suburban family Dave and his

gang adopt fake accents as part of their disguise to mislead any subsequent police investigation. Whilst other members of the gang feign
Irish and West Indian accents, Dave assumes the Scottish vernacular
of his father: 'It's funny, but when I was a nipper, people always used
to say to my old man – who's Scotch – people like this smarmy scum-
bag, that they never understood the Jock accent. Funny thing is, when
I do these little jobs, they always get the message loud n clear and no
mistake' (*E* 87). Drew Milne suggests that it is not only the villains
who are hiding behind these accents but also Welsh's own complicity
in the scene's ethnic stereotyping:

> Although there is some literary irony in the deliberate cheapness of the
> effects involved, the confusion between the social use of adopted accents
> and the literary artifice of almost explicitly racist representation pushes
> irony to a level of cynical banality. The problem of voice as a marker of
> local identity is played with by the character's own narration but the
> effect is to trivialise the estrangement of classes in the politics of
> accents.[32]

After taking ecstasy and meeting Samantha at a club, however,
Dave's somewhat caricatured villainy dissolves in a moment that confirms Simon Reynolds' account of *ekstasis*, a freeing of the self from its
socially conditioned limitations: 'I never felt like this before. I felt like
someone. Someone different' (*E* 110). (He will later bond, in a fight
with Newcastle United casuals, with a Geordie who is also on Ecstasy.)
As Dave's love for Samantha grows he agrees to help her track down
Sir Bruce Sturgess and hack off his limbs. However, when Dave tells
Samantha he is assisting her because of his love she counters:

> Didn't anybody ever tell you that there ain't no love in this world? It's all
> money and power. That's what I understood: power. I grew up learning
> about it. The power we ran up against when we tried to get our com-
> pensation, our justice from them: the industrialists, the Government,
> the judiciary, from the whole fucking clique of them that run things.
> The way they fucking closed ranks and stuck together. It would've done
> you proud, Dave. Ain't that what you and your Firm's all about, in your
> own toytown way? The power to hurt. The power to have. The power to
> be somebody, to be so feared that nobody'll ever fuck you around? Ever?
> But it's misguided though, Dave, cause there will always be somebody
> to fuck you around. (*E* 125–126)

The novella ends when Dave befriends Sturgess in a gay bar and
then lures him to Samantha. She chainsaws Sturgess' limbs off whilst

Dave holds the door of his lock-up closed as the police try to gain entrance. The unified state of the romance closure is secured when they mouth 'I love you' to one another. There is once more perhaps a very standard and troubled sexual politics operative in the story's imagination as Sturgess' corruption gets underlined by his homosexuality. To this end, Northrop Frye illustrates that romance plots invariably confront some monster who represents the ultimate form of lack or horror. The prize for vanquishing the monster is the 'victory of fertility over waste land'.[33] It would be feasible to regard the monstrosity of Sturgess' capitalism and profit-driven mindset concerning tenazedrine as evidence of his soul's corruption: 'The tragedy had been one he assessed in terms of pounds: the monies lost to the company' (E 131). Yet the story seeks to compound his monstrosity with not only his paedophilic tendencies but also his homosexuality, as when Dave rages: 'Samantha ain't got no arms, ain't got no mum or dad, was brought up in a fucking home, all because of some fucking rich old queer-beast' (E 141). It is possible to push the conventional gender politics still further and to suggest that standard gender politics also unconsciously project Samantha as the ultimate monstrosity. Although Dave was previously a thug his violence was conducted according to various criminal codes (however misconceived) and it is notable that at first he recoils in horror at Samantha's plan to dismember Sturgess. However unconsciously, the romance logic of the story suggests that it is the monstrous agency of an independent and assertive woman which leads Dave astray when he could have rededicated himself to his partner and son – the final victory, in a reversal of Frye's terms, of the waste land over fertility. The fact that Dave's narrative is rendered in the first person whilst Samantha's is told in the third person also discloses an effort to distance the overarching emplotment of the novella from her actions. So again, whilst 'Fortune's Always Hiding' seeks to forge an equal and emancipated alliance between its central characters, it also invokes some of the more reactionary gender politics of the romance form which trouble the desired, ecstatic unity.

'The Undefeated: An Acid House Romance'

The first person narratives of 'The Undefeated' alternate through chapters headed Heather and Lloyd. Heather is trapped in a boring office job and a soulless, loveless marriage. Heather's professional life has suffered due to being considered subordinate to her husband: 'Hugh and I left university at the same time and went to work for different local authorities. He's now the manager of a building society and I'm exactly where I was six years ago' (*E* 171). Equally, her home life is paradoxically a fundamental alienation of belonging: 'I'm slipping away from him, slipping away from this world he wants me to inhabit: his world, which is not our shared world . . . It's not our shared world cause I'm his, his property and he won't relinquish it easily' (*E* 178).

Heather satirises Hugh's endorsement of mainstream values by tracing a mock curriculum vitae from Hugh as student – 'Committed to: the liberation of working people from the horrors of capitalism' – to Private Sector Manager Hugh: 'Committed to: maximising profit through cost efficiency, resource effectiveness and expanding into new markets' (*E* 215–216). At her parents' house Hugh disparages the socialist politics of her father, which, he maintains, need to be replaced with what he calls a 'responsibility-orientated society' (*E* 191). Heather's response gives the lie to the idea that Welsh's work is politically disinterested, and is also imbued with an unerringly accurate prophetic quality (remember this is 1996): 'You're New Labour. Tony Blair Labour. Which is the same as Tory, only Major's probably further left than Blair. Blair's just a snidier version of Michael Portillo, which is why he'll do better than Portillo will ever do' (*E* 190).

Although Heather is prescribed the officially sanctioned drug Prozac, it is taking Ecstasy with her friend which precipitates the symbolic rebirth of romance: 'I had let go of fear' (*E* 230). Heather leaves Hugh and buys new music and books in confirmation of her transformation. After Heather and Lloyd meet at a club he also undergoes a profound change in lifestyle: 'ah'm changin the keks everyday and cleanin under the helmet' (*E* 261). Eventually, Heather issues Lloyd with the ultimatum that she will only see him if he stops his excessive drug taking – which he does and they end the novel in love and together. Chris Mitchell argues that this non-chemically induced communion lends the novella 'a peculiarly conservative twist – that the natural high of love is better than a chemical one'.[34] However, it also reiterates that Welsh does not simplistically regard Ecstasy or any drug as an end in itself but rather as only a part of a process to rebuild a decimated social life at both personal and more broadly political levels. And it is in 'The Undefeated' that Lloyd's defence of ravers offers the most impassioned, defiant and socially contextualised articulation of the politics of Ecstasy culture in Welsh's work:

> We are social, collective fucking animals and we need to be together and have a good time. It's a basic state of being alive. A basic fuckin right. These Government cunts, because they're power junkies, they are just incapable of having a good fuckin time so they want everybody else tae feel guilty, tae stey in wee boxes and devote their worthless lives tae rearing the next generation of factory fodder or sodgers or dole moles for the state. It's these boys' duty as human fuckin beings tae go oot clubbin and partying wi their friends. (*E* 213)

Lloyd's remarks mirror Welsh's own view that it is not drugs but the dominant capitalist system itself which has ruptured the daily fabric of society and community:

> Drugs policy needs changing: to reclaim the entrepreneurial spirit towards creativity, expression and enjoyment of life for its own sake, rather than simply personal profit. It's both a reaction against the narrow individualism as defined by the political right (the reduction of the individual to a mere consumer who makes qualitatively meaningless choices from a selection of trinkets presented to them by those who hold power) and a move towards the collective interactions destroyed by 1980s industrial closures and community devastations, anti-union legislation and even the Taylor report into football stadia which means that the only way working-class people can now meaningfully interact is in clubs, at raves and at parties. (*T&H* 4)

Ecstasy and the carnivalesque

Aside from Welsh's effort to dissect the socio-political underpinnings of Ecstasy culture, he also stresses, alongside his attempts to intellectualise, the sheer physical pleasure involved. Welsh asks: 'Is it a big shattering New Age thing? Or is it just a more sophisticated way to get off your tits and have a good time?'.[35] However, if we return to the Bakhtinian carnivalesque drive in Welsh's work, this reassertion of the body and physicality equally bespeaks a dissident politics. It is perhaps in the carnivalesque, which informs much of Welsh's work and its transgressive potential, wherein *Ecstasy* can be redeemed in radical terms that do connect with the more subversive elements of rave culture. Bakhtin opposes the utopian, collective resonance of the carnivalesque body to the clearly patrolled boundaries and strictures of 'the private, egoistic, "economic man"'.[36] The corpulent excesses of *Ecstasy*, its plethora of both functioning and malfunctioning bodies and its effusion of a physicality that overwhelms the division between self and other, actuate the carnivalesque rejection of fixed and immutable identities and social categories:

> Grotesque realism images the human body as multiple, bulging, over- or under-sized, protuberant and incomplete. The openings and orifices of this carnival body are emphasized, not its closure and finish. It is an image of impure corporeal bulk with its orifices (mouth, flared nostrils, anus) yawning wide and its lower regions (belly, legs, feet, buttocks and genitals) given priority over its upper regions (head, 'spirit', reason) . . . it is always in process, it is always *becoming*, it is a mobile and hybrid creature, disproportionate, exorbitant, outgrowing all limits, obscenely decentred and off-balance, a figural and symbolic resource for parodic exaggeration and inversion.[37]

Tellingly, in 'Lorraine Goes to Livingston', the attack by Glen, Lorraine's co-worker at the hospital, on the state is undertaken in terms of his juxtaposition of dominant yet lifeless and static corpus – 'posturing' –with a radical and unrestrained physicality:

> He felt that you had to party, you had to party harder than ever. It was the only way. It was your duty to show that you were still alive. Political sloganeering and posturing meant nothing; you had to celebrate the joy of life in the face of all those grey forces and dead spirits who controlled everything, who fucked with your head and livelihood anyway, if you weren't one of them. You had to let them know that in spite of their best efforts to make you like them, to make you dead, you were still alive. Glen knew that this wasn't the complete answer, because it would all still be there when you stopped, but it was the best show in town right now. It was certainly the only one he wanted to be at. (*E* 26–27)

Nonetheless, Gary's acknowledgement that the dominant order of society will still be there when the music stops also confirms that the Bakhtinian carnival is a temporary overturning of hierarchies despite its optimistic spirit.

> As opposed to the official feast, one might say that the carnival celebrated temporary liberation from the prevailing truth and from the established order; it marked the suspension of all hierarchical rank, privileges, norms, and prohibitions. Carnival was the true feast of time, the feast of becoming, change and renewal. It was hostile to all that was immortalized and complete.[38]

Similarly, Welsh concedes that more often than not contemporary drugs use is a short-term means of escaping a dominant, overarching system but which in its own way invokes a call for that ruling order to be changed:

> There can be little doubt that increasing levels of social inequality and poverty and a decreasing number of employment opportunities will lead to an increase in the misuse of opiates, alcohol and other downers, as people seek temporary respite from social pressure. The phrase "getting out of it" springs to mind. Surely if "it" was better, then so many people wouldn't need to get out of it so often.[39]

Finally, then, Welsh is clearly not the mindless drugs advocate that he is sometimes painted to be. He is much more interested in the politics and communities which the Ecstasy culture generated, offering some hope and alternative to a deadening social mainstream. The state's own highly political attack upon the rave scene itself discloses that for a time it focused and galvanised a whole gamut of popular discontents and radicalism. In Bakhtin's terms, *Ecstasy* indicates that the carnivalesque may normally merely suspend the dominant order of society temporarily as a means of social control rather than social critique. But it also suggests that in the 1990s, at a time when the mainstream left embraced the dogma of the governing right, the carnival's usual function can be pushed to its limits as rave culture did form part of a struggle against the power of the state and its denial of oppositional constituencies to itself. As Stallybrass and White assert: 'the most that can be said in the abstract is that for long periods carnival may be a stable and cyclical ritual with no noticeable politically transformative effects but that, given the presence of sharpened political antagonism, it may often act as *catalyst* and *site of actual and symbolic struggle*'.[40] As a collection, *Ecstasy* articulates both the subversive, disruptive energies of the carnivalesque yet also its ultimate limitations in terms of both class and gender. Correspondingly, the meretricious manner in which the book was conceived also helps convey the economic and entrepreneurial elements of rave culture that run counter to its more utopian impulses. Welsh's deliberate invocation of the romance form does indicate a willingness to engage further with female experience and desire and whilst this remains highly problematic due to much of *Ecstasy* being underpinned by ultimately masculine codes, it does adumbrate his efforts to articulate female subjectivity in *Glue* and, in particular, *Porno*. In his next book, *Filth*, however, Welsh redeploys grotesque realism and the carnivalesque to thoroughly dystopian ends to confront further both the power of the state and an imploding masculinity that seeks to obliterate all forms of otherness and female agency.

Notes

1 Cited in Jennifer Berman, 'An interview with Irvine Welsh', *Bomb Magazine* 56 (1996), 61.
2 Jenny Turner, 'Love's chemistry', *Guardian*, G2T (31 May 1996) 17.
3 Pat Kane, 'Infernal desires: *Ecstasy*', *New Statesman* (7 June1996), 37.
4 Nick Curtis, 'Drug-fuelled romances: Scottish fiction', *Financial Times* (8 June1996), 12.
5 Tim Adams, 'Just say no', *Observer*, Review (2 June1996), 14.
6 Cited in Andy Beckett, 'Irvine Welsh: the ecstasy and the agony', *Guardian* (25 July 1998), 6.
7 Cited in Steve Redhead, *Repetitive Beat Generation* (Edinburgh: Rebel Inc, 2000), 142.
8 Turner, 'Love's chemistry', 17.
9 Cited in Be Thompson, 'The interview: Irvine Welsh', *Independent on Sunday* (2 June1996), 14.
10 Simon Reynolds, *Energy Flash: A Journey through Rave Music and Dance Culture* (London: Macmillan, 1998), xxii.
11 Reynolds, *Energy Flash*, xxvii–xxviii.
12 Cited in Kevin Williamson, *Drugs and the Party Line* (Edinburgh: Rebel Inc, 1997), ix.
13 Kane, 'Infernal desires', 37.
14 Kane, 'Infernal desires', 38.
15 Sarah Thornton, *Club Cultures: Music, Media and Subcultural Capital* (Oxford: Polity Press, 1995), 11.
16 Thornton, *Club Cultures*, 12.
17 Matthew Collin, *Altered State: The Story of Ecstasy Culture and Acid House* (London: Serpent's Tail, 1998), 314. Palumbo was a former City trader and the son of Lord Palumbo, a millionaire property tycoon and a former chairperson of the Arts Council.
18 Hillegonda Rietveld, 'Repetitive beats: free parties and the politics of contemporary DiY dance culture in Britain' in George McKay, ed., *DiY Culture: Party and Protest in Nineties Britain* (London: Verso, 1998), 252.
19 Irvine Welsh, 'From America', *Daily Telegraph* (31 Mar 2003), accessed at www.telegraph.co.uk (Apr 2003).
20 Cited in Mark Fisher, 'Talking 'bout E's generation', *Observer*, Review (9 Oct 1994), 6.
21 Scott McCracken, *Pulp: Reading Popular Fiction* (Manchester: Manchester University Press, 1998), 75.
22 See Northrop Frye, *The Secular Scripture: A Study of the Structure of*

Romance (Cambridge: Harvard University Press, 1976), 129–131. I am deeply indebted to David Salter for his discussions of the socio-symbolism of romance literature with me.

23 Northrop Frye, *Anatomy of Criticism: Four Essays* (London: Penguin, 1990), 186.

24 McCracken, *Pulp*, 75.

25 David Salter, '"Born to thraldom and penance": wives and mothers in Middle English romance' in Elaine Treharne, ed., *Writing Gender and Genre in Medieval Literature* (Cambridge: D.S. Brewer, 2002), 42.

26 Salter, '"Born to thraldom and penance"', 42.

27 Salter, '"Born to thraldom and penance"', 44.

28 Janice Radaway, *Reading the Romance: Women, Patriarchy and Popular Literature* (London: University of North Carolina Press, 1991), 147.

29 Nick Curtis, 'Drug-fuelled romances: Scottish fiction', *Financial Times* (8 June1996), 12.

30 Tania Modleski, *Loving with a Vengeance* (London: Anchor Books, 1982), 48.

31 The novella's title borrows a line from West Ham United supporters' adopted song 'I'm Forever Blowing Bubbles'.

32 Drew Milne, 'The fiction of James Kelman and Irvine Welsh: accents, speech and writing' in Richard J. Lane et al., eds, *Contemporary British Fiction* (Oxford: Polity Press, 2003), 166. Indeed, the rendering of the 'normal' Cockney accent of Dave's character is far from convincing and at times makes Dick Van Dyke's performance in *Mary Poppins* seem like a gritty piece of social realism.

33 Frye, *Anatomy of Criticism*, 193.

34 Chris Mitchell, 'Love is a many splintered thing' is found at: www.spikemagazine.com/spikeecs.htm (Jan 2000).

35 Cited in Matthew Collin, *Altered State: The Story of Ecstasy Culture and Acid House* (London: Serpent's Tail, 1998), 282.

36 M. M. Bakhtin, *Rabelais and His World*. Trans. Hélène Iswolsky (Cambridge, Mass: MIT Press, 1968), 19.

37 Peter Stallybrass and Allon White, *The Politics and Poetics of Transgression* (London: Methuen, 1986), 9.

38 Bakhtin, *Rabelais and His World*, 109.

39 Cited in Williamson, *Drugs and the Party Line*, xii.

40 Stallybrass and White, *The Politics and Poetics of Transgression*, 14.

5

Filth (1998)

After the adverse reaction to *Ecstasy*, Welsh was avowedly more considered with his next novel: 'I had to be a lot more careful with the
book *Filth*. I feel a lot more confident as a result. I've taken a lot more
care. And I know, I just get that feeling that it's back up to the standard of the first three'.[1] Yet not everyone was convinced. For Roger
Scruton *Filth* was 'the worst novel of the year',[2] whilst Stuart Maconie
dismissed the novel in the context of what he deemed the vacuity of
the Cool Britannia project and a wider failure of British culture:

> As for Irvine Welsh, well, it always looked more like word-processing
> than writing, but surely now the game's up for the foul-mouthed
> chancer? Compare his most recent novel, the dire, unfunny, remorse-
> lessly vulgar *Filth* to, say, Don DeLillo's *Underworld* and it is clear that
> while American literature's concerns are politics, history, adultery,
> money and war, Welsh's go no further than a tapeworm and the c-word.[3]

However, this chapter will examine precisely how *Filth* does
address issues of power, the state and social conflict in contemporary
Britain. The novel charts the disintegration and eventual suicide of
Detective Sergeant Bruce Robertson, a hard-drinking, drug-taking,
homophobic, misogynist, racist, rapist and sociopathic Edinburgh
police officer. *Filth* centres on Robertson's investigation of the poten-
tially racially motivated murder of Efan Wurie, a journalist whose
father is ambassador for Ghana.[4] Ultimately it transpires that Robertson's unwillingness to investigate the murder thoroughly is due neither, as it first seems, to his debauched lifestyle nor his careerist
preoccupation with damaging his rivals' chances for an upcoming
promotion that he covets, but to the fact that he is the murderer. The
revelations about Robertson's crime and his guilty past emerge as his

venomous first person narrative is increasingly interrupted in the text by the voice of a tapeworm which inhabits his bowels and slowly and painfully offers self-analysis and conscience. The tapeworm's discourse first emerges in the form of worm-shaped speech bubbles which intrude over the surface of Robertson's main narrative and then eventually assume narrative control and prompt Robertson's confrontation with his crimes and his past. This emergent conscience is necessary as Robertson distils some of the most reactionary and repressive aspects of mainstream British society – indeed, Welsh has stated that:

> *Filth* was a difficult book to do because just like *Marabou Stork Nightmares* you have a character who is very difficult to live with, whatever you think of him. He's got this personality, he's a very hard character to live with. When you get somebody who's right out like that you can make comments about society, about power relationships, about authority. The Bruce character was not the classic authoritarian personality. The classic authoritarian personality is very servile to their bosses, and really fascistic to their subordinates whereas he is very manipulative and controlling to both, you know he hates his bosses and his subordinates equally, he is even handed, which is quite unusual for somebody in that position. Organisations tend to breed authoritarian personalities – it's their hierarchical nature. He's that kind of maverick. What I really hate is the idea that in the mainstream where the cops are the good guys, the Bruce Willis-type characters, they've always got to be this subversive slight character who doesn't go by the rules but all they're actually doing is saving the world from the 'Arabs' or the 'Communists' or aliens or whatever. They make the world safe for the subordinates, so they're all respectable figures. So I wanted to take somebody who was a real reactionary, respectable figure doing the things that most authoritarian personalities do subconsciously, using his power in that organisation, very nakedly, very much in an aware way. It's somehow covering up for something, a spoiled idealism, that things should and can be better.[5]

In disrupting the Bruce Willis-type maverick yet good cop who naturalises the protection of the dominant interests of society, Welsh acknowledges the influence of Abel Ferrara's 1992 film *Bad Lieutenant* about a corrupt and malevolent American police officer ultimately searching for some kind of redemption:

> when I wrote *Filth* I had this idea that I would do the same thing only with environmental health officers working for the council – but like really dirty bastards working for the council . . . so instead of *Bad*

Lieutenant, Bad Environmental Health Officers. But I thought I can't fucking do that, you've got to have some corrupt fucking cop – I mean, if an environmental health officer has fucked up you get food poisoning, but if a cop has fucked up you can go down for years, you know. So I wanted to get to the fucking soul of corruption there, that's what I was trying to do. To me society is a conflict, not a consensus.[6]

Furthermore, Welsh also makes subversive use of the detective thriller in *Filth* to turn the genre's formal logic of pursuing crime towards a questioning of the very legitimacy of the police and the state.

Watching the detectives

Sally Munt styles the conventional male detective hero as 'the controlled centre surrounded by chaos, and an effective reading must involve identification with this mediator of action, truth, and finally pleasure and relief through closure'.[7] But in spite of this conventional account of the genre, the idea of a detective struggling with a darkness both within and without is not new but rather builds upon the formative ethical anxieties of the hardboiled detective tradition itself, which has, even in its most canonical form, always dealt with a confusion and tension between good and evil. Since its inception, the form has grappled not with moral certitude but within a blurring of social codes and identities. By way of example, Dashiell Hammett's hero, Sam Spade, is introduced as 'a blond satan' on the first page of *The Maltese Falcon* (1930),[8] a complex mix of both light and dark, whilst Raymond Chandler's main protagonist was originally named Malory and then subsequently Marlowe, evoking both a pure, chivalric heroism and a modern heart of darkness.[9] The influence of German Expressionist theatre on the atmospherics of *film noir* and the cinematic adaptation of hardboiled thrillers by writers such as Hammett and Chandler neatly and visually reinforces this point, as central to its technique was the use of lighting and shadow to evince not merely the encroaching of evil upon good in the twentieth century but also the intermingling of both categories.

With regard to Scottish fiction, *Filth* also rewrites William McIlvanney's detective novels based upon his character Laidlaw, who provides a decent, upstanding working-class figure involved in the maintenance of law and order. Indeed, Bruce Robertson's name itself suggests that the text will subvert a Scottish tradition of maverick

heroes given that it inverts Robert the Bruce. Laidlaw, as his name
suggests, provides a means of ensuring, if you like, that the law is laid
down but in an apparently oppositional way. But Laidlaw also designates himself 'a wrack of paradox' and draws a correlation between
himself and the criminals he uncovers: they are often 'the same terrible force talking to itself'.[10] And despite Laidlaw naturalising the operation of law, what is most evident is that one of the things he must
investigate is himself. Hence, the hardboiled thriller deals not with
the maintenance of a clearly defined boundary between right and
wrong but rather is produced out of a fissure incorporating both
detective and criminal within a fractious problematic of moral and
masculine identities.[11] So it is not so much the case that *Filth* corrupts
a tradition in which the detective is enduringly benevolent and secure
in his empowered masculine and authorised identity regulating the
rule of law. Rather Welsh supersaturates or overdetermines the formative ambivalences of the hardboiled form and its insecurities. In fact,
one does not need to look only to an American hardboiled tradition to
verify that crime fiction is not a straightforwardly righteous form
which always ratifies the dominant interests in society. The formal
structure of *Filth*, wherein a first person narrator investigates a
murder which it transpires he has himself committed, mirrors the
subversive dynamic of Agatha Christie's British Golden Age novel
The Murder of Roger Ackroyd (1926). Even in the most seemingly conservative of popular genres, then, proof can be found that techniques
such as the unreliable narrator with its radical undermining of
authority, truth and power are not the preserve of high cultural mod-
ernist texts.[12] Thus, Scott Bradfield's dismissal is perhaps unfounded:
'Welsh's avid, counter-cultural readers deserve more than a lot of
phoney, Agatha Christie-style plot-twists'.[13] So although Robertson
declares that 'A good polisman always knows where to look' (*F* 41), the
novel's trajectory redirects Robertson's gaze from its effort to criminalise others – whether the working class, women, ethnic minorities
or homosexuals – and focuses it upon himself and the state apparatus
of which he is a part. The police, the state and its justice system are all
put on trial or at least under thorough investigation in *Filth*.

   The novel's subversive gaze also criminalises the heart of genteel,
establishment Edinburgh – despite Robertson's efforts to project
crime firmly on to the city's outlying working-class housing schemes:

> Ignore the schemies: these cunts are a law unto themselves. As long as
> they stey oot ay the city centre, they can kill each other as much as they

like on cheap bevvy, fags, drugs and high-cholesterol food. Zero tolerance of crime in the city centre; total laissez-faire in the schemie hinter-
lands. That's the way forward for policing in the twenty-first century.
Tony Blair's got the right idea: get those jakey beggars out of the city centres. Dispossessed, keep away. (*F* 273)

Similarly: 'This city of ours is truly beautiful and we like this part
where there is not a scheme in sight. Why could we not simply move
all the scum to the middle of nowhere, like Glasgow, where they
would blend in more effectively? Come to think of it, that's exactly
what we did do, when we built the schemes. Sent them far, but not far
enough' (*F* 327). The chapter 'Infected Areas', in which his doctor first
informs Robertson that he has worms, makes explicit the connection
between the true corruption of the city and its elitist, law-abiding
façade, and features Robertson making the newspapers as a local hero
for attempting to save a man dying in the street from a heart attack at
the same time as his inner heart of darkness becomes ever more
apparent. Moreover, the tapeworm metaphor is especially prescient
given Edwin Muir's comment on the veneer of modern, bourgeois
Edinburgh that 'presents outwardly the face it had a hundred years
ago, while within it is worm-eaten'.[14]

Nonetheless, some critics suggest that Welsh does not merely set
up Robertson's reactionary, hypocritical politics for analysis but is
also complicit in its excesses. Alan Taylor, for example, criticises
'books like *Filth* which aim by inversion to show society's ills and end
up encouraging readers to rejoice in them'.[15] Notably, in the novel's
prologue – in which a first person narrator, whom we later learn is
Robertson, describes murdering Efan Wurie – the very language
employed does invite the reader's participation or complicity. The text
describes how, when Wurie is beaten with a claw-hammer, 'his blood
fairly skooshes out' (*F* 2) – the adverb 'fairly' here ambiguously denot-
ing not just the rate of the blood loss but also implying a certain justice in this act. Equally, the prologue's language seeks to implicate the
victim in the murder. The phrase – 'he can't resist my blows' (*F* 2) –
prosaically describes Wurie's inability to fend off Robertson's attack
yet also insinuates a kind of enticed acquiescence in keeping with the
seductive irresistibility of violence in the scene. But rather than dismiss this as pure voyeurism, Welsh's technique forces us to confront
the lure of power and to unpack its beguiling aesthetics. As so often
in Welsh's work, Robertson's character operates as a Brechtian alien-
ation-effect which, in offering a timeline in the shift from Thatch-

erism to Blairism in British society, starkly unmasks the mechanics of the British state. Instead of positioning him as a rogue anomaly, Welsh is keen to imbricate Robertson's oppressive views within the context of a dominant and coercive social system:

> I wanted to write about institutions . . . I noticed all the cases against the police, like racism and sex discrimination; there seems to be one every day in Britain. All these things came out about 'canteen culture', and I wanted to write something about that, the misogynistic, racist, misanthropic sort of culture that people get involved in. And I thought, well, what if we have somebody who can hide in that kind of culture? The challenge was to try and write a character that represented everything that I detest in a way, but then to try and empathise with him . . . There had to be a voice of reason kicking against the psychopath . . . and the tapeworm became that. It's like Bruce's conscience because he believes he's flawed in some fundamental way, maybe even genetically flawed, and it's a good thing to believe, you know, because it frees you of all responsibility to behave in a decent, moral way. I think the tapeworm is a nagging conscience that tells him he should be getting on, thinking more, you know, and it's a more sympathetic voice to offset Bruce's completely over-the-top behaviour . . . What I've done is taken every negative statement I've heard somebody make, and turn them into a character . . . I think there's a power, you know, when somebody says these quite taboo things without being the slightest bit self-conscious. It's a power, a strange kind of seduction. They're fearless and uncontained by morality, and because of that there is this paradoxical attraction towards them, you know, towards Bruce who actually believes his conscience is some sort of infestation that he's got to be ridded of.[16]

A sorry state

Perhaps the most grievous allegation of racism casting a shadow over the institutions of the state at the time of *Filth*'s composition concerned the murder of Stephen Lawrence, who had been brutally stabbed by a gang of white youths in east London on 22 April 1993 and then bled to death in front of the police officers who arrived on the scene. In July 1997 the incoming New Labour government appointed Sir William Macpherson to head an official inquiry into the police response to and investigation of Stephen Lawrence's murder. In a landmark moment Macpherson's inquiry eventually concluded that the Metropolitan Police as an organisation was 'institutionally racist'.[17] However, as Paul Gilroy shrewdly observes, the charge of institutionalised or systemic racism also absolved individual officers of culpability:

> The learned judge's well-publicised adjustments to the concept of insti-
> tutional racism acknowledged that prejudice was present but empha-
> sised the idea that it was 'unwitting'. He identified institutional racism
> with collective organisational failures but provided a definition of what
> counted as racist that was so narrowly and tightly drawn that it excluded
> almost everybody and left the sources of these mysterious failures inac-
> cessible to all but the management consultants.[18]

A large part of the dissident political force of *Filth* resides in its refusal to dismiss racism as either a problem of rogue individuals in an oth- erwise equitable system or as an abstract and impersonal structural fault to which individual officers are helplessly bound despite their better intentions. Instead the novel excoriates both the institution and those who maintain its oppressive culture. Gilroy's critique also inti- mates how under the corporate speak of Blairism the Macpherson report at its most strategic seems to regard racism as less a brutal real- ity with concrete social effects and more a conundrum for effective management practice.[19] Similarly, Welsh believes that Thatcherism and now Blairism have led to a 'managerial ideology dominating insti- tutions, where there are no governing principles. Getting results is the only important thing'.[20] The enervating orthodoxy of Thatcherite and Blairite economics and the dehumanising credo of power, profit and results ultimately govern Robertson's actions as much as his racism, sexism or homophobia. Having bludgeoned Wurie to death Robertson ends the prologue with the rationalisation – 'It's just a job that had to be done' (F 2) – a chillingly sterile inanity that is then echoed in the opening mantra of the novel proper: 'Woke up this morning. Woke up into the job' (F 3).[21] And the first chapter, aptly entitled 'The Games', details the daily manipulative means by which Robertson relates to his colleagues in a working environment he per- ceives as structured by power relationships: 'The games are the only way you can survive the job' (F 3). To this end, one of the most dis- turbing and sinister aspects of *Filth* is the fact that whilst Robertson falls apart and eventually commits suicide, his colleague, Ray Lennox, who is just as racist and corrupt yet more calculating and strategically innocuous, gains the promotion to Detective Inspector due to his capacity to attune himself to the new management doctrine, to learn the rules of the new game: 'You see Bruce, you have tae learn a new script. It's like all that equal opps bullshit: just spout that at the cunts and do it with conviction' (*F* 379).

In many ways, Robertson becomes a victim of his own doctrine. His standard motto throughout the novel – 'same rules apply' – which he uses to justify his multifarious oppression of others, itself crystallises the dominant ethos of an era of deregulation wherein the only code left is that of power and profit. It is a profound indictment of the ideology of Thatcherism that a conscience should be viewed as a parasitic 'infestation' (*F* 231) to be shed. Notably, Thatcher did seek to imbue her monetarism with moral purpose – 'Economics are the method; the object is to change the heart and soul'[22] – but the soulless void at the heart of *Filth* provides a caustic commentary on the social implications of this philosophy. At the core of Robertson's mindset is merely his internalisation of monetarist doctrine, as illustrated by his thoughts on 'justifiable inequality' (*F* 78), or that 'life is one big competition' (*F* 195), and 'destruction is natural in the human spirit' (*F* 229). Upon seeing his colleague, Clelland, who has been hospitalised after being overcome by the horror he has witnessed in the job, Robertson muses: 'natural selection mate, natural selection. The twisted, broken people go to the wall and you are one of them my friend. Same rules. Clell always was a weak, sensitive, commie poof under that jokey exterior' (*F* 282). Correspondingly, when Cliff Blades falls to pieces after his arrest – having been framed for making obscene phone calls to his own wife by Robertson who was the real perpetrator – Robertson muses sadistically: 'He deserves to die, to be forced into committing suicide and dying. Like Clell. Aye, if I had my way that would happen with the fucked up: a sort of psychic natural selection' (*F* 232). The irony of this posturing is that it actually presages his own breakdown and demise.

In fact what is most striking about Robertson's supposedly tough guy persona is how fundamentally weak his opinions and actions are. Robertson briefly admits as much when confronted by the widow of a heart attack victim whom he had attempted to save: 'Just looking at her there, at her distress, just for a second, we wish we were stronger. I wish I was somebody else' (*F* 327). The novel makes plain that in a dominant culture of aggressive self-interest it is sympathy and compassion which require infinitely more strength and will than strong-arm populism. Robertson first becomes aware of the presence of something inside himself during the chapter 'Equal Opportunities', a realisation that unsettles his racist and misogynist dismissals of social

equality: 'It's like there's something in me, I can almost feel it growing, getting stronger' (*F* 50). Tellingly, Robertson fights off his panic
by retreating into the shell of his hard man persona and concentrating on his plans to discredit all his promotion rivals: 'The cunts here'll
never fuckin know, they'll never fuckin ken cause I'm better than that,
better than all of them, stronger than the fuckin lot of those cunts put
together' (*F* 50). It is left to the tapeworm to disclose the past which
Robertson's power-hungry present would repress. He actually hails
from a working-class, Midlothian mining village, a community that
he not only psychologically seeks to eliminate in his present but also
one that he actually helped decimate as a member of the police force
which suppressed the Miners' Strike in 1984.

The enemy within

On 19 July 1984 Thatcher made the following pronouncement on the
striking miners: 'We had to fight an enemy without in the Falklands.
We always have to be aware of the enemy within, which is more difficult to fight and more dangerous to liberty'.[23] Elsewhere Thatcher has
referred in speeches to her fight against 'enemies of democracy both
within and without'.[24] The clear implication is that the British state
had declared war upon those elements of society deemed to be recal-
citrantly resistant to the New Right mainstream. One of the functions
of the tapeworm's elucidatory and compassionate narrative in *Filth* is
to subvert the Thatcherite ravings of the main text from within, as
indicated in the book's very form wherein Robertson's voice is blotted
out by the winding coils of the tapeworm's discourse that visually
irrupts from the centre of the main body of the text. The parallel
between Thatcherism's struggle with perceived internal subversives
and Robertson's wrestling with what he considers a treacherous par-
asite is made explicit when Robertson drinks whisky to 'burn out the
enemy within' (*F* 152) and in his ruminations on the worm as 'the
alien monster. I know it's up there though, inside of me, twisting and
growing, biding its time, like an Arthur Scargill in the healthy body
politic of eighties Britain, the enemy within' (*F* 171).

   Bruce's decision to turn his back on his mining family background
and to join the ranks of the police and state forces to quell the strike
and its objectives is informed by his belief that 'power was everything
. . . Only the winners or those sponsored by them write the history of
the times. That history decrees that only the winners have a story

worth telling' (*F* 261). By contrast, particularly since the end of the
Second World War, there has been a challenge to the dominant idea
that history and the writing of history concern only the great and the
powerful. This counter-history, or 'history from below' as it is termed,
is promoted by the work of historians such as E. P. Thompson and
Christopher Hill who affirm that it is ordinary people who make history but whose agency and struggles are ignored or expurgated by the
dominant historical narratives of the powerful. In *Filth* an ethical
voice of the oppressed emanates, quite literally, 'from below' in the
form of the tapeworm's narrative that emerges from Robertson's
bowels. Its voice returns a repressed history of communal struggle
and social belonging supposedly vanquished by the competitive individualism of contemporary society.

In the chapter 'Coarse Briefings' the tapeworm starts to assume
narrative control for longer periods of the text and its nascent consciousness, which grows out of a basic urge to eat, initially appears to
endorse Bruce's unthinking Thatcherite ravaging: 'this consumption,
all this chomping and chewing, it provides me with more evidence of
my existence than thought does. This is the only real way I can inter-
act with the environment I am in' (*F* 70). Yet the worm also becomes
conscious that it has a 'soul' which demands contact with something
beyond the self. By contrast, Robertson (in tellingly economic terms)
concedes that in order to achieve what he has 'the price is your soul'
(*F* 262), and that: 'You can't afford a conscience in this life, that has
become a luxury for the rich and a social ball and chain for the rest of
us' (*F* 109). The tapeworm's desire for communion with 'something
bigger perhaps something that is a part of me' (*F* 192) is heightened
by the development of a second worm in Robertson's guts (*F*
230–231). However, this 'soulmate' is purged by Robertson's medica-
tion. The incommensurability of Robertson's and the tapeworm's
worldviews is foregrounded in the aftermath of Robertson musing,
having slept with Blades' wife, Bunty, that: 'The problem with hoors
is not so much the getting into their keks, but the keeping them at
arm's length afterwards' (*F* 300). The tapeworm's narrative interjects:
'I miss the Other. I miss that soul so much. How can you live like this
Bruce, like the way you've made us live, alone in this world? We need
to be together Bruce, together in our own societies and communities.
How can you do this to us?' (*F* 301). Ironically, the tapeworm, whose
voice is distinguished by its compassion and sociality, self-depreciat-
ingly thinks of its host: 'You must be leading a far more interesting

life than myself, a primitive organism confined to dull, unexciting ritual' (*F* 139), when it is actually Robertson whose soul is stifled by his deadening regime.

Of course if Thatcherism was purely a negative, delimitating ideology that oppressed everyone equally it would never have survived as long as it did. It also provided a large cross-section of the British population with a renewed and galvanised sense of identity in the midst of profound and often threatening social change. The empowerment and security which Robertson's views afford his sense of self helps demonstrate what Stuart Hall saliently deems Thatcherism's 'authoritarian populism': 'Thatcherism's "populism" signals its unexpected ability to harness to its project certain popular discontents, to cut across and between different divisions in society and to connect with certain aspects of popular experience'.[25] For example, when Robertson assaults a passer-by on a drug-fuelled and brothel-cruising holiday in Amsterdam, he is reminded:

> It's that front-line feeling; that rush when you're at a picket line or at a big game and you've got your truncheon and shield and the whole force of the state is behind you and you're hyped up to beat insolent spastic scum who question things with their big mouths and nasty manners into the suffering pulp they so richly deserve. It's a great society we live in . . . I hate them all, that section of the working class who won't do as they are told: criminals, spastics, niggers, strikers, thugs, I don't fucking well care, it all adds up to one thing: something to smash. (*F* 160)

If Robertson's persona and views here seem preposterously over the top, it is worth remembering comments such as that by the Thatcherite Sir Alfred Sherman in January 1984: 'if the unemployed get lower benefits, they will be quicker to start looking for work . . . As for the lumpen proletariat, coloured people and the Irish, let's face it, the only way to hold them in check is have enough properly trained police'.[26] So Thatcherism grants Robertson a means of self-aggrandisement by constructing a populist political subject of dominant Britishness which founds itself on the denigration of otherness. Significantly, Robertson is a keen consumer of the tabloid press yet also feels superior to its other readers, as when a shopkeeper attempts to engage Bruce about the copy of the *Sun* he has just bought: 'This disgusts me as I'm not like the rest of the festering plebs who read the *Sun*. I'm more like somebody who writes the thing, edits it even. Know the difference, you pleb, always know the fuckin difference'

(*F* 25). Welsh succinctly satirises Robertson's pretensions by having him later declare of the *Sun*: 'it's a pleb's paper, I only buy it for the tits, the telly and the fitba' (*F* 200). Reading the tabloid press gives Robertson a sanction for his despicable politics and also allows him to feel an identity of interest with the powerful in society. This delusory enablement gives the lie to Neville Wakefield's claim that such popular reading activity is not merely mass deception but a knowing and ironic process informed by a deeply 'postmodern sensibility'.[27] Indeed, the actual social ramifications of the tabloid press are made plain when the *Sun*-reading Robertson is confronted by a group of Liverpudlians, who, like most of the working-class people in their city, refuse to read that paper due to its reporting of the 1989 Hillsborough football tragedy in which ninety-six people died (*F* 176–180).[28]

As the tapeworm's voice of conscience takes hold of Robertson's thoughts it tells him: 'Just moving around inside you I can feel all your ghosts. You've internalised them Bruce' (*F* 242). Robertson typically strives to forestall his creeping memories by launching into a rant about the Miners' Strike at work. But the worm's effusion of thoughts about Robertson's family background interrupts his polemic and precipitates a statement in support of the trade union movement and its democratising goals that he quickly tries to erase:

> If unions had never broken the laws, we wouldnae have any democracy . . . in the first place, I say, wondering why the fuck I'm coming out with all this wank . . . I correct myself, – But there are people within the unions now who don't give a fuck about democracy. Maggie sorted them out, but they're still there, just waiting for that Tony Blair spastic to show signs of weakness and let them back in. That was why things got so messed up with the last Labour government. These bastards held sway. Scargill and the likes. That's why we had to sort them out. (*F* 245)

And just as for Robertson's hard man cop persona to function he must repress a large part of himself, his own past, so too, it is implied, Thatcherism's identity rested upon the jettisoning of a large part of Britain's own history and culture. As Robertson's identity is stalked by these ghosts unleashed from his tapeworm conscience, he increasingly refers to himself as 'we'. On one level, this satirises Thatcher's personal appropriation of the royal 'we', perhaps most comically demonstrated upon the birth of her first grandchild, Michael, in February 1989 when she announced to waiting television cameras: 'We are a grandmother'. More seriously, though, it also helps trace the collapse of the Thatcherite populist subject, the Great British 'we' that the New Right project sought to construct. As Stuart Hall imparts: 'Thatcherite populism is a particularly rich mix. It combines the resonant themes of organic Toryism – nation, family, duty, authority, standards, traditionalism – with the aggressive themes of a revised neo-liberalism – self-interest, competitive individualism, anti-statism'.[29] The foundering of Robertson's own identity helps elucidate Thatcherism's irreconcilable contradictions as the fantasies of his happy family life and his dutiful professional commitment to the law are overwhelmed by the manipulative and degraded reality of his pursuit of power and personal gratification: 'we're falling apart' (*F* 254). This disjuncture is perhaps most apparent in the sections of the novel dealing with his wife Carole.

Carole

The short chapters featuring what at first appears to be Robertson's wife are typographically divorced from the main narrative by being in bold type. In the first of these episodes, 'Carole', Robertson utilises his fantasy wife's voice to conjure a devoted domestic unity: 'I really know my man . . . I wrap my arms around myself and imagine that we're together. In a sense we are together because nothing, space, time, distance, whatever, can break the delicious communion between us' (*F* 42–43). This idyll is then contrasted, in 'Still Carole', with the corrosive social and domestic disruption of the miners and their socialist politics:

> I'm remembering when I first met Bruce's parents. They were good people, from a mining village in Midlothian. This was before they were corrupted by that Scargill, who split up families and turned everyone against each other. Bruce doesn't bear any grudges though, even though they were cruel to him and rejected him, their own son. That's what these people want though: to split up the family. It's not important to them but the way I see it, if you haven't got family then you haven't got anything. (*F* 166)

But as Raphael Samuel, Barbara Bloomfield and Guy Boanas divulge, it was actually the miners and their supporters who staged 'a defence of the known against the unknown, the familiar against the alien, the local and the human against the anonymous and the gigantesque'.[30] Robertson's fantasy family castigates Thatcherism's own pretensions of being the guarantor of traditional family values whilst simultaneously lacerating the fabric of society and community necessary to maintain those very values. In the chapter 'More Carole', it surfaces that Robertson has been abusing his daughter, even as he uses his wifely persona to repress the fact: 'I'm looking forward to seeing Bruce again, so we'll be back together as a family; me, Bruce and our little girl Stacey. She has to accept the wrong she's done and the hurt she's caused with her silly little lies' (F 211). It is in the following chapter, 'Private Lessons', in which Robertson is enacting his masochistic fantasies with a prostitute that he first starts referring to himself as 'we': 'We are compelled to obey. We? Me. I' (F 223).

The reader becomes increasingly aware that the 'we' shared by both Robertson's narrative hereafter and the 'Carole' interludes is a compendium of his own mental disintegration. In 'Carole Remembers Australia' Robertson uses his imagined wife to justify his own serial infidelities: 'He explained to me why he went with that prostitute back in Australia. He needed to be with someone. It meant nothing. I failed Bruce by not being there for him. I was with my mum' (F 239). Additionally, Robertson seeks to justify his own evil by having 'Carole' relate how his being was shattered by happening upon a tortured man named Costas, whilst working undercover in the Sydney police force, whom he was forced to shoot to put out of his misery due to the severity of his mutilation: 'I think that image of Costas became a symbol for extreme possibilities of evil. That's why Bruce is how he is' (F 241). Nevertheless, any nascent sympathy for Robertson is immediately dissipated in the next chapter, 'Worms and Promotions', in which Robertson gleefully recalls the lies that he attempted to feed to his wife: 'I used to tell her a pile of shite when I was knocking off Madeline, this half-Abo bird I used to leg out there. I made up a lot of bullshit about working undercover' (F 242). Finally, in 'More Carole?', the usual bold type imaginings break off into the present of the narrative as Robertson, publicly masquerading as his wife in women's clothes and make-up, is accosted by the gang of youths who originally assaulted Efan Wurie. The preposterousness of Robertson's delusions become evident when he tries to fob off the gang with a claim that he is working undercover before pronouncing: 'We're a family' (F 343). The gang place a plastic bag over his head and kidnap him. This jolt of reality finally spurs Robertson to confront his compensatory transvestite façade and his sister-in-law's news that Carole and his daughter have left for good:

We're remembering how this all started; that when Carole first left
with the bairn we used to set the table for two and then we started wearing her clathes and it was like she was still with us but no really . . .
Carole, why did you dae it, with that fuckin nigger, those whores they
meant nothing tae me . . . your fuckin big-moothed hoor ay a sister . . .
fanny like the Mersey tunnel . . . and the bairn . . . oh God . . . God . . .
God . . . we want to live . . . all we're asking for is some law and order.
(*F* 343)

One way of understanding Robertson's psychic construction and
inhabitation of an imagined wife is offered by Jacques Lacan's dictum
that 'woman does not exist'. By this statement, Lacan does not mean
that women do not actually exist, but rather that according to the dominant cultural codes of our patriarchal society they are never represented as themselves nor can they represent themselves as subjects.
Instead they function within patriarchal language and culture merely
as objects upon which male subjects project their fears and anxieties.
Lacan deploys the punning neologism, *le sinthome*, in place of *le symp-
tome* (thus combining the French words for 'symptom' and 'man'), to
reinforce his thesis that woman is the symptom of man.[31] That is, a
support for the male subject's consistency yet also a point of radical
inconsistency. Under such conditions woman as a representational
object becomes a mystificatory fetish that is used to bolster a male
subject and shore up its insecurities. As Rob Lapsley and Michael
Westlake aver: 'It is not so much that male fantasy willfully misrepre-
sents women as that it uses women as a metaphor for what does not
exist'.[32] Hence, for Robertson ultimately all women commingle into a
fantasy designed to mask the fracture and gaping lack of his own
identity: 'All my life I felt that I was meant for greater things but there
was always something holding me back, some missing piece in the
jigsaw. That missing piece, I can see now, is the love and understanding of a wonderful woman' (*F* 325). It is through his imagined
female, 'Carole', that Robertson seeks to impose some 'law and order'
upon his disintegrating masculinity, to legitimate and structure his
dissolving self. In terms of his fantasy life as his own wife, Robertson's opprobrium is complete after he escapes from the gang by
falling from a building and is eventually discovered by his colleagues
wearing his female clothes.

Pigs and filth

Robertson's fractious and unstable 'we' also communicates the antin-
omies of his class identities. During the class reconstitution of
Thatcherite and Blairite Britain and the solidification of the monetarist state, some workers became consumers, some citizens became
shareholders and then stakeholders, whilst others became a seditious
enemy or disenfranchised underclass. The state's sustained assault
upon the trade union movement and organised labour sought to rupture traditional forms of class solidarity by pitting members of the
working class against one another. Within this context of profound
social change and the collision of class identities under Thatcherism,
Welsh's use of ideas of the police as 'pigs' and 'filth' is also propitious
in light of Peter Stallybrass and Allon White's engaging Bakhtinian
cultural history of the pig. For Stallybrass and White the pig is a
deeply ambivalent and ambiguous creature which diffuses and con-
fuses social boundaries and categorisations: it is 'the site of competing definitions and desires'.[33] Stallybrass and White relate how the pig
troubled the demarcation between human and animal in classical
reason:

> Not only did the pink pigmentation and apparent nakedness of the pig
> disturbingly resemble the flesh of European babies (thereby transgress-
> ing the man-animal opposition), but pigs were usually kept in peculiarly
> close proximity to the house and fed from the household's leftovers. In
> other words, pigs were *almost*, but not quite, members of the household
> and they *almost*, but not quite, followed the dietary regimes of humans
> . . . Whereas animals which ate grass or berries could be thought of as
> part of a different habitat and different food system, the pig overlapped
> with, and confusingly debased, human habitat and diet alike. Its mode
> of life was not different from, but alarmingly imbricated with, the forms
> of life which betokened civility. It is precisely 'creatures of threshold'
> which become the object of fear and fascination.[34]

So one reason why the term pig is often uses as a recurrent form of
abuse is not merely due to a sense that pigs are low, bestial others but
rather, more significantly, because they belie an anxious insecurity
about the hybrid intermingling of seeming incompatibilities. As
Stallybrass and White affirm:

> From early records of Greek and Latin slang, where . . . *porcus* and *pocel-*
> *lus* were used to describe the female genitalia, through to modern uses
> of 'pig' to mock the police, the fascist and the male chauvinist, pigs seem

to have borne the brunt of our rage, fear, affection and desire for the 'low'. Bakhtin's major advance in 'thinking pigs' was to recognize that the pig, like the fair itself, had in the past been *celebrated* as well as reviled. It was precisely the ambivalence of the pig, at the intersection of a number of important cultural and symbolic thresholds, which had traditionally made it a useful animal to think with.[35]

The use of the term to designate the police developed out of the response of the urban working class to resist their own status as despised slum dwellers in urban 'filth' and squalor. Stallybrass and White demonstrate:

> At the same time the pig was appropriated by the city underworld to describe the 'filth' from above, a particularly urban 'world upside down' political strategy which removed any trace of affectionate ambivalence from its symbolism. In the early nineteenth century the police (and especially the 'feared plainclothes man') were first called 'pigs' or 'grunters'. [36]

In Welsh's novel the metaphor of pigs and filth subtly elucidates contemporary Britain's convulsive disruption of social identities as impacted in Robertson's own character. Robertson himself seeks to recast the term's derogatory inflection by claiming that pig stands for 'Pride, Integrity and Guts' (*F* 62). But even as he attempts to construct a clearly patrolled boundary between himself and the supposed criminal working-class filth that he so demonises, it is manifest that Robertson is actually riven by a hybrid confusion of definition which continually threatens to overturn his elevation of his self. His efforts at disavowal are most succinctly encapsulated when he comments after snorting cocaine: 'This is washed down by Glenmorangie to get the taste of diseased druggy scum out of our nostrils' (*F* 238).

Comparably, when Robertson happens upon Alan Loughton, a former member of the strike committee from his own village who is now a beggar, in Edinburgh city centre on a night out, he instantly seizes upon the opportunity to mock Loughton mercilessly. Yet Loughton manages a seemingly indecipherable reply which prompts the following:

> There's two words though, that I, we, I, we can make out.
> Filth.
> The other is bea
> No fuckin way a jakey, a purple-tinned cunt is fucking with my head.
> It's me, Bruce. There are no others. I'm not the one he's on about.

Loughton. A nothing. A nobody. A set of fucking dormant social problems waiting to be cleaned up. That's the real filth, that's the real
garbage. (*F* 319)

The unfinished second word from which Robertson's narrative fear-
fully recoils is 'beast' and with it the tapeworm's voice finally unlocks
the buried secrets of Robertson's past.

'I come from a lot dirtier, filthier places than doon a fuckin pit'

As a child Bruce felt continually neglected by his father, Ian Robertson, but cannot understand why. Robertson's feeling of rejection
manifests itself in a refusal to eat food, which angers Ian further to
the point where he forces Bruce to eat the coal that he spends his
working life digging from the earth: 'Your mother would look away as
Ian Robertson pulled you up to the fireplace and pointed at the coal in
the bucket. – Ah've been fuckin diggin this site aw day for you! Eat!
But you still couldn't eat the food. Then he'd pick up a lump of coal
and make you eat it' (*F* 292). When Bruce's brother, Stevie, is born he
immediately usurps Bruce's place in the family. The tapeworm's discourse assumes narrative control, despite Robertson's efforts to prevent it, to relate how Robertson's jealousy eventually led him to
murder Stevie when both brothers were sent out to steal coal during
the 1972–1974 miners' strike. Having pushed his brother to the
bottom of a coal mountain, Robertson then precipitates a landslide
which buries and kills Stevie: 'You don't mean to move the coal, but
you still experience a strange elation as well as a crushing fear as it
starts shifting and comes sliding down on Stevie, sealing him in' (*F*
355). Indeed, the typographical arrangement of Robertson's interjec-
tion neatly indicates a psychological shift within his consciousness
from denial to an acceptance of the verity of the worm's account:

That is not true
That is not
true. (*F* 355)

Although the murder is passed off as an accident, the tapeworm
describes Ian Robertson's knowing reaction: 'This thing killed him,
your father screams, this bastard spawn ay the fuckin devil killed ma
laddie! You look straight at him. You want to deny and affirm his
assertions all at once. You're no ma son! You've never been ma fuckin
son! You're filth!' (*F* 355). Bruce is sent away to live with his alcoholic

grandmother and subsequently loses touch with his father Ian and mother Molly, who visits him occasionally with the family's new daughter but stops when another son is born. His grandmother confirms that Ian is not his real father but claims that his actual father is now dead. Bruce is later befriended by one of his grandmother's ex-partners, Crawford Douglas, who not only inducts Robertson into the masons but also reveals to him the secret of his paternity. It transpires that before Ian and his mother, Molly Hanlon, married, she was raped and became pregnant. Hailing from an Irish immigrant family, the Catholic Church pressurise Molly into having the baby and she and Ian decide to bring their wedding date forward and to bring the child up as their own. His biological father is tried and convicted for this and many other offences as a serial rapist of both men and women. His biological father suffered from acute schizophrenia, depression and anxiety attacks and is known in the prison system as the Beast, as well as appearing in newspaper headlines as 'The Face of a Beast'.

The young Bruce finds salvation briefly in his love for a disabled girl named Rhona, despite the taunting of the other local youths who refer to them both as 'The Son of the Beast and the Spastic' (*F* 372). But yet another tragedy ensues when Bruce and Rhona are playing in a golf course and Rhona is killed by a bolt of lightening which strikes her callipers. Robertson feels responsible for Rhona's death too. Moments before the lightening, he had picked up the pin from the golf green and thrown it like a javelin, thereby, as the police inform him later, removing a target other than Rhona for the lightening which always strikes the highest point. When Robertson leaves for London and joins the police he gets married to Carole and they have their daughter, Stacy. But the normality is only a façade, as the tapeworm explains: 'You were normal. Only, there came the anxiety attacks. The depressions. The desires' (*F* 386). In the chapter, 'Home Is the Darkness', Robertson recounts his cathartic visit, thanks to a fellow mason prison warden turning a blind eye, to the prison where his rapist father is incarcerated and where he beats him to a pulp: 'My own father. The one who never abused me, never forced me to eat coal, never called me the spawn of the devil. But he was still the one I hated most' (*F* 387).

These revelations help explain Robertson's vile ruminations in an earlier scene in the novel when raping the daughter of a defence lawyer that he despises: 'A mining family. Ha! I come from a lot dirtier, filthier places than doon a fuckin pit' (*F* 94). Equally, the *leitmotifs* of blackness and filth become recodified by the reader's awareness of Robertson's need to denigrate all the threats to his self as a homogeneous, hostile otherness, whether it is the 'black, shiny, filthy coal' (*F* 245) that Ian Robertson made him eat, the blackened flesh of his brother Stevie as he lies buried under the coal, or the skin of his wife's new partner and of his victim Efan Wurie. In turn, the hatred expressed by the then anonymous murderer in the prologue conveys how the innocent Wurie becomes a frantic projection of both Robertson's brother and his wife's lover: 'You pushed me away mister. You rejected me. You tricked me and spoiled things between me and my true love. I've seen you before. Long ago, just lying there as you are now. Black, broken, dying. I was glad then and I'm glad now' (*F* 1). Another instance of the denigration of this homogenous other through which Robertson gains self-empowerment is proffered by the scene in which he is investigating a burglary at an old woman's house: 'That old coal fire looks comfortable. The coal is placed in a nice brass bucket. One lump or two, or twenty-thousand falling around you? The filthy, dirty coal and the minging cunts that dig it. You dig it baby? You dig that coal brother' (*F* 11). Here his dead brother, miners and indeed black people – given Robertson's painful attempt at 'jive' – all conjoin as the inferior object of his mirth. Yet, as indicated above, Robertson's own sense of himself as a 'pig' and as 'filth', his own pinioning at the collision of conflicting social identities, perpetually frustrates his effort to construct a superior and sequestered subjectivity, as is evident when he cracks up in his car in front of Amanda Drummond:

> I'm not so good at my job now . . . not so good . . . I've been in it too long
> . . . in Australia I was the best . . . my family don't talk to me . . . cause
> of the strike . . . they're a mining family . . . Newtongrange . . . Monk-
> tonhall . . . they don't talk to me. They don't let us in the house. My
> father. It was my brother. It was the coal, the dirt, the filth. The dark-
> ness. I hate it all. They won't let us in the hoose. Our ain fuckin hoose.
> We tried. We really fuckin well tried . . . ah wis only daein ma fuckin job
> . . . polis, eh. It was only the strike . . . There's something wrong with us
> now. Something bad. Something . . . inside. (*F* 339)

A cop out?

So the emotional and physical starvations of Robertson's childhood are presented as informing his later aggressive consumption and materialism, his self-aggrandisement and his self-implosion: 'Can you taste the filth, the dirt, the oily blackness of that fossil fuel in your mouth as you choke and gag and spit it out? Do you still hear his voice in your head urging you to eat? . . . Now you can consume to your heart's content or your soul's destruction, whichever comes first' (*F* 295). For some critics the disclosures about Robertson's past are a kind of cop out, an attempt to excuse, or at least explain, his actions in a manner which reaffirms the status quo by default in directing attention away from the power and corruption of the state institutions in the novel. Neil Cooper finds that 'this is an old-fashioned politically correct piece that points the finger at today's bogeyman figure, only to excuse him care of a tortured childhood'.[37] Phil Baker argues that '*Filth* ends in inverted sentimentality, *grand guignol* and sick-joke excess'.[38] When the tapeworm loses its soulmate, the other worm, it asks of Robertson and perhaps self-referentially of the book itself: 'How can I forgive you? But forgive you I must. I know your story' (*F* 260). In this respect, the novel's narrative seeks to produce a sense of compassion and forgiveness through the telling of Robertson's story. But it is a magnanimity of which Robertson is himself incapable. Having arranged for Carole and Stacy to visit him, Robertson hangs himself from the rafters of his attic by jumping down into his hallway when they open the front door, so that both witness his death. To this end, he wears a T-shirt with 'YOU CAUSED THIS' emblazoned on it. His final thoughts render his Thatcherite philosophy in its terminal exegesis: 'I've won and beaten the bastards but what price victory' (*F* 393). The tapeworm finally goes the way of its soulmate by sliding out of Robertson's body with his excrement – but not before it grants a final castigation of his uncaring, sociopathic doctrine: 'like the Other I am gone, gone with the Host, leaving the screaming others, always the others, to pick up the pieces' (*F* 393).

While the novel does provide an individualised account of Robertson's past and present it interlaces this psychic journey with a keen sense of social and political context. Once more Welsh's work attests to the concept of *displaced abjection* and Welsh's own belief that pain is passed on, that suffering often produces more suffering and victims. For although he hates 'privileged cunts' (*F* 49), Robertson finds in Thatcherism and aggressive individualism a means by which to surmount temporarily his own sense of innate inferiority through the obliteration of others. As the tapeworm confides with regard to Bruce and his biological father:

You were different to that monster. They wanted you to be the same, right from the start, you were the one thing an isolated, terrorised people could kick out at. That was the role you took on. But you're different Bruce, you're different from him . . . But the impulses are still there. The impulse to hurt and control, in order to try and fill the void inside. You think of the man who sired you. You are repulsed and proud. The urge to hurt, demean and control is great in you. To somehow get back at them. You consider politics as a career. How wonderful it would have been to start a war. To send thousands of people to their deaths. You idolise Thatcher over the Falklands. You try to imagine the buzz she must have felt when the word 'rejoice" came from her lips. (*F* 389)

One other means of short-term empowerment is the embrace of a dominant, oppressive masculinity. As in *Marabou Stork Nightmares*, Welsh again offers a kind of zero condition of masculinity in which there are only two options available: either to participate fully in a hyper-masculine psychosis or to undergo self-annihilation. Stefan Herbrechter notes: 'Whereas *Trainspotting* can be read as a negotiation of sexual identity and difference that explores the variety of identity positions available within the realm of sexual consumption, in . . . *Filth*, Welsh zooms in on the extreme masculinist position in order to further dissect and advance its psychotic self-dissolution'.[39] Welsh has asserted that, in the midst of the social flux traced in *Filth*, he does feel a broad sympathy for anyone entrusted with attempting to suture that rupture: 'In some ways, the novel's a bit unfair to the police because they have been trying to put things right. They are in the impossible position of having to police antiquated laws; drugs laws, homelessness laws. The social fabric has been ripped up and the police are not the appropriate organisation to try and hold all that together'.[40] In his next novel, *Glue*, Welsh attempts to use different modes of masculinity and male friendship to try and fasten those loosening social connections.

Notes

1 Cited in Steve Redhead, *Repetitive Beat Generation* (Edinburgh: Rebel Inc, 2000), 141. The film rights to the book were quickly sold to Miramax, Welsh commenting: 'I can see – given the way they want to do it – it's quite a commercial movie, quite a slick thing, quite "hardcore" but done very glossy' (cited in Redhead, *Repetitive Beat Generation*, 143).

2 Roger Scruton, 'Modernists and monsters', *The Times* (10 Dec 1998), 41.

3 Stuart Maconie, 'Fool Britannia', *The Times*, Metro Section (26 Dec 1998), 24.

4 In Bruce's irksome punning discourse he becomes 'a Effen Worry' (*F* 228).

5 Cited in Redhead, *Repetitive Beat Generation*, 144.

6 Cited in Aaron Kelly, 'Irvine Welsh in conversation with Aaron Kelly', *Edinburgh Review* 113 (2004), 9.

7 Sally Munt, *Murder by the Book? Feminism and the Crime Novel* (London: Routledge, 1994), 1.

8 Dashiell Hammett, *The Four Great Novels: The Dain Curse – The Glass Key – The Maltese Falcon – Red Harvest* (London: Picador, 1982), 375.

9 Malory is an illusion to Sir Thomas Malory, author of the chivalric *La Morte D'Arthur* (1485), whilst Marlowe echoes the name of the protagonist in Joseph Conrad's *Heart of Darkness* (1902).

10 William McIlvanney, *Laidlaw* (London: Hodder and Staughton, 1977), 9, 214.

11 It is also noteworthy that in Ian Rankin's Scottish detective novels the name of his central character, Rebus, discloses his embroilment in this interpretative riddle given Sigmund Freud's use of the term *rebus* to denote the coded and enigmatic nature of dreams (see Freud, *The Interpretation of Dreams*. Trans. James Strachey. Ed. James Strachey and Alan Tyson (London: Pelican, 1953)). Another variant of this trope would be Colin Dexter's detective Morse, a name which again evokes ideas of coding and encrypted meaning.

12 I provide a fuller account of the politics of the crime form in my book *The Thriller and Northern Ireland since 1969* (Aldershot: Ashgate, 2004).

13 Scott Bradfield, 'A touch too Scotological', *The Times* (30 July 1998), 39.

14 Edwin Muir, *Scottish Journey* (Edinburgh: Mainstream, 1979), 21.

15 Alan Taylor, 'Thieving, rape, drugs. And that's just the police', *Observer* (9 Aug 1998), 34. Francis Gilbert, in his interview with Welsh, seems to find the author himself complicit in Robertson's attitudes and actions: 'However, for all his condemnation of DS Robertson's behaviour – "I'd jump off Tower Bridge if I thought I was like him" – Welsh seems to admire, and even have affection for, the sheer nastiness of the character. He calls him "Bruce" and when we talk about a scene in which Bruce forces himself upon a young girl, an uneasy smile is never far from Welsh's lips' (Francis Gilbert, 'Where there's muck', *The Times*, Metro Section (25 July 1998, 16).

16 Cited in Wendy Cavenett, 'A star is bored', *Independent* (11 Jul 1998), 20.

17 The full Macpherson report can be accessed at: http://news.bbc.co.uk/ hi/english/static/special_report/1999/02/99/stephen_lawrence/report /default.htm.

18 Paul Gilroy, *There Ain't No Black in the Union Jack: The Cultural Politics of Race and Nation* (London: Routledge, 2002), xxii.

19 Gilroy claims of mainstream anti-racism activity: 'It became equality of opportunity, was trivialised in the poetry of management science, and then contained in the theatrical inclusiveness that was regularly staged to create the impression of more solid shifts' (Gilroy, *There Ain't No Black in the Union Jack*, xxx).

20 Cited in Gilbert, 'Where there's muck', 16.

21 Perhaps the most obvious contemporary cultural example of a violence justified through a blank professionalism is provided by the tag-line of Quentin Tarantino's film *Reservoir Dogs*: 'Let's go to work'.

22 Cited in Martin Holmes, *The First Thatcher Government, 1979–1983: Contemporary Conservatism and Economic Change* (Brighton: Harvester Wheatsheaf, 1985), 209.

23 Cited in Ian Gilmour, *Dancing with Dogma: Britain under Thatcherism* (London: Simon & Schuster, 1992), 76.

24 See Robin Harris, ed., *The Collected Speeches of Margaret Thatcher* (London: Harper Collins, 1997), 228.

25 Stuart Hall, *The Hard Road to Renewal: Thatcherism and the Crisis of the Left* (London: Verso, 1988), 141, 6.

26 Cited in Gilmour, *Dancing with Dogma*, 117.

27 See Neville Wakefield, *Postmodernism: The Twilight of the Real* (London: Pluto, 1990).

28 Amongst other insidious allegations, the *Sun* claimed at the time that some Liverpudlians present both urinated upon and robbed their own dead.

29 Hall, *The Hard Road to Renewal*, 48.

30 Raphael Samuel, Barbara Bloomfield and Guy Boanas, *The Enemy Within: Pit Villages and the Miners' Strike 1984–5* (London: Routledge and Kegan Paul, 1986), 22.

31 See Jacques Lacan, *Le Séminaire: Livre XI* (Paris: Éditions du Seuil, 1978).

32 Rob Lapsley and Michael Westlake, 'From *Casablanca* to *Pretty Woman*: the politics of romance' in Anthony Easthope, ed., *Contemporary Film Theory* (London: Longmann, 1993), 199.

33 Peter Stallybrass and Allon White, *The Politics and Poetics of Transgression* (London: Methuen, 1986), 63.

34 Stallybrass and White, *The Politics and Poetics of Transgression*, 47.

35 Stallybrass and White, *The Politics and Poetics of Transgression*, 44–45.

36 Stallybrass and White, *The Politics and Poetics of Transgression*, 46.

37 Neil Cooper, '*Filth*', *The Times* (21 Sep 1999), 44.

38 Phil Baker, 'An unfair cop', *Sunday Times* (2 Aug 1998), 8.

39 Stefan Herbrechter, 'From *Trainspotting* to *Filth*: masculinity and cultural politics in Irvine Welsh's writings' in Russell West and Frank Lay, eds, *Subverting Masculinity: Hegemonic and Alternative Versions of Masculinity in Contemporary Culture* (Amsterdam: Rodopi, 2000), 112.

40 Cited in Gilbert, 'Where there's muck', 16.

6

Glue (2001)

During the composition of *Glue* Welsh stated an intention to move away from the dark themes pursued to such bleak ends in *Filth* but also intimated that a straightforwardly affirmative novel was for him an impossible task:

> The book I'm doing now, I wanted to do a more upbeat, happier book after *Filth* but I'm writing all this nice positive stuff and I'm thinking well fucking hell I don't really believe it. I come back up here to Edinburgh and talking to my pals and people and everybody's getting shat on in so many different ways. You've got to represent that in what you're doing. You can't just write an upbeat book. The next one is really pissing me off because I wanted to do something positive and hopefully it will have upbeat and hopeful elements in it but I just don't seem to do upbeat and hopeful very well.[1]

The novel revolves around the experiences of four life-long friends from the schemes of Edinburgh, Billy Birrell, Andrew Galloway or Gally, Carl Ewart and Terry Lawson. And the critic Matt Thorne does find in the relationships between these central consciousnesses in *Glue* something of a departure for Welsh thematically – particularly in terms of masculinity: 'the novel has remarkably little violence, with Welsh, this time round, choosing to emphasise what brings men together rather than what drives them apart'.[2] In terms of Welsh's prior work, there is also a major shift in terms of form as *Glue* jettisons the radical typographical and technical experimentation with narrative and voice that so characterises novels such as *Marabou Stork Nightmares* or *Filth*, or the decentred and fragmentary cadences of *Trainspotting*, and indeed the frequent use of surrealism and fantasy throughout his *oeuvre*. Instead Welsh's avowed aim was a more con-

ventional and linear structure documenting the lives of his central figures and their families:

> Some people like the text to be broken up. They like weird things to
> happen. *Glue* has no effects. It's a straight narrative. There's no talking
> babies or exploding squirrels. There's no plan on what novel I plan to
> write next. I never know what I'm going to do one minute to the next. I
> don't have a master plan. I finally wrote a proper book.[3]

The idea of Welsh resolving to write a 'proper book' may appear
something of a retreat given that his earlier works offer such a profound challenge to the assumptions of the conventional novel, its
class bias, its social exclusions and attenuated bourgeois focus.
Equally, it is much closer in ethos to the social documentation in realism, a genre that Welsh declaredly avoided from the outset. Perhaps
one reason for this change of emphasis and aesthetic is that the material covered by *Glue* – the friendships and hardships of the housing
schemes of Edinburgh – is increasingly remote from his own lived
experience as a famous writer. In a sense, the formal technique and
perspective of *Glue* has a more superintending and overarching
regard for a terrain that was once immediate and directly experiential.
Welsh conceived of *Glue* quite directly as an attempt to return to the
same ground as *Trainspotting* whilst also conceding a very different
focalisation or point of view on his own behalf in relation to the book's
substance. He asserts in conversation with Christopher Kemp of
salon.com that

> it's very much character-based rather than plot-based. I didn't really
> have a plot for this one. I just thought, well, I did want to get back to the
> feel of *Trainspotting*, the idea that you've got these characters that are,
> sort of, sparking off each other and they generate the story from there
> . . . Normally, I like to have characters that are living in a short time
> frame in the novels, and put them in a position whereby they're having
> to overcome something. Like Renton has to overcome his heroin addic-
> tion in a short time frame of about a year. Roy Strang of *Marabou Stork
> Nightmares* has to come to terms with his rape and being in a coma.
> Bruce Robertson from *Filth* has the murder and the mental breakdown
> and the tapeworm. It's like throwing stones at somebody over a short
> period of time and you get that kind of incendiary feeling that you're in
> their world. But *Glue* ended up a lot more expansive.[4]

So although the effort to write a 'proper' novel at some level discloses
an increased distance between Welsh and his primary materials, that

distance also, more positively, facilitates a critical and evaluative engagement both socially and historically with the by now familiar terrain of his work. This novel therefore offers an overarching time-line for tracing the social malaise into which many of Welsh's other characters often find themselves thrown *in media res* without histori-cal or cultural templates for comprehending their experience. *Glue* grants a much more reflective historical sweep in its handling of social upheaval. Welsh avers:

> I think my writing is a response to the changes of the last ten years and how they affect working-class communities in general. When I look at the stuff of some writers that I admire, say Jimmy McGovern, one of the main themes is betrayal – unions, welfare state, churches, extended and nuclear families, how those institutions have failed the working-class by failing to protect them from global capitalism and the disintegrating society. I kind of take all that as given and I'm more interested in what the 'Thatcher's Children' generation of forty and under of the working class get up to – how they survive in the current economy and society.[5]

The novel is divided into four component parts: 'Round About 1970: The Man of the House'; '1980ish: The Last (Fish) Supper'; 'It Must Have Been 1990: Hitler's Local'; and 'Approximately 2000: A Festival Atmosphere'. Each section is broached by a short chapter: 'Windows '70'; 'Windows '80'; 'Windows '90' and 'Windows '00'. As well as punning on the well-known Microsoft operating system, these sections offer portals through which to view the development of the characters across these four decades. Where *Filth* offered a diagnosis of shifts within state power across the 1980s and 1990s, *Glue* focuses directly upon the working-class experience of social convulsion. Clearly, working with Jimmy McGovern and the Liverpool Dockers themselves in producing the screenplay for the television drama about their strike has had an impact upon Welsh. For betrayal is struc-turally and thematically central to *Glue* – in terms of not only the main characters' fears of betraying one another but also the selling out of certain sets of communal values and codes. These collective mores are most clearly distilled in the Ten Commandments espoused by Carl's father, the trade unionist Duncan Ewart:

1. NEVER HIT A WOMAN
2. ALWAYS BACK UP YOUR MATES
3. NEVER SCAB
4. NEVER CROSS A PICKET LINE

    5. NEVER GRASS FRIEND OR FOE
    6. TELL THEM NOWT (THEM BEING POLIS, DOLE, SOCIAL,
        JOURNALISTS, COUNCIL, CENSUS, ETC.)
    7. NEVER LET A WEEK GO BY WITHOUT INVESTING IN NEW
        VINYL
    8. GIVE WHEN YOU CAN, TAKE ONLY WHEN YOU HAVE TO
    9. IF YOU FEEL HIGH OR LOW, MIND THAT NOTHING GOOD
        OR BAD LASTS FOR EVER AND TODAY'S THE START OF THE
        REST OF YOUR LIFE
   10. GIVE LOVE FREELY, BUT BE TIGHTER WITH TRUST. (G
        407–408)

The main events in the novel which put these core values under intense strain and which propel the main dramatic impetus of the novel are Duncan Ewart's death and the suicide of Gally, who has contracted the HIV virus through his heroin use. In terms of technique the increased crisis in these values is represented formally in the novel as it opens with third person accounts of the parents and families of the central characters before moving into first person portrayals of those key protagonists and then finally withdrawing into a third person narrative that dispassionately charts the tensions of their friendships and disparate experiences. Welsh explains his narratorial perspectives in the following terms:

> The focus starts on their parents, not them. They're not full characters yet. 1980 and 1990 establish the relationships, really. Then I move from the first person to the third person when I get to 2000, not only because you can give the impression that things are beyond their control – things are happening *to* them – but you move things along a lot faster. They're older, and things are out of their hands. I wanted it to seem like things were moving faster, out of control, with the technology and society in general . . . The two main influences in Scotland were probably Presbyterianism and Socialism. Both those things really went down the tubes in the eighties with secular society and the collapse of trade unions, the movement of the Labour Party to the right – but the moral codes have come from those two things. What's replaced them is the cult of the individual. Consumer capitalism isn't a moral code like Christianity or Socialism; it's just a descriptive statement, a set of relationships. People still espouse those old codes, but they maintain the right to shelve them if it's not in their particular interest.[6]

In this context Duncan Ewart's death has therefore a much wider significance – along with the status of his value system, as the Ten Com-

mandments obviously invoke a profound social authority or religious
(and patriarchal) authority – as it implies the passing of older forms
of working-class community and experience. It was noted in the discussion of *Trainspotting* that one of the few traditional forms of community available to the characters was the funeral, which in itself
signals the dying out of collective value systems. In *Glue* the four
friends finally get back together at the hospital where Duncan is dying
due to a stoke so that again there appears only to be a community
structured around death, around a sense of its own untenability. Yet
there are more positive aspects in *Glue* and a palpable sense of
renewal coupled with a faith that the values which Duncan's ethos
embodies are not completely overthrown. Indeed, the coming
together of the friends at the novel's close also allows a reconciliation
of issues concerning Gally's suicide as the three surviving mates have
varying perspectives on that event which eventually reach a catharsis.
This final elaboration of the novel's key event constitutes the main
dynamic formally and Welsh offers his own account of *Glue*'s purpose: 'To me, it's about miscommunication. They've had a bereave-
ment, these four, but they haven't handled it very well. There's
unfinished business. Each of them has different bits of information,
but they haven't put it together'.[7]

(One nation) stuck in a groove?

For some critics the approach is highly successful, for example Adam
Higginbottom describing Welsh's *Glue* as 'easily his best book since
the one that made his name'.[8] However, on BBC2's *Newsnight Review*,
Philip Hensher dismissed the novel as sub-Dickensian and substandard: 'basically, this is *The Old Curiosity Shop* with chemicals. It's
really quite badly written in lots of ways'.[9] On the same programme
Ekow Eshun was similarly disparaging and likened it to a schemie
version of the apotheosis of Americanised saccharine sitcom emotion: 'It's Irvine Welsh does *Friends*, really. We all grow up together
. . . we all love each other through thick and thin. It's got this ambition to be this grand sweeping novel . . . but he can't do grand scale'.
Eshun continues: 'I think Irvine Welsh's strength and weakness is
that he writes about what he knows. So he writers about Edinburgh
versus Glasgow, about male friendships. I don't think he can really
write about the state of Scotland. What he can describe is the sensibility of Scotland, what it feels like to live in certain estates'.

The introductory chapter of this study of Welsh's fiction observed that historically the conventional novel served to help produce certain kinds of national community and identity and argued further that the value of Welsh's work was to expose this ideology of national unisonance as a bourgeois worldview. The dissonance of his work refutes the claim of a bourgeois narrative register to represent everyone, to speak for all. So by constructing *Glue* according to this grand scale, Welsh is in danger of playing into his critics' hands, of attempting – and failing – to encapsulate, as Eshun would have it, 'the sensibility of Scotland'. However, this national claim is not really Welsh's purpose. *Glue* is quite an apt title in that the novel seeks to adhere to – in the sense of both holding together and remaining loyal and committed to – the key themes of working-class experience that have informed his work. *Glue*, then, bonds the raw materials of his disparate books into a broad historical tribunal that strives not to affirm the national community but rather to pass judgement upon its inequalities.

For some critics the more positive aspects of *Glue* indicate the influence of devolution upon Scottish culture and society, particularly in terms of a new sense of confidence and diversity. Matthew Hart, commenting upon the central father–son relationship of Duncan and Carl, perceives a much wider scope in the novel's ultimate cultural import: 'despite its Oedipal structure, it's clear that Welsh . . . sees *Glue* as an allegory of the nation – one that, this time, ends happily in New Caledonia, friends gathered round the big multi-cultural mixing desk of devolutionary Scotland'.[10] Nonetheless, in relation to nationality itself, Hart discerns a tension between traditional national attachments and more global and popular cultural energies to which the characters have access:

> Welsh wants to have it both ways; Scotland, that antisyzygetical nation, insists on it. The Scotland that we see in *Glue* is both newly confident and newly irrelevant. Welsh's characters are unabashed national stereotypes, yet we see them abroad in both mind and place, drawn to the international affinities of music, sport, and pharmaceuticals. Welsh has so far shown no sign of wanting to escape the triple Scottishness of language, setting, and type; but the Scotland he portrays is unimaginable without other criss-crossing elective affinities, running counter to the nation. In *Glue*, the nation is non-negotiable: a monument to modernity that postmodern chancers can neither overcome nor gainsay.[11]

But is not so much a case of the nation being a static, even anachronistic, model of community outwith the hybrid spaces of postmodernism. Rather Welsh's work indicates forcefully that postmodernity
constitutes a collision between the existing exclusions and inequalities of nationhood and emergent forms of domination and power.
When Carl is travelling back from a rave in Australia to be at his dying
father's bedside he passes through Heathrow Airport in London and
thinks: 'Britain. No, it's England, it's not Scotland. Britain never really
existed. It was all some PR con in the service of the Empire. We've different empires to serve now, so they'll tell us that we're something
else. Europe, or the fifty-first US state or the Atlantic Islands, or some
shite like that. It's all fuckin lies' (*G* 489). Carl's thoughts here on
Britishness position nationality directly in relation to global circuits of
power and multinational capital that are in perpetual states of transformation and readaptation. Hence, the idea of a new, plural and
diverse Scotland – a New Caledonia as Hart would have it – is
debunked by an awareness of the socio-economic disadvantage maintained by the newly devolved nation and its imbrication in these
global networks of power. In fact, *Glue*, as with Welsh's other texts,
indicates that postmodern buzzwords such as hybridity and diversity
are euphemisms masking the realities of socio-economic division and
disadvantage. As Carl puts it: 'The great injustices continued and all
society seemed to do about it was obscure the cause-and-effect relationships around them, setting up a smokescreen of bullshit and
baubles' (*G* 548–549).

Schemie windows

The novel opens in Gally's family home with the short chapter, 'Windows '70', which is imbued initially with the late 1960s' and early
1970s' optimism about the then new housing schemes and their
replacement of the tenement housing of 'Auld Reekie'. Through the
windows of their high-rise home Gally's father, Davie Galloway, surveys his 'fiefdom' and opines that: 'This was the way to live' (*G* 3).
Although narrated in the third person, the chapter often deploys free
indirect style to fuse the language of narration with characters'
thoughts and impressions and is an instance wherein Welsh's style
comes closest to James Kelman's technique. Whilst the novel as a
whole continues Welsh's concentration on masculinity and male
friendships and this opening chapter makes a very specific male ter-

ritorial claim through Davie Galloway's aforementioned 'fiefdom', it is also noteworthy that both in this opening scene and at key moments throughout the text, Welsh attempts to underline these dominant masculine perspectives with female contraventions. Amidst Davie Galloway's optimism and his promise to buy Andrew a new bicycle, his wife Susan's consciousness interjects: 'Where was the money coming from for a bloody bike? Susan Galloway thought, shivering to herself as the blazing, sweltering summer sun beat in relentlessly, through the huge windows' (*G* 5). Where *Marabou Stork Nightmares* and *Filth* offered a critique of a dominant and imposing masculinity's reduction of women to mere objects by embodying that very process and refusing an autonomous space for female characters, the approach in *Glue* is different in that it is the agency of the female characters that is asserted as a means of disrupting the masculine assumptions of the novel. Hence, the following chapter, 'First Day at School', which introduces the childhood of Terry Lawson, focuses upon his mother Alice in a scene in the beer garden of a pub where Terry's father walks out on her, Terry and his sister Yvonne. The third person narrative juxtaposes the casual and affable greetings that his father gives to his acquaintances in the pub with the 'exploded' world of Alice who ends the scene 'soundly crushed' (*G* 12).

The introduction to Carl Ewart's family and the values of his father comes in 'The Works', a chapter in which Duncan, a factory worker and trade union shop steward, stands up for the rights of Billy's father Wullie Birrell. A manager had declined to let Wullie leave work even though his wife Sandra was in labour. Duncan's intervention is successful and the following chapter, 'Two Royal Pests', establishes the bourgeoning friendship between the Ewart and Birrell families as Wullie comes to thank Duncan at home. Wullie and Duncan share a working-class code that they feel still possesses social relevance. Yet this homosocial bonding session is once more undercut by a female voice as Duncan's wife Maria interjects: 'If you want tae give yir sons some kind ay code tae live by, what about try not tae line the pockets of the brewers and the bookies too much' (*G* 26). Similarly, the optimistic faith in the new housing schemes is troubled by ominous realities: 'Duncan loved those big warm tiles under the carpet. You put your feet under that fireside rug and it was sheer luxury . . . Then as winter set in and the first bills came through the post, the central-heating systems in the scheme clicked off; synchronised to such a degree it was almost like they were operated by one master switch'

(*G* 27). The chapter is also noteworthy for its communication of Duncan's humanity and compassion. Although he forced the factory line manager, Abercrombie, into a humiliating climbdown over Wullie, Duncan also empathises with him: 'One thing Duncan's father had told him was to try not to be too quick in passing judgment on others, even your enemies. You never knew what kind of shite they had going on in their own lives. There was something about Abercrombie, something crushed, and by something a lot bigger than that day's events' (*G* 23). Additionally, it transpires that Duncan and Maria were going to tour America in a hired car, pursuing their shared love of popular music, until Carl's unplanned arrival. Against this familial commitment is juxtaposed the following chapter, 'The Man of the House', which stylistically moves into the first person narration of Andrew Galloway. The narrative commences with a faint echo of the opening line of Dickens' *A Tale of Two Cities* – 'It was the best of times, it was the worst of times' – in an early adumbration of Gally's tragic fate: 'It wis when it wis one ay the best times whin ah'm kneelin oan the flair n ah hud the *Beano* oan one ay the big chairs soas that naebody could bother me n ah've got a chocolate biscuit n a glass ay milk' (*G* 28). The entire first paragraph is just one sentence as Gally's young mind attempts to come to terms with the fact that his father is being taken away by the police to serve a jail sentence, though not before he tells Gally he is now 'man ay the hoose' (*G* 30).

Adolescent concerns

Part two of the novel – '1980ish: The Last (Fish) Supper' – moves into the central characters' teenage years but again opens with a short snapshot, 'Windows '80'. Therein, amidst the masculine focus of the novel, Sandra Birrell meditates upon her son Billy as 'tough and private' (*G* 34) and bespeaks her isolation from her husband Wullie. Although this second part on the novel deals with – and is at some level complicit with – adolescent male preoccupations, its opening is the counterpoint of 'an abyss' (*G* 35) of female solitude and alienation. The distanced third person narrative of this section then dissolves into the first person of 'Juiced Up', which details Terry Lawson's decision not to stay on at school – he boasts that he has had sex with all the available girls there. Instead, earning him the nickname Juice, he works on the lemonade lorries which deliver to the schemes. He is unconcerned at foregoing the possible benefits of further education and prefers the immediate prospects offered by his daily rounds on the scheme: 'the main thing fir me is fanny' (*G* 40). As with *Marabou Stork Nightmares* and the reductive 'sameness' accorded both Roy and his victim, Terry's sense of women is merely an extension of his own rapacious masculinity: 'Thir jist like us. Fuckin worse, if the truth be telt' (*G* 45).

Billy Birrell's character is introduced in 'Sex as a Football Substitute', which sets him up as more motivated and sporting than the others and prefigures his career as a boxer. It also details the friends' involvement in a robbery at a wireworks factory with Alex Setterington, the casual from *Marabou Stork Nightmares*, the psychotic Doyle brothers and another thug Marty Gentleman.[12] Billy's first person narrative also depicts a scene – which echoes a classroom scene in William McIlvanney's *Docherty* – in which Gally is chastised by their headmaster, Blackie, for arriving late for school and for speaking improperly by using the word 'aye': 'Eyes are what you have in your head you stupid boy! We speak the Queen's English here' (*G* 82). When Blackie asks what would have happened if Jesus had been late for the Last Supper Carl replies: 'Eh would've goat fuck all tae eat' (*G* 85). Blackie then starts beating Carl until Billy physically restrains him. However, the result is that they all get corporal punishment for their actions. The scene is notable for not only intimating the future boxer Billy's physical presence and controlled strength but also for is validation of Duncan Ewart's code of backing up your mates.

The relationship between masculinity and violence is explored further in the chapter 'The Sporting Life', which details the four friends' involvement in football casuals' culture. The chapter's title offers an ironic reworking of *The Sporting Life*, the 1963 film based on a David Storey's novel of the same name, which deals with the life of a Northern English working-class rugby league player. Here the sport participated in by the friends is a random and casual violence perpetrated in Edinburgh city centre and on the terraces of Easter Road. In fact the book as a whole affords Welsh's most considered appraisal of the casuals phenomenon. The fact that casuals culture demarcates a paradigm shift in football and in culture more broadly is indicated by Billy Birrell's reaction to the fact that casuals do not wear their team's shirts or scarves. He initially believes that: 'Only a coward doesnae wear thir colours . . . ye wear them wi pride, even against aw the odds' (*G* 86). For Billy supporting a team entails a strictly observed and clearly demarcated display and assertion of communal solidarities and belongings. By contrast, the casuals dress in 'smart casual' designer clothes not only because it makes it easier to infiltrate opposing groups of fans and to start violence but also because their creeds are style and looking good. As Roy Strang comments in *Marabou Stork Nightmares*: 'Big-time soccer violence in Scotland had always been aboot really thick Weedgies who never went to church knocking fuck oot ay each other to establish who had the best brand of Christianity. We were big news because we were different; stylish, into the violence just for itself, and in possession of decent IQs' (*M* 137). In mocking Rangers fans for what he perceives as their anachronistic ideology and religious and communal belonging, Roy deploys a telling commercial analogy in describing the blunt ethos of the casuals:

> Their badges and their buntings; Ulster and aw that wanky shite, needy an excuse, a silly toytown reason to muster up the kind ay force we'd learned tae love fir its ain sake, tae have on tap. They were yesterday's thing. They looked around nervously as we walked in our groups throughout their midst. We had nae colours; we wir here tae dae real business. No for the fitba, the bigotry, the posturing, the pageantry. That was just shite tae us. We wir here oan business. (*M* 171)

The casuals assemble not around older working-class loyalties and territorial spaces but instead around designer clothing, trendy brand names and displays of conspicuous consumption. In one scene Billy's brother, Rab, recoils in horror when he realises that his parents have bought him a replica Hibs top as a present, whilst the top casuals Lexo and Ghostie often send people home for wearing the wrong designer labels such as 'Schemie Hilfiger' (*G* 357). And by the time the novel reaches the present the casuals have removed themselves from footballing contexts to more gentrified locales: 'these days you *were* more likely to find some of the old crew in the Fringe Club than at Easter Road' (*G* 357–358). The casuals mark a shift from people being involved in football violence being branded as hooligans to hooligans themselves as brand. Naomi Klein has argued that the colonising imperatives of consumer capitalism and its major multinational brands ensure that 'no space has been left unbranded'.[13] Klein continues:

> Many brand-name multinationals . . . are in the process of transcending the need to identify with their earthbound products. They dream instead about their brands' deep inner meanings – the way they capture the

spirit of individuality, athleticism, wilderness or community. In this context of strut over stuff, marketing departments charged with the managing of brand identities have begun to see their work as something that occurs not in conjunction with factory production but in direct competition with it.[14]

Where supporting a football team once designated an affiliation that had a set, often working-class and industrial locale, a communal identity and symbols that unified a very specific territorial claim, the casuals inhabit a mobile, mutable *milieu* traversed by the circuitry of multinational capital, consumerism and money.[15] It is through this creed of style, pleasure and commodity that the four friends and the other casuals become a 'team' (*G* 87). Writing in 1988, Simon Frith contextualised the nascent phenomenon of 'casuals' in the following way:

> Pop music has become an ideological issue again (the BBC banning records with the same bizarre logic as the 1960s) because the problem of leisure and unemployment has arisen just as the leisure *industry* is being acclaimed as the solution to Britain's economic problems. The transformation of electronic goods into consumer goods, the development of cable TV, video recording, home computers, and so on, have put an economic premium on people's leisure tastes (and, in some respects, threatened state and oligopolistic manipulation of those tastes). Pop's leisure significance is thus being fought for again – hence, Britain's newest youth subculture, the 'casuals,' whose aggressive, stylistic celebration of leisure goods and 'life-style' conceals both continuing dole queues and continuing 'hooliganism' – the street-corner menace now comes from such nice, clean-cut Tory-looking boys and girls.[16]

The casual clothing sported by the casuals and the casualness of their violence also chimes with another form of casualisation: the casual ties that link contemporary de-industrialised employment and a service economy promoting flexible or casual labour and working conditions. These casualised economic conditions themselves decimate organised labour and the traditional working-class values ascribed to Duncan Ewart and his trade unionism. To that end, Duncan himself is eager to accuse the state of its own kind of casual violence. He posits in relation to the media obsession with football casuals that: 'They've aw been demonised oot ay all proportion tae take people's minds off what this Government's been daein for years, the *real* hooliganism. Hooliganism tae the health service, hooliganism tae education' (*G* 187). *Glue*, as with *Marabou Stork Nightmares*, offers the casuals as casualties too, as victims and not just perpetrators.

Damaged/damaging masculinities

Although *Glue* strives to find more progressive and positive forms of masculine attachment it retains an awareness of the dangers of male bonding as compensation for the loss of identity in late capitalism. Welsh asserts:

> Scotland is one of the most repressed societies. It completely sustains that kind of misogynistic behaviour. The pubs, dark inside . . . a completely masculine environment. And then there's this militaristic, football thing, and adults in positions of trust . . . that sense of affirmation within your peer group is such a strong and powerful part of the culture. It's unfortunate that it's been used in such a destructive way, and is becoming more and more destructive. The only places people can meet collectively, now, are through gangs and groups of friends. It's very difficult for people to do it anymore through other collective ways like trade unions, football.[17]

So whilst the four friends become a 'team' with other young men in the casuals network, in *Glue* Welsh maintains an ambivalence about this kind of association: 'I like to look at the good things and the bad things about male culture. There are lot of great things about male culture, but there's also the slightly twisted, fascistic part when you get a bunch of guys together. They do turn into nutsos sometimes, the whole group intoxication thing'.[18] In the chapter 'Clouds' the main characters follow up their violence in the streets with an evening's drinking in Clouds nightclub. Another fight ensues in the club and in the melee Gally lets a knife he is carrying be used by another character, Polmont, to badly lacerate someone's face, before the knife is returned to him. It later transpires that Polmont did this partly due to the recent death of his mother from cancer and simply decided to take his frustrations out on someone else. Though Gally is wracked by guilt he cries 'tears that nae cunt'll see' (*G* 126) in private in a demonstration of the repressed nature of masculinity that Welsh is seeking to diagnose. The incident also begins to unravel the Ten Commandments espoused by Duncan Ewart as Gally decides to take the blame for the stabbing because it would violate the code to grass on the actual perpetrator. Remembering his father's comment as he was taken away to prison that the young Gally was now man of the house, Gally realises as the police apprehend him that 'thir isnae a man ay the hoose any longer' (*G* 137). For Carl in particular this signals the untenability of his father's value system in the contemporary world.

He rages: 'Ma auld man's useless rules. Ehs patter's just goat ays intae bother at school, wi the likes of Blackie, for standing up for masel and tryin tae back up other cunts thit dinnae thank ye fir it . . . One ay ehs rules is thit ye eywis back up yir mates. Fine. Then eh says ye never grass anybody. Well, how kin ye dae baith wi Gally? How kin ye back him up without grassin oan Polmont' (*G* 140–141). The fact that Gally is prepared to go to prison for someone who does not care about him or his family seems, for Carl, to confirm that these core values are now obsolete, as they are open to abuse in the contemporary world. He later ruminates: 'But that was the problem with a moral code, everyone had to subscribe to the same one for it to work. If a few people took the piss and got away with it, everything collapsed' (*G* 547).

The patriarchal nature of the rules is also indicated when Terry invokes them to ensure Carl lies on his behalf to cover up his multiple infidelities to his fiancé Lucy. For all the novel's examination of the more negative aspects of male bonding, however, James Campbell detects more commonly an assertion of the New Lad image which has spawned so many men's magazines, television programmes and cultural forums from the 1990s onwards: '*Glue* has an epic scale; it charts the rites of passage from boyhood to ladhood (no Welsh character has progressed beyond the latter)'.[19] Michael Bracewell contextualises the New Lad in the following manner:

> the Laddism Nouveau of the early 1990s found its voice in an iconography of beer, babes and bacon sandwiches. Laddism was a generational return to the gender stereotyping of the early 1970s (talk about 'like punk never happened'!) and foregrounded a devout anti-intellectualism. It put forward a mixture of hedonism and nihilism which was essentially apolitical, but which thrived upon an infantilist nostalgia for adolescence.[20]

There is a sense in which the timeframe of *Glue*, stretching through the 1970s to the present, facilitates not only an understanding of the main characters' development but also an indulgence in adolescent boyhood and early masculinity that offers no apologies for its excesses and immaturity and which permeates the novel as a whole. This more regressive dimension becomes apparent in the third section of the novel – 'It Must Have Been 1990: Hitler's Local' – which recounts the friends' trip to the football World Cup in Italy in 1990 and a subsequent foray to the Munich Beer Festival in the same year. To that end, one of the starting points for the assertion of the New Lad in Britain generally was the song and video for the English football team's World Cup campaign. 'World in motion' was written by New Order and marked the beginning of a football-music crossover which informed the spirit of magazines such as *The Face* and the *New Musical Express*. In turn, this crossover facilitated a more widespread realignment of masculine expressions in the popular cultural realm so that so-called New Men's magazines such as *GQ*, *Esquire*, *FHM* and *Loaded* offered supposedly adult versions of comics such as *Roy of the Rovers*, *Goal* and *Shoot* – or indeed the adventure texts that are so formative for Roy Strang's sense of his masculinity in *Marabou Stork Nightmares*. Notably, the apotheosis of New Lad magazines, *Loaded*, was, according to its own publicity, written for men who read Nick Hornby. And by extension, aspects of Welsh's own work formed the basis of this new marketing of masculinity. When at the 1990 World Cup Terry declares: 'Ah dinnae gie a fuck aboot the fitba or gittin tickets; if Scotland loast every game six-nil or if they won the fuckin World Cup itself, it wid make nae fuckin difference tae me at aw. Ah'm here fir the shaggin' (*G* 207). Terry's character, then, suggests that all these other identifications – football, nationality, socialising and so on – are only really sublimations of an underlying and primal masculine imperative that seeks to justify itself only in terms of its own unrestrained inexorability. However, in Welsh's defence, the rampant Laddism of the four friends' time abroad is undercut by the first chapter of the novel's third section. Again a female perspective is utilised to undermine the assumptions of the main male narratives and Maria and Sandra also offer a context in which to place that masculinity:

> The mothers shared a concern for their sons. The world now had a greater superficial wealth than the one they grew up in. Yet something had been lost. It seemed to them a crueller, harsher place, devoid of values. Worse, it seemed that young people, despite their fundamental decency, now had to buy into a mind-set which made viciousness and treachery come easy. (*G* 186)

Furthermore, 'Windows '90' also grants amidst the hedonism of the four lads' holiday in Germany a vantage point from which to castigate the social decay of the schemes: 'there was no community spirit left, it was a dumping ground for social problems and it had gone downhill' (*G* 184). It transpires that the now unemployed Wullie has spent his redundancy on buying the Birrell's council flat with the positive result that 'Sandra was sleeping again, without alcohol or pills' (*G* 184). Wullie, however, feels increasingly useless, as does Duncan who has also been laid off: 'Redundancy seemed to be a term which meant more than just the loss of a job . . . Like Wullie, Duncan was finding life hard without a job, struggling to pay off the mortgage on their small house in Baberton Mains' (*G* 185).

Business Birrell

Through the partying in Munich the contrasting experiences of the four friends over the previous decade does become apparent and it serves to enhance the social context established by the predicament of Carl's and Billy's parents. Billy has turned professional as a boxer and has earned himself the nickname Business Birrell on account of his clinical, no nonsense performances. Similarly, Carl has inherited his father's love of music and is achieving increasing fame as a house music DJ under the moniker N-SIGN. For Billy both he and Carl are embracing new social and economic opportunities that seem to dismiss the traditional values which he associates with their (now unemployed) fathers: 'Aw we're gittin is the same respect that oor faithers goat for bein tradesmen, for workin in a factory. Now people like that, punters that were once seen as the salt ay the earth, are taken for mugs' (*G* 192). Through his boxing connections he becomes involved with an Edinburgh crook and entrepreneur, David Alexander Power, who wants to involve Billy in his plans to redevelop Edinburgh city centre with trendy clubs and bistros and offers him the chance to open his own establishment – The Business Bar:

> Me, having my ain bar, my ain business. Sounds good. It's the only way to make money, having your ain business, buying and selling. And having money is the only way to get respect. Desperate, but that's the world we live in now. Ye hear the likes ay Kinnock n the Labour Party gaun oan aboot the doctors n nurses n teachers, the people that care for the sick and educate the kids and everybody's nodding away. But they're thinking aw the time, ah would never dae that kind ay joab, just gie me money. It's drastic, but you'll never change it. You try to be decent tae people close tae ye, but everybody else can piss off, n that's the wey ay it. (*G* 206)

So communal values and social justice now appear to Billy to be relics of the supposedly bygone age that is projected on to his parents. The fact that he is a boxer is apt in its typification of this new creed of rugged, self-protective individualism. Although his trainer Ronnie frequently uses the collective pronouns 'we' and 'us' in describing their workouts, Billy inwardly muses upon the more stark and solitary reality of boxing: 'Nope, sorry Ron, we're always alone in the ring' (*G* 190). The colonising imperative of the market and free enterprise is made explicit with a wry irony as Billy's nickname Business Birrell ultimately becomes associable with him – both for himself and others – due to his commercial interests rather than his boxing. In a way, it is business which subsumes his other characteristics and means of expression and identification, claiming his very name as its own. Everything, for Billy, is dictated by this economic imperative:

> You needed respect, and the only way you could get it in Britain if you weren't born with a silver spoon in your mouth, or had the right accent, was through having money. You used to be able to get it in other ways, like his old man, or Duncan Ewart, Carl's dad. But not now. You see the contempt punters like that are held in now, even in their own communities. They say it's all changed, but had it fuck changed. (*G* 505)

Carl also perceives opportunity in his new found wealth and fame as a DJ to escape the limitations of the class system in Britain: 'Any cunt whae disnae huv a silver spoon in thir mooth or isnae prepared tae be an arse-licking wanker cannae live within the law back thair' (*G* 340). Nonetheless, unlike Welsh's earlier work where the acid house scene seemed a more sustainable alternative to punk, which had seemingly gone mainstream and dissipated by the time Welsh started writing, dance culture in Britain is treated with more critical judgement. Whilst at a rave in New South Wales Carl rages polemically:

> Australia was different, it really was the last frontier. So many heads had ended up here, after the dream had been smashed by the riot police and the black-economy drug-dealing nutters the Thatcher years had thrown up. Britain felt old and shoddy, strangely even more so with its New Labour and its modernisation, its wine bars and coke-snorting media and advertising ponces everywhere. It only took one glum 'time gentlemen please' to send the citizens of Cool Britannia scuttling home for the last bus or Tube before the stroke of midnight. That old fist of repression still lurked under the smarmy banality of everyday life. (*G* 385)

In this context, Phil Thornton offers an incisive revision of the achievements of dance culture:

Many claims have been made for acid house, most of them false. In the end, acid didn't change much at all, it just gave a false sense of reality, a drug-induced mirage that old barriers had been broken down: black and white, rich and poor, gay and straight, north and south, we were all one, all on one. The 90s were supposed to have been a reaction against the excesses of the preceding decade, when in fact for some they soon became what the 70s had been to the 60s; a mass collective comedown and a realisation that vague hippie ethics and escapist drugs had nish [no] effect on the state of the world.[21]

Notably in *Glue* many of the gangsters and criminal gangs involved in the redevelopment of Edinburgh of which Billy is a part are former casuals. So where *Ecstasy* and *Marabou Stork Nightmares* offered the dance and ecstasy scene as a new, more progressive buzz for casuals, this novel again inculcates the drive and lure of the market. Terry Lawson too decides that only a 'mug' would still believe in the moral code espoused by Duncan Ewart and his generation. In one scene he is involved in robbing a house in Edinburgh's affluent Grange district, which belongs to an academic who wrote a book on the new security state in Britain arguing that private-security firms run by gangsters are taking over from the state. As a consequence, and as a matter of principle, he has no alarms at his home. For Terry the academic's principles are his opportunity: 'That wis the Tories' biggest achievement: tae make huvin principles cost ye. Private health care, cooncil-hoose sales, mortgages, flogging the nationalised industries, if ye dinnae join in and tow the line yir a mug, even if aw thir daein is helpin them tae stick thir hand in yir poakit fir the rest ay yir puff' (*G* 238). Terry's opportunism, however, extends not only to strangers but also to his friends as it transpires that he has been seeing Gally's former wife Gail: 'Sometimes ye cannae help it if yir best mate's a mug' (*G* 247).

Although things have not gone well for Terry in the intervening years – he lost his beloved lemonade delivery job as the lorries become obsolete due to the opening of large supermarkets and has drifted between jobs and scams – Gally has suffered most out of all the mates. Having been released from prison after serving time for the knife attack which was actually perpetrated by Polmont he eventually marries Gail purely because she falls pregnant. But their marriage is a disaster and she soon begins an affair with – of all people – Polmont. As Gally's life starts to fall apart he finds solace in the heroin habit that will eventually lead to him contracting AIDS. Worse follows when Gail taunts Gally about her relationship with Polmont and, in trying to punch her, Gally's elbow strikes his daughter Jacqueline instead. He is jailed for this offence and in prison mires himself in self-loathing:

> The one ah hated most though, it wisnae her, or even him. It wis me: *me*, the stupid, weak mug. Oh, ah battered *that* cunt awright. Battered um wi everything: alcohol, pills, smack. Punched waws until the bones in ma hands broke and they swelled up tae the size ay baseball gloves. Burned filthy, red-brown holes intae ma airms wi cigarettes. (*G* 215)

For all the New Lad excesses of the trip to Munich, Gally's character offers a searing critique of particular kinds of irresponsible, self-regarding masculinity. Just as his own father became 'an unwelcome stranger' (*G* 212), Gally realises: 'When ah wis growin up, the worst thing my Ma could say tae me was that ah wis as bad as ma faither. Ah telt maself ah'd never, ever be like him . . . Then ah wis inside n aw' (*G* 212). Upon his release Gally is increasingly withdrawn, embittered and hopeless and stares fixedly at the samurai sword and crossbow on the wall, resolving to: '*Take care ay it, take care ay that unfinished business*' (*G* 211). The day before Gally commits suicide by jumping from Edinburgh's George IV Bridge, Polmont is attacked and critically injured by a crossbow and the reader is left guessing as to what exactly happened. When Gally is diagnosed with AIDS in the chapter 'Training' it is evident that his world has collapsed: 'In the disintegration ay reality, yir vision becomes a diffused scan, followed by a desperate focus on the extreme and the mundane. Ye'll grasp at anything, no matter how daft, that seems tae provide the answer: tryin so hard tae find significance in it' (*G* 211). This is also an apt self-referential key to the fourth and final section of the novel, as the remaining three friends all try to piece together and find meaning and significance in their fragmentary sense of events and of their former togetherness.

Friends reunited

The narrative returns to the third person in delineating the scattering lives of the central characters and it is perhaps apposite that the introductory section – 'Windows '00' – features Gally's father, Davie Galloway, a figure who was been absent throughout the text and very much an outsider to his own son and family. For the narrative itself detaches experientially from the events in order to provide an overview of the scattered friendships and misconceptions which the main characters harbour. Also aptly, Davie Galloway is working as a security guard and has a cold, mediated view of the scheme: 'Looking out from the control centre across this large housing scheme, Davie Galloway considered that the monitors were his windows to the world, the black, grey concrete world outside. Monitor six was his favourite, the overview camera sweeping beyond the tower blocks and over the river' (G 350). Much of the final narrative itself attempts a sweeping survey of lives that have lost control. The exception to this technique is Carl's first person narrative and his consciousness becomes the guiding force in the final section of the novel as he flies back from Australia to be at his dying father's hospital bed. As he travels back to Scotland he sets the events of Gally's suicide in a perspective which helps explain the disparateness of the remaining friends' lives: 'We kept away from each other because we reminded each other of our failure as mates. For all our big talk, our friend had died alone' (G 490). After Gally jumped off George IV Bridge in full view of his mates Carl feels:

> That was the last time it was special. After that we kept away from each other. It was as if we learnt about loss too young and wanted to take ourselves away from each other before the others did it first. Even though we wirnae really that far fae each other; me, Billy, Terry and I suppose Gally became the four corners ay the globe after that night. (G 492)

Only Carl had been aware that Gally had contracted AIDS and amidst the hedonism of Munich felt there was also something else wrong with him, some damaged or 'dirty' inside (G 345). Carl's way of dealing with the guilt of his friend's suicide is to become the international playboy through his jet-setting DJ life as N-SIGN. Billy pursues his boxing career until he is diagnosed with a thyroid problem that saps him of energy and leaves him physically unable to move in what becomes his final bout. However, Billy himself reveals there is another reason for the abrupt end to his career: his final opponent looked exactly like Gally and this is why in the most crucial fight of his career: 'Billy's body had gone and was not moving for him' (G 502). But he has his Business Bar to fall back on and as he moves increasingly up the social hierarchy he shuns Terry and physically kicks him out of the bar in one scene. Terry he feels is not just 'a waster' but also a malevolent figure whom he believes does not have the emotional capacity of himself or Carl: 'He wished he hadn't cut Terry off like that, all those years ago, but the man was a liability . . . You suspected that if it wasn't Gally, he'd find some other justification to be a cunt' (G 501).

Whilst Billy has climbed the social ladder, Terry has encountered ladders of a more real kind in his new job as a window cleaner. He is forced into employment after his mother, who is sick of catering to his lazy lifestyle at home, finally departs having left him a note which reads: 'Tell the council I've committed suicide. God knows, I felt like it often enough . . . PS. Don't try to find me' (G 354). Terry feels that he has been made the scapegoat for what happened to Gally and is highly resentful of Carl's and Billy's affluent lifestyles. When he goes to Gally's mother's house to offer help in babysitting Gally's daughter he is rebuffed:

> He once saw Billy in his big flash car, Mrs Galloway getting out, and Billy helping her with her shopping. Aw aye, Birrell's little practical help would be welcome of course, that would do nicely. But Birrell was a 'capital sporting personality' and now a successful businessman. Even Ewart, that drug-addled cunt, was a top deejay and rumoured to be a millionaire. Naw, you needed a scapegoat, and in this age the guy left behind in the scheme fitted the bill. (G 500)

Nevertheless, despite Terry spending most of the novel celebrating an uncaring, manipulative and sex-obsessed masculinity, he too is forced into self-reflection when thinking of the collapse of his marriage and his estrangement from his son Jason:

> Jason. He picked the name. That was it. He'd said to Lucy that he'd never be like that old cunt, the bastard that left him and Yvonne, that he would be a good faither. He'd become so obsessed with making himself appear different from the fucker, he'd not noticed it had all been superficial characteristics he'd worried about and that they'd turned out like two peas in a pod. (G 499)

The critic James Campbell argues that despite such moments the novel and its narrative technique is hampered by a superficiality and a fundamental lack of empathy and understanding:

> Given Welsh's descriptive talent, there is curiously little feeling for life beyond the schemes (even they are sketchily described). He shares this lack with his characters, for whom other people barely exist. No matter how far afield they travel, Terry, Carl and Gally will never develop the faculty of recognising value in outsiders; others remain the Other.[22]

And in particular, for Campbell, 'no species is more exotic than women'.[23] However, as indicated above, *Glue* does seek to undermine its admittedly pervasive male focus with the voices and experiences of women who are subject to the negative and reactionary sides of that masculinity. This is apparent too in the fourth section of the novel when Terry and Billy's brother meet Charlene and her friends on a night out and Rab establishes a relationship with her. Charlene had been abused as a child by 'that fucking thing' (*G* 388), her father, who still beats and abuses her mother. Charlene confronts her father in a pub – that bastion of male comfort – about the abuse and also challenges the men drinking with him to disown him – which they duly do. Another female perspective is introduced – somewhat improbably – towards the novel's close when Terry befriends an American pop singer whilst cleaning her hotel window. The singer, Kathryn Joyner, has had enough of being manipulated by her record company, manager and agent, and decides to forgo the celebrity lifestyle for a night's drink and drugs with Terry and Rab. This experience affords her access to certain fulfilments which she perceives are lacking in her celebrity life:

> They'd shown her something though, something useful and important, during those last few days of drug-addled nonsense. Strange as it was, they cared. They weren't world-weary or blasé. They cared about things; often stupid, trivial things, but they cared. And they cared because they were engaged in a world outside the constructed world of the media and showbusiness. (*G* 513)

But there is a danger here of repeating a common bourgeois trope – and it is a trait for which Welsh often criticises writers such as Martin Amis – of indulgently and condescendingly representing the working class as having an authenticity or naturalness and spontaneity lacking in the middle and upper reaches of a philistine and reified society. In such terms, the working classes become an exotic repository of the real for the supposedly cultured and sophisticated. There is also something telling in the combination of the schemes and celebrity – the shape of both Kathryn Joyner and the millionaire DJ Carl. It perhaps offers a means for Welsh to reconcile his own celebrity with the primary materials of his work, so that Carl and Kathryn Joyner become mediatory figures liminally poised between schemie and celebrity cultures. Just as the plot seeks to conjoin Carl's celebrity lifestyle with those left on the schemes, so too the novel's author seeks new means of re-entering a terrain that was once familiar from a position that is now outside or at least in between cultures and classes.

Despite their contrasting experiences since Gally's death, the three friends finally unite at the hospital where Carl's father is dying. And whilst all three had expressed doubts about the viability of Duncan Ewart's Ten Commandments, Carl – when asked by his father to remember them – surmounts his initial disdain and retains them: 'Aye, they really worked for you, he thought. But just as this thought formed in his head, it was overwhelmed by a surge of passion from his heart which lifted right through him, stopping at the arc in the roof of his mouth. Words were spilling out of him, like shimmering golden balls of light, and they were saying, — Of course I will, Dad' (*G* 537). The scene is one of the few instances in Welsh's work of the intergenerational transmissions of values, of the sense that communal, familial and social solidarities are resilient and can withstand contemporary pressures and attacks. Unlike *Trainspotting*, there is a sense of regeneration and solidarity amidst death and tragedy: 'through Duncan's death something hung in the air between them. There was just *something*, some kind of second chance, and even Carl seemed to sense it through his grief' (*G* 539). This coming together also achieves a kind of exorcism of the guilty ghosts that have haunted the three since Gally's death and it also finally resolves what actually happened when Polmont was attacked. Billy discloses that Gally had approached him to accompany him to Polmont's house that night but he declined and now feels he did not try to talk him out of what occurred. But it is left to Terry to reveal that it was he who went with Gally – not, as Carl and Billy initially think, to back up his mate – but for the purely selfish reason that he feared Polmont would tell Gally that he was sleeping with Gail. In the end it was Terry who shot Polmont with the crossbow in an attempt to keep him quiet and it was Gally who phoned the ambulance that saved Polmont's life. To lessen Terry's remorse Carl informs the others that Gally had AIDS and that this was ultimately the reason for his suicide. The final chapter – 'Reprise 2002: The Golden Era' – jumps forward a couple of years to confirm that the reconciliation is lasting. Carl has returned to Edinburgh to record his music there – including a bizarre collaboration with Kathryn Joyner that rejuvenates her career – and Terry is present asking for a favour: 'Carl braced himself, sucking air into his lungs. A wee something. There was always a wee something. And thank fuck as well' (*G* 556). The 'wee something' in question becomes apparent in Welsh's next novel, *Porno*, which reprises the characters from *Trainspotting*. *Glue* notably prepares the ground for this return as Renton, Spud, Begbie and others are slowly introduced into the childhood and adolescent experiences of the four friends. In terms of *Glue* itself, whilst it concerns itself with the major themes of Welsh's *oeuvre* – social fragmentation and deprivation, economic change, masculinity – it affords one of his more affirmative treatments of these subjects and is imbued with a strong sense of resilience and solidarity against at times overwhelming odds. In the words of Gally, 'Ye always gie a fuck' (*G* 220).

Notes

1   Cited in Steve Redhead, *Repetitive Beat Generation* (Edinburgh: Rebel Inc, 2000), 145.
2   Matt Thorne, 'Fanny peculiar – review of *Glue*', *Independent on Sunday* (6 May 2001), 12.
3   Cited in Alexander Laurence, 'Irvine Welsh: Scottish and still alive', *Free Williamsburg* 13, www.freewilliamsburg.com/july_2001/interviews.html (July 2001).
4   Christopher Kemp's 'Irvine Welsh' is found at www.salon.com/people/conv/2001/07/09/welsh (Oct 2003).
5   Cited in Redhead, *Repetitive Beat Generation*, 142.
6   Cited in Dave Welch, 'Irvine Welsh', www.powells.com/authors/welsh.html (Sep 2003).
7   Cited in Welch, 'Irvine Welsh'.
8   Adam Higginbottom, 'Irvine Welsh: a man of substance?', *Independent on Sunday* (29 Apr 2001), 20.
9   *Newsnight Review*. BBC2. Broadcast 20 Apr 2001.
10 Matthew Hart, 'Substance abuse: *Glue*', *Postmodern Culture*, 12: 2 (2000), 164.
11 Hart, 'Substance abuse', 163.
12 The break-in features an obligatory dog torturing scene to which readers of Welsh's work are now accustomed.
13 Naomi Klein, *No Logo: No Space, No Choice, No Jobs* (London: Flamingo, 2001), 73.
14 Klein, *No Logo*, 195.
15 A really lively and informative cultural history of the casuals is provided by Phil Thornton's *Casuals: Football, Fighting and Fashion – The Story of a Terrace Cult* (Lytham: Milo Books, 2003).
16 Simon Frith, 'Art ideology and pop practice' in Cary Nelson and Lawrence Grossberg, eds, *Marxism and the Interpretation of Culture* (Chicago: Uni-

versity of Illinois Press, 1988), 471.

17 Jennifer Berman, 'An interview with Irvine Welsh', *Bomb Magazine* 56 (1996), 59–60.

18 Cited in Welch, 'Irvine Welsh'.

19 James Campbell, 'Scratch 'n' sniff', *Guardian*, Review (28 Apr 2001), 14.

20 Michael Bracewell, 'Farewell to the nineties', *Independent on Sunday* (28 Nov 1999), 11.

21 Thornton, *Casuals*, 225.

22 Campbell, 'Scratch 'n' sniff', 14.

23 Campbell, 'Scratch 'n' sniff', 14.

7

Porno (2002)

In *Porno* Terry Lawson has channelled his long-standing interest in sex and women into organising shag parties in pubs after closing time with many willing participants. One of these sessions is inadvertently caught on a closed circuit security camera in the pub and the group decide henceforth to routinely film these events in this amateur way. As the *Trainspotting* characters return to Leith, with Sick Boy and Renton's financial help Terry and his group are able to move into producing a pornographic film for commercial sale, which makes it all the way to the Cannes Adult Film Festival. Despite being under pressure from his publisher to produce a *Trainspotting 2* for some time Welsh waited until *Porno* to reprise the characters of Renton, Sick Boy, Begbie, Spud and Diane (though in preparation for this return the *Trainspotting* crew are filtered through the experiences of the four friends in *Glue*).

Porno deals with the *Trainspotting* characters a decade on from the events of his first novel. In part, Welsh was wary of the heightened commercialisation of *Trainspotting* after the success of the film, as the product became a central part of the commodity culture that its subject matter is intended to indict:

> It went mainstream. It probably shouldn't have happened. It is maybe not the kind of material that should go mainstream but it did . . . It does get appropriated. At first it was my book. Then it was Danny's film. Then it was Ewan's film. And now it's even gone beyond that. When people say *Trainspotting* they think of Richard Branson, it's right into the heart of consumerism. That's the reason I didn't do *Trainspotting 2* then.[1]

When asked for the purposes of this study about his motivations for finally reprising the characters, Welsh offered two explanations.

Firstly, that 'the characters were just such a part of my heart, and I felt such a part of them – that I could not bear to be apart from them'. The second answer was 'mega, mega, mega-bucks'.[2] Welsh freely admits that a side of him is tempted by the lure of massive commercial success but it is not his overriding concern artistically:

> Well, I do want to write fucking Harry Potter, and live on the money and capitalise on it all, and buy Hibs – part of me does actually want all that, but not enough to actually fucking write about it, you know what I mean, it's a fantasy, not enough to fucking write about it. I mean I know I've got a fucking minor Harry Potter franchise with the *Trainspotting* characters, but that's another world.[3]

Another reason for the delay in returning to the *Trainspotting* cast, aside from a desire to resist being perceived as immediately capitalising upon the commercial success of the brand, was the fact that it required a fundamental reacquaintance with the original material. Welsh conceded: 'In order to write this one I had to re-read the original, and I had a bit of a problem with the dialect . . . When I was writing the first one it was like a song in my head, but when it came to reading it back I had a few setbacks'.[4] It was observed in the discussion of *Glue* that Kathryn Joyner and to an extent the internationally famous DJ Carl offer a means of re-engaging from a celebrity vantage point with Welsh's raw materials of the schemes, which is perhaps strategic for the writer himself and his more distanced handling of a milieu which was once immediate. So too in *Porno* Sick Boy must refamiliarise himself with Leith on his return from London, Renton journeys back from Amsterdam and Begbie following his years in prison emerges to find a place that he can no loner recognise. Most particularly, the character of the student, Nikki Fuller-Smith, who is very much outwith the scheme culture, being English, upper-class and female, proffers a mediating figure for recomprehending a strange, even exotic terrain. Nikki becomes involved in the sex club through her university friendship with Billy Birrell's brother and associate of Terry, Rab. Nikki considers her interest in him thus: 'Rab doesn't really like drinking with the other students too much. He's social and affable enough with them, but you can tell he thinks they're wankers. I agree. I want, not so much into Rab's keks, but into his world' (*P* 56). In a sense the novel itself seeks a renewed access to this environment and slowly Nikki, perhaps self-referentially in a similar fashion to Welsh as author, starts to attune to the cadences of the working-class characters' existences: 'It must be the company I'm keeping, but I find myself starting to think like a local' (*P* 273). As early as May 1999 Welsh had expressed difficulties in writing about the social concerns and experiences of his earlier work and was dissatisfied with the kind of stories he was producing: 'To be honest, they are crap. I think I'm going to throw them away. I've exhausted any autobiographical content, and there isn't anything socially significant in my life now'.[5] So both *Glue* and *Porno* strive to reconcile a growing and fairly understandable disjunction between Welsh's lifestyle as a successful writer and the social context inhabited by his characters.

Moreover, *Porno* pursues stylistically the more conventional approach to narrative exhibited by *Glue* and its eschewal of the experimental formal forays in Welsh's other work. However, *Porno* also possesses a dramatic propulsion that is redolent of Welsh's powerful and established storytelling capacity as it traces the uneasy alliances and subterfuges of the characters as they pursue fame and fortune in the porn industry. With regard to linguistic register, it is significant that both Renton and Sick Boy's thoughts and speech are extremely hybrid and often denoted in a largely Standard English that discloses their time away from Leith in Amsterdam and London respectively, but this more standardised register also characterises the book's narration as a whole. It is only in Spud's placatory and affirmative rhythms and Begbie's syncopated psychosis that the Leith demotic of *Trainspotting* is retained.

During the writing of *Porno*, Welsh anticipated that its subject matter would be controversial: 'It's going to be hardcore. All the freaks will like this one. All the literati will think, "Oh, he went all immature again."'[6] Drew Milne argues that Welsh's work employs a 'sensationalist mode of narrative, intimate with genres such as pulp fiction, pornography and popular music. Welsh is not uncritical of the sensation-seeking immediacy he portrays, but much of the critique is left implicit . . . [in] a populist postmodern blend of William Burroughs and Quentin Tarantino'.[7] Welsh's decision to meld his return to *Trainspotting* with the subject of pornography is interesting in relation to Will Self's critique of Danny Boyle's cinematic reworking of Welsh's first novel. For Self the ultimate logic of the film version of *Trainspotting* unfolds itself as voyeurism and pornography: 'When drug voyeurism is allied to a nifty soundtrack and freaky imagery it becomes a form of pornography. The connection between the orgasm

and the hit of heroin is no mere accident in this context . . . the punters who get a kick out of watching it, are directly exploiting someone's pain for their pleasure'.[8] Welsh is trenchant in his rebuttal of
accusations of voyeurism in his work, tending instead to refract the
admonition back upon many of his accusers: 'it's precisely the bour-
geois-types that are perceiving in that way. They're recognizing that
voyeurism in themselves'.[9] Yet Welsh's own textual readaptation of
the terrain of his first novel intriguingly utilises pornography as a lens
through which to mediate the experiences of his own characters in
Porno and it becomes the mode by which they in turn order their experiences of one another.

However, just as in his writing about drugs Welsh is more concerned with the social and communal context of consumption rather
than the sensationalising of narcotics, so too this engagement with
pornography and the sex industry strives to evaluate the dominant
trends of contemporary culture and society. The original etymology of
pornography, according to the *OED*, pertains to writing or depiction
of not merely sex but specifically prostitutes. *Porno* is written in a
manner that retains this attachment of pornography to commerce,
economic relations and exploitation. To this end, Nikki works in a
sauna, where she has to masturbate and perform oral sex upon the
punters, to earn the money with which to subsidise her university
degree. For Nikki this employment lays bare capitalism in its most
naked form: 'I'm thinking about how much I need the job, and how
far I'll go to keep it. That's the thing with sex work, it always comes
down to the most basic of formulas. If you really want to see how capitalism operates, never mind Adam Smith's pin factory, this is the
place to study' (*P* 88). Hence, utilising sexual metaphors of corruption, John King deems the novel to be a stringent indictment of 'rampant capitalism and its nonce-like big brother globalisation'.[10]

In addition to deploying pornography as an allegory of economic
and power relations, Welsh also intends that the novel pinpoint paradigm shifts in the lived sexual politics of contemporary society. Part
of the inspiration for the novel's theme derives from his own awareness of changes in sexuality that have occurred since his own time in
Leith and which become evident upon his returns to his former
stomping ground. He observed during the writing of *Porno*:

> If you look at sexuality, it used to be this whole thing, the porn industry
> – it used to be this idea in the seventies that if someone got paid off from
> a factory, they had this problem with sexuality – they couldn't get it up

– but the next generation who have known nothing but the dole, it's completely different. Just shagging, shagging, shagging all the time, shagging and porn. It's actually the yuppies who don't have time to do that kind of thing, so that's switched around from the time in the eighties when all the middle-classes were enjoying sex and all that, and the working-classes 'manhood' was more threatened. It's completely switched the other way now.

That's an area of interest I want to reflect in the writing next. It's just one of those changes, nobody's really noticed it, it's just talked about in terms of burn out and yuppie fatigue. But it's not, it's actually more to do with globalisation and casualisation. People who are in work have no time for anything else but work. They have no mental space to accommodate anything else but work. Whereas people who are outside the system will always find ways of amusing themselves. Even if they are materially disadvantaged they'll still find ways of coping, getting by and making their own entertainment. There's so much happening. If you come up to Edinburgh and go drinking with your mates and they tell you they've been sitting in a lock-out in the pub making porn movies and all that kind of stuff, you think to yourself well I don't really want to do that, I don't want to get my kit off and dive in and have pictures on the internet with my big white arse covered with pimples. You think to yourself I'm not really engaged in that kind of thing – if I had stayed up here in Edinburgh, if I'd stayed working, maybe I'd have just got into that kind of stuff. You wouldn't feel awkward and voyeuristic, rather it would just be a natural thing being pissed at the end of the night and the security cameras on everybody.[11]

If sex and sexuality are, in the above terms, among the most avowedly 'natural' or authentic expressions of human feeling then pornography actually serves to problematise rather than channel the supposedly direct or organic access to human nature. Pornography is the apotheosis of the reification and stylisation of human experience, as pleasure is transmitted not through the act itself but rather its reworking through technological media. It is significant that these activities should be captured on security cameras. Closed circuit television has become a ubiquitous means by which working-class people in particular are increasingly subject to state surveillance and regulation. Michel Foucault argues that power is not merely prohibitive but instead continually traverses and produces itself amongst all things. Power, for Foucault, is 'a productive network which runs through the whole social body'.[12] So power, in Foucault's terms, is not merely about repression or coercion but also permits us certain supposed enablements and fulfilments. Foucault specifically argues that there is a deep and symbiotic relationship between power, knowledge and pleasure. The term 'closed circuit' surveillance is entirely apposite in this context of the binding networks of Foucauldian power, as the members of the sex club in *Porno* believe that they are permitted access to this systemic pleasure of scrutiny and regulation. Power in a sense produces an erotics of surveillance and contemporary culture is awash with such putative pleasures as evidenced by the contemporary trend for so-called reality TV and exemplified by *Big Brother*. In a society where people are more surveyed than at any time in history, we are bombarded in popular culture with a range of images and experiences which furnish an illusion of cognitive autonomy in which we are watching Big Brother and not vice versa. Hence, Nikki's claim that porn is 'mainstream' (*P* 347) discerns how culture and society as a whole are suffused by the dynamics of power, surveillance and voyeurism. Consequently, for the Machiavellian Sick Boy, porn is not so much an instrument in itself but rather the measure of a society where empowerment is attained or at least conjured through witnessing the disempowerment of others: 'Pornography sneezes and popular culture catches cold. People want sex, violence, food, pets, DIY and humiliation. Let's give them the fuckin lot. Look at humiliation television, look at the papers and the mags, look at the class system, the jealousy, the bitterness that oozes out of our culture: in Britain we want to see people get fucked' (*P* 179). Furthermore, Sick Boy directly relates the power sought by such voyeurism to our thrall to the images of commodity culture and consumerism:

> We need tits and arse because they have got to be available to us; to be pawed, fucked, wanked over. Because we're men? No. Because we're consumers. Because those are the things we like, things we intrinsically feel or have been conned into believing will give us value, release, satisfaction. We value them so we need to at least have the illusion of their availability. For tits and arse read coke, crisps, speedboats, cars, houses, computers, designer labels, replica shirts. That's why advertising and pornography are similar; they sell the illusion of availability and the nonconsequence of consumption. (*P* 450)

Sick Boy

The novel opens with Sick Boy's vitriolic and virtuoso first person narrative. He is characteristically using and abusing a wide range of people, particularly women – from those he pimps to the rich and upwardly mobile professional classes. Sick Boy, or Simon as he prefers these days, is dissatisfied with his current home in Hackney which he feels is no place for 'an upwardly mobile thirty-six-year-old entrepreneur' (P 4) like himself. (He adds 'Simone de Bourgeois' to his list of aspirant, self-afforded monikers.) Where *Trainspotting* offered a number of randomly numbered chapters titled *Junk Dilemmas* as means of indicting the deadening seriality of the characters' underclass subsistence, *Porno* renders Sick Boy's monologues in chapters of numbered *Scams* and thus reduces his materialist opportunism to the same enduring rote of late capitalism's quotidian barrenness. Initially the only connection with his former home Edinburgh comes in the form of the gay porn which he regularly sends to Begbie in Saughton prison where he is serving out a sentence for manslaughter – as a means of annoying and undermining him and yet also, more generally, 'part of my little war against my home city' (P 24). Having lost his job as a barman in a lap-dancing club, Sick Boy gets the opportunity to escape London – and his estranged wife Mandy and son Ben – and continue this 'little war' when his Auntie Paula offers him her pub, the Port Sunshine, in Leith for £20,000 on the generous terms that he can pay this sum off as he earns it. Sick Boy's plan is to refurbish and gentrify the pub, banishing what he perceives as its undesirable locals and regulars: 'You can feel the gentrification creeping up from the Shore and forcing house prices up and I can hear the tills ringing as I give the Port Sunshine a tart-up from Jakey Central to New Leith café society' (P 45). Sick Boy is enthralled by the new Leith which is supplanting the formerly working-class districts of the port area: 'the Royal Yacht Britannia, the Scottish Office, renovated docks, wine bars, restaurants, yuppie pads. This is the future, and it's only two blocks away. The next year, the year after maybe, just one block away. Then bingo!' (P 47). Sick Boy constructs a series of aggrandising scenarios for himself and imagines being interviewed by the *Evening News*: 'Simon, what is it about Leith that makes people like yourself and Terence Conran, archetypal London success stories want to invest so heavily in the area?' (P 60). His replies include: 'I want to reinvent her as a sexy, hot young bitch and pimp that dirty wee hoor oot for aw she's fuckin worth. In a word: business. I want Leith to be about business. Whenever people hear the word "Leith", I want them to think, "business". Port of Leith, Port of Business' (P 60–61). Just as Billy Birrell became synonymous with business in *Glue*, so too in this passage Leith loses its identity and specificity to the peremptory logic of the commerce and the flow of capital.

Sick Boy is horrified to see his former acquaintance Spud enter the Port Sunshine and orders him to leave – having refused his request for drugs: 'I almost regretted my words as Spud looked incredulously at me for a second, let the hurt sink in and then skulked out in a broken silence. Fortunately, the rush of shame was instantly replaced by a surge of pride and relief as yet another lame duck hobbled out of my life' (*P* 82). In taking ownership of the Port Sunshine Sick Boy believes that his upwardly mobile persona finally has a real founda-tion as he buys into the gentrification of the new Leith and plays a part in a decimation of the older working-class area, thereby also erasing and exorcising a large part of his own personal history. Upon hearing of Terry's amateur porn club he offers the upstairs room of the Port Sunshine and seizes upon what he feels will be a scam that will really earn him some big money. He helps fund the project by involving himself with the Leith Business Against Drugs organisation – despite dealing and using narcotics. He befriends the organisation's driving force, Paul Keramalindous, a yuppie advertising executive, and during an evening in the Port Sunshine shows him some of the pornographic films the gang have been making and encourages him to take cocaine. He subsequently films Keramalindous taking the cocaine on the pub's security cameras. With this footage as blackmail, Sick Boy then extorts money from the Leith Business Against Drugs campaign to help finance the porn project. Most compellingly for Sick Boy, he tracks Renton down to Amsterdam – having been alerted to his presence there when Carl Ewart plays at Renton's club – and involves Renton's capital in the project as partial payback for his betrayal a decade previous. However, the reader is aware that Sick Boy intends to gain a more cutting revenge – 'Renton is getting paid back with interest' (*P* 138) – both financially and by setting Begbie upon Renton once his economic usefulness to Sick Boy is ended. One of the most ingenious aspects of the financing of the movie emerges from a chance meeting with Spud's Glaswegian friend Dode. Dode is a loy-alist Glasgow Rangers supporter who boasts that his bank allows him to choose his own PIN number so that he never forgets it. Spud and Sick Boy swiftly deduce that the magic number is 1690 – that sacred year for British Protestantism, hence the slogan 'Remember 1690' – and prove their intuition correct when they steal his bank card and successfully withdraw money from his account. Sick Boy realises this is probably widespread practice amongst Rangers supporters and he successfully defrauds the Ibrox ticket office and Rangers supporters of large amounts of cash by accessing accounts and utilising the 1690 code.

It transpires that the equally entrepreneurial Renton co-owns a successful club in Amsterdam and has a German girlfriend. He has stopped taking drugs and regularly goes to the gym and practises karate. The muscles on his once junk-ravaged body are now 'chunks of rock' (*P* 87). In a way, Renton's character has become the filmic image of itself, it has been transformed into the image of Ewan McGregor which was used so widely to advertise the movie and which replaced David Harrold's original skeleton mask cover of *Trainspotting* the novel in subsequent reprints. Renton's transmogrified physique also signals a reassertion of the male body, of a physically expressive masculinity, which was wrought into such crisis and abjection in *Trainspotting*. At the beginning of Welsh's debut novel, as Sick Boy and Renton watch the Jean-Claude Van Damme video, Sick Boy is described as 'looking like a hunted animal. There's nothing in his eyes but need' (*T* 4). This moment defeats the conventional scopic gaze of masculinity as power, since Sick Boy's eyes are the site of dependency not subjective autonomy and empowerment. Sick Boy's gaze is marked by a constitutive lack or absence rather than the self-affirming presence conventionally associated with masculine subjectivity under patriarchy in a manner that prefigures the entire novel's dissection of male abjection. The phrase 'looking like a hunted animal' is also wonderfully ambiguous and constitutes a crisis of masculinity in terms of both subject and object. Is Sick Boy being watched or surveyed as a hunted animal or is he himself gazing as a hunted animal would do? In each case masculinity is insecure and threatened, uncomfortable being both subject and object of a gaze. Masculinity, in Welsh's first novel, fails to adapt itself to new sets of gender and economic relations. In *Porno*, however, pornography serves to reassert the male gaze as the traditionally hegemonic subject enjoying the sexual spectacle and also visually celebrates the male as empowered object (reinforced by the display of the phallus as ultimate signifier of that male power). As indicated in the discussion of casuals' culture in *Glue*, Welsh's later work illustrates how masculinity has become more assured in its role not only as subject but also as object of desire, pleasure, commoditisation and stylisation. Tellingly, New Lad magazines such as *Loaded* often featured male stars on the cover rather than the traditional woman-as-object, suggesting a more confident sense of the status of masculinity which may be now displayed, consumed, emulated. Nonetheless, as with the concerted effort to provide counter-narratives by female characters, Nikki seeks to rewrite the conventional misogyny of pornography and to unfold a more progressive and liberating cultural space for herself and the other female actors in the movie.

Nikki

Nikki and Rab use the knowledge that they have gleaned from their film course at university to write the screenplay for the film and to insist upon a more provocative and challenging movie than the standard porno formula. The title of their screenplay – *Seven Rides for Seven Brothers* – reworks the 1954 film musical *Seven Brides for Seven Bothers* which involves what is essentially the kidnap of women for marriage in a confirmation of women's subordinate status. The porn version features seven oil rig workers who use their shore leave to win a bet that they can all not only have sex but also satisfy their particular sexual predilections. So, despite Nikki's intent, it does appear a very male-dominated project. Nonetheless, with regard to Nikki's character, Burhan Wazir maintains that in *Porno*: 'Welsh establishes himself as something of a Renaissance man, expertly, and, for the first time, writing sympathetically about women'. For Wazir, Nikki is 'the most well-rounded character yet to surface in a Welsh novel'.[13] The polyphony of both *Trainspotting* and *Glue* had sought to offer female voices which undercut the primarily male concerns of those novels and Nikki's character does signal an attempt to provide a more sustained and accomplished extension of that process. In terms of the representation of women, Welsh has always insisted that he is not someone who avoids writing about women but rather is sensitive to the problematics that it entails:

> it's not so much I can't write women characters, it's a question of being very wary of doing it. It's about acknowledging that you're not a woman, and acknowledging the other-ness ... of how women characters think, feel, react and all that. I don't think women and men do think, feel, react differently. But again, it's this whole imperialist thing. You've got to be aware of the issues and acknowledge the possibility of that other-ness. So, it's been a tentative process, for me, writing about women characters.[14]

Nikki's narrative introduces her as an upper-class and English student who is having an affair with a university lecturer Colin Addison.
When it is revealed that her 'essence' (P 14) prompts her to end the
relationship this does not seem to augur well for hopes of a more progressive gender politics in the novel as it is a somewhat perfunctory
moment of essentialising women: it is not Nikki's intellect, reasoning
or even a physical feeling that make this decision but a highly vague,
exotic and inscrutable femininity. But despite being something of a
Ladette who continually assaults the feminist principles of her flatmate Lauren, Nikki does offer a counterpoint to the Laddishness of
Welsh's male characters: 'Age makes most girls into women, but men
never really stop being boys. That's what I admire about them, their
ability to wallow in silliness and immaturity, which is something I
always strive to imitate. It can be tiresome though, if you are constantly on the receiving end of it' (P 17).

In the chapter, ' . . . ugly . . .', Nikki is filled with 'hateful self-
loathing' (P 66) as she stands in front of a mirror comparing her body
to magazine images. Her thwarted desire is to be famous on television and in magazines. One of the targets for Nikki's unhappiness is
her former school friend Carolyn Pavitt, who is now an Olympic
medal-winning gymnast who regularly appears on television sports
quizzes. Nikki resolves that pornography is the solution which will
finally allow her to make her mark, become a celebrity and someone
who is in control of her own life and body. She also embarks upon a
relationship with Sick Boy and senses that she has achieved autonomy of her own life and goals: 'My heart's racing now because I've got
him now. He's mine, and that means, well, what does that mean? It
means it's my film, my gang, my money: it means everything' (P 236).
However, in an illustration of Welsh's capacity to weave voices in and
out of another, continually modifying and shifting the perspective,
Nikki's moment of resolution is dramatically undermined by the fact
that it is immediately preceded by a Sick Boy monologue that claims
sole possession of the whole project: 'my scam, my move, my scene'
(P 230). Nikki becomes increasingly disenchanted with Sick Boy's
demands and the viability of her own philosophy of pornography as
self-empowerment. One scene in the film with a fellow female actress
and a dildo takes place in a boxing ring surrounded by a large group
of male onlookers: 'For the first time since I started this, I feel as if
I'm being used, I feel dehumanised, like an object as those ugly men
from the pub surround the ring, their faces contorted as they bay and

scream. At one point I can feel the tears rolling down my cheeks' (*P* 293). Although Sick Boy promises – 'I'll never put you through some-thing like that again' (*P* 294) – he continually presses her against her wishes to comply with what he regards as the need for obligatory anal sex scenes. Nikki refuses and alleges that he is prepared to become a 'rapist' (*P* 348) in making the film by forcing the female actresses to do things against their will. Despite refusing to do anal sex and becoming increasingly alienated from Sick Boy, Nikki still maintains a sexual relationship with him because she finds him 'irresistible' (*P* 393).

Nikki's investment in their relationship is also undercut by the pri-vate thoughts of Sick Boy's narrative which makes it clear that he is using her: 'relationships are all about power and now is the time to cool it with her' (*P* 225). Nikki finally realises that 'I've given myself over to a total bastard' (*P* 370) when she and the others see the fin-ished product. In addition to claiming that he co-wrote the screenplay and taking all the production credits, Sick Boy has edited the film to make it appear that Nikki does have anal sex: 'For me the sense of dis-appointment and betrayal is absolutely fucking sickening' (*P* 369). As with her former school friend Carolyn, Sick Boy has become for Nikki a symptom of a wider social malaise that infects every corner of con-temporary life:

> I'm heading up into town, trudging through a strong, bitingly cold wind, thinking that we live in such boring times. That's our tragedy: nobody except destructive exploiters like Sick Boy, or bland opportunists like Carolyn, has any real passion. Everybody else is just so beaten down by the crap and mediocrity around them. If the word in the eighties was 'me', and in the nineties 'it', in the millennium it's 'ish'. Everything has to be vague and qualified. Substance used to be important, then style was everything. Now it's all just faking it. I thought they were real, Simon and the rest of them . . . It hits me like an iron fist in the chest that in this global communications village somehow, in some way, my father's going to see me getting a butt-fuck I didn't actually get. I hate the idea of having anal sex; as a woman it's a negation of your feminin-ity. Most of all, I loathe being a fake. (*P* 374)

Both Sick Boy and Renton offer parallel and mutually reinforcing figures for taking advantage of this dominant culture of faking it and spin. Renton acknowledges that he and Sick Boy are 'twisted soul brothers': 'I suppose he was a bit like me, we both knew that deca-dence was a bad habit for council tenants. A ridiculous habit in fact.

The *raison d'être* of our class was simply to survive. Fuck that; our punk generation, not only did we thrive, we even had the audacity tae be disillusioned' (*P* 365). Similarly, Sick Boy identifies in Renton a trait that both characters seemed to have shared since *Trainspotting*: 'No matter how involved he seems, there's a part of the bastard always on the outside, taking everything in' (*P* 134). Given that both Sick Boy and Renton return to the locale of *Trainspotting* to make money, behind all of this there may again stand a self-referential and perhaps slightly guilty figuration of Welsh himself since *Porno*'s publication coincided with the remarketing of *Trainspotting* ten years on from its original publication with the release of the *Trainspotting 2* DVD box set and a reissue of new soundtrack CDs. Both Sick Boy and Renton regard the new Leith as an opportunity to connect themselves to an entrepreneurial culture of style, gentrification and capital. Notably, Leith – as part of its rebranding – was used as the location of the 2003 MTV Europe awards ceremony. Part of Welsh clearly enjoys the opportunism of Sick Boy but is also under no illusion of the impact upon most of the Leith working class: 'I like the idea that basically a dirty bastard can make some money out of it – but you've got to be realistic: for every dirty bastard that does, there's five that go down'.[15]

From the local to the global

For Welsh the gentrification of Leith is part of a global dynamic which is sundering already decimated working-class communities still further and which seeks the extension of bourgeois leisure, civics and commerce into areas hollowed out for exploitation by de-industrialisation:

> I think in virtually every city the task, the quest, after the war was to get the middle classes out to the suburbs and away from the city. Now the quest is to colonise the city – it's the same here as it is in Chicago, as it is in London: get the fucking working classes and the schemies out of the road. That's the process: it's every city's project to get people with money living in the city, a second wave movement. And actually, in its own stupid fucked up way, is so out of date. In America, the whole thing is they want a middle class audience for everything, for their football and that, but what they don't realise is the middle classes don't actually fucking go to the green field sites cause they've all moved back into the city. So the new demographic is to build these fucking stadiums back in the city. These stupid fucked up cunts are so short sighted – even in their

own terms they're failing. The offensive thing about it, as far as I'm concerned, is that this big middle class game plan of kick the schemies out
and build a by-pass or whatever, its whole conceptual icon, the United
States of America and McDonald's corporate hamburger culture, has
actually failed on its own terms: now its like get the stadiums back into
towns, build them in the cities because that's were the middle classes
are now, all their bars, all their restaurants, where they play at being
working class. That's the thing about middle-class leisure time: it's to
play at being working class. I wrote for *Loaded* where middle class men
play at being working class. So this is what really offends me about it,
it's not even the ruthless opportunism of it, it's the short-sightedness of
it.[16]

By returning to Leith and taking over the local pub the Port Sunshine
with his plans for international celebrity and commercial gain, Sick
Boy provides an allegory of this wider situation in which the local is
transplanted and exploited by the global dynamics of multinational
capitalism. The new 'business' Leith is a stylised rebranding of a
former established working-class community as the area is reduced to
a commodity within chains of global exchange. The assertion of a new
Leith can be comprehended in terms of Fredric Jameson's contention
that: 'neo-regionalism, like the neo-ethnic, is a specifically postmodern form of reterritorialization; it is a flight from the realities of
late capitalism, a compensatory ideology, in a situation in which
regions (like ethnic groups) have been fundamentally wiped out—
reduced, standardized, commodified, atomized, or rationalized'.[17] The
reparcelling of areas such as Leith is underpinned not by an assertion
of its own community but rather by the micro-restructuring of global
capitalism as it extends itself ever further. Against both Renton and
Sick Boy's highly commercialised and commoditised rediscovery of
Leith as a new economic unit is juxtaposed Spud's humane, social
and historical recovery of his locale.

Spud's character is reintroduced in the chapter 'Counselling', in
which it emerges that he is still hopelessly addicted to heroin. In addition to his drugs' problems Spud is also keenly aware that there are
profound changes taking place that put his fundamentally generous
spirit under threat: 'the modern world hus a kind ay natural selection
and it's no really the sort ay gig where ah fit in. Cats like me have
become extinct. Cannae adapt, so cannae survive' (*P* 63). Feeling that
he is part of a culture and a community that is been extirpated, Spud
resolves – despite the mocking of others – to write a book about Leith:

'Some cat should write the *real* history ay the famous auld port, talk tae the punters that were around; like the auld cats that worked the docks, yards n bonds, drank in the boozers, hung oot wi the Teds, the YLT, the CCS, right through tae the present' (*P* 75). His relationship with Alison (who appeared in *Trainspotting* and who is an unsuccessful target of Sick Boy's advances in this novel) and their son is falling apart but Spud gains resolve from the fact that Leith's own motto is 'Persevere'. In the chapter 'Leith Will Never Die' Spud's research in Edinburgh public library allows him to challenge the official history and rebranded the present of Leith through his own experience of his community. Just as *Glue* sought to regalvanise the core working-class values of Duncan Ewart and to offer a history of working-class experience that is so often buried or forgotten, so too Spud gains insight into a history of working-class revolt and dissidence that is forgotten by the postmodern present.

> Aw that info, as that history, even if it's selectively written by the top cats tae tell their tales, on one roll ay film. But ah reckon thit thir's other stories thit kin be teased oot . . . Leith, 1926, the General Strike. Ye read aw that n what they aw said then, n ye pure see what the Labour Party used tae believe in. Freedom for the ordinary cat. Now it's like 'get the Tories oot' or 'keep the Tories oot', which is jist a nice way ay sayin 'keep us in, man, keep us in, cause we like it here'. (*P* 257)

As John King argues: 'Sex, violence, drugs – big business peddles these money-spinners, claiming freedom of choice, and even though Sick Boy and Renton know the truth, they blank it out. Only Spud – junkie, gypo, scruff – makes a stand as he researches a book on Leith's local history, concentrating on the old characters who made the place what it was'.[18] Spud is able to set his own previous depoliticisation in context and his discovery of a lost past that was radically different from the present also, quite hopefully, indicates that the seemingly endless seriality of the late capitalist now which spans all of Welsh's work is not immemorial or unshiftable: 'It's funny though, man, but they political gadges aw seem like they come fae posh hames, students n that. No thit ah'm knockin it, but ah think, it should be the likes ay us that agitate for change, but aw we dae is drugs. No like in the General Strike n that. What happened tae us?' (*P* 259). Equipped with this knowledge, the newly politicised Spud informs Begbie: 'it's aw changing, man. Yuv goat the Scottish Office at one end and yuv goat the new Parliament at the other. Embourgeoisement, that's what the intellectual cats call it. Ten years' time, there'll be nae gadges like me n you left doon here' (*P* 261). However, Begbie resents the insinuation (and reality) that he is working-class, referring instead to himself as a 'businessman' (*P* 261).

Indeed, Spud's growing awareness of the interrelation between local change and global historical conditions contrasts markedly with the internecine rage of Begbie who channels his sense of unfairness into violence against the Leith community. Notably, despite being released from jail, Begbie feels a 'prisoner' (*P* 128) on the outside and is incapable of comprehending the changes taking place in Leith – including his business partner Lexo's decision to open a Thai restaurant on the site of the second-hand furniture shop that they once co-owned. It is also related that his conviction for manslaughter emanated from his need to punish someone for Renton's betrayal in *Trainspotting* – and having killed his victim he then stabbed himself to ensure he was not convicted of murder. Whilst playing pool in a pub with Second Prize and waiting for Spud to arrive Begbie also kills Chizzie, a sex offender from Saughton prison whom he recognises. So Spud and Begbie offer diametrically opposed responses to the globally determined economic change occurring in Leith: Spud's reaction is an increased politicisation facilitated by his new-found comprehension of the history and community of the locale, whilst Begbie retreats into highly localised violence and a rejection of political consciousness (he feels books are dangerous because they put ideas in people's heads). The only other character to act in a kindred manner to Spud is Curtis, a mild mannered and gentle associate of Spud's who is continually teased about his stammer. But when Terry ruptures his penis during the filming of a scene in the movie and no replacement can seemingly be found, Sick Boy by chance is urinating beside Curtis in the toilets of the Port Sunshine and cannot help but notice how massively well-endowed the shy Curtis is. Curtis goes on to star in the film but when the gang arrive in Cannes for the Adult Film Festival he merely wished that Spud and his other pals were there to enjoy the fun, whilst everyone else – notably, Sick Boy – is caught up in the celebrity, glamour and financial opportunities. John King asserts that Spud and Curtis:

> stay true to their core values, refusing to sell their souls – unlike Sick Boy and Renton, who, though decent at heart, have embraced the capitalist con. They are on the make, surfing the Thatcherite/new Labour wave to fame and fortune, a rip-off world run by yuppies bankrolled by

rich mummies and daddies, an air-conditioned nightmare in which the older boys have to bury their punk beliefs if they are to compete and earn themselves a pension. The old folk looming in the background are a reminder of what lies ahead if they fail: a local rather than a global world, where the type of peas on the menu is more important than the strength of the landlord's cocaine, a whole way of life squeezed into a small corner of a pub destined for 'refurbishment'.[19]

Spud does indeed seem an endangered species. After his history of Leith is rejected by a publisher he decides in his despair that the best thing he can do for Alison and his son is cash in his life insurance policy: 'the world wid be a better place without useless, scruffy, junky Murphy' (P 381). Because the insurance company will not pay out in the event of a suicide, Spud decides to provoke Begbie into killing him by goading him about the manslaughter cover story, the subsequent murder of Chizzie and, most of all, the fact that Renton gave him his share of the money. As Begbie beats him to a pulp Spud thinks of Alison and his son as a means of enduring the pain but these thoughts in turn lead him to a renewed desire to live. Fortunately, Alison and his son arrive in time to save him from the death which Begbie is intent on inflicting upon him. A badly beaten Spud does achieve a reconciliation with Alison and his son in hospital.

Porn plots

The main dramatic impetus of the novel's closure derives from the expectation that one of the gang will attempt to rip off the rest and Sick Boy is determined that it will be Renton who suffers this time. As Sick Boy enjoys the celebrity status he is granted in Cannes he is nevertheless anxious about Renton's whereabouts. Renton has rekindled his romance with Diane, who was a schoolgirl in *Trainspotting* but who is now Nikki's flatmate and working on a postgraduate thesis of workers in the sex industry. Renton has promised to arrive in Cannes after he has extricated himself from his life and relationship in Amsterdam. But alarm bells start ringing for Sick Boy when he attempts to use a credit card to pay for an expensive meal with Nikki and is told that there is no longer any money in his account. Sick Boy cannot track down either Renton or Diane on their mobile phones, though Nikki assures him that Diane is merely away visiting her family. In a state of panic Sick Boy finally rings Begbie to tell him that Renton is back in Edinburgh and to try and find him and keep him there until

Sick Boy returns. During the conversation Begbie spots Renton across the street from him but as he runs to accost Renton he is knocked down by a car and critically injured. It transpires that Renton and Diane have taken all the money from Sick Boy's movie accounts – around £60,000 – and are fleeing to San Francisco, and Renton and his Dutch associates also have the master copies of the film. To make matters worse Sick Boy receives a phone call from Edinburgh to inform him that Customs and Excise have closed down the Port Sunshine and confiscated all his porn. Whilst returning to Edinburgh from Cannes Sick Boy sees Renton and Diane in the airport in London but they pass through check-in before Sick Boy can reach them. He is implacable despite Nikki's reassurances. Finally, the next day Nikki too has gone and left the following note: 'I'm off to visit Mark and Dianne. You won't find us, that I guarantee. We promise to enjoy the cash. . . . PS: When I said you were the best lover I ever had, I was exaggerating but you weren't bad when you tried. Remember, we're all faking it. PPS: As you said about the British, watching people get fucked has become our favourite sport' (*P* 481).

So once more, and this time on a much grander scale, Sick Boy has been duped by Renton and has also fallen victim to the ruthless materialistic creed that he espouses. The only pleasure left to Sick Boy is to visit the comatose Begbie in hospital and to continue his campaign of undermining his psychotically male associate's sexuality. Sick Boy uses a marker pen to write abuse such as FAGGOT ASS and other insults on Begbie's plasters. He even works up the courage to call him Beggar Boy for the first time ever to his face: 'I look down and his hand is like a vice around it. And when I look up, his eyes have opened and those blazing coals of enmity are staring right into my lacerated, penitent inner self' (*P* 483). The symbolism of this scene is striking. Whilst the infectious and infecting dominant entrepreneurial culture has permitted Renton to escape Edinburgh once more, Sick Boy and Begbie – both self-professed businessmen – are entrapped in a mutually destructive embrace. The same business culture which affords opportunity to a few, condemns and entraps many others. But as with Ewart's voice in *Glue*, Spud's voice in *Porno* suggests that there are more dissident possibilities beyond and resistant to that dominant culture. To this end, John King sees Welsh's later work as an 'attack on the corporate machine' and regards his most recent three novels as a trilogy: '*Filth, Glue,* and *Porno* operate beyond the narrow imagination of the literary establishment. They speak directly to the reader, operating in the sort of pubs and clubs where the thought police never tread'.[20] Although the logic of late capitalism seems all-pervasive in Welsh's earlier work, the history from below which begins with the tapeworm in *Filth* finds voice in Duncan Ewart's codes and ethics in *Glue* and Spud's history of Leith in *Porno*, producing collectively a more affirmative awareness that the increased economic exploitation of working-class people can also stir renewed politicisation and resistance against all odds.

Notes

1 Cited in Steve Redhead, *Repetitive Beat Generation* (Edinburgh: Rebel Inc, 2000), 140–141.

2 Cited in Aaron Kelly, 'Irvine Welsh in conversation with Aaron Kelly', *Edinburgh Review* 113 (2004), 17. The reader should perhaps bear in mind that both interviewer and interviewee were extremely drunk by this point in the conversation so the comment should not be taken entirely seriously.

3 Cited in Kelly, 'Irvine Welsh in conversation with Aaron Kelly', 10.

4 Jeremy Watson and Gillian McCormack, 'Posh Welshie cannae dae the voices nae mair', *Scotland on Sunday* (14 Apr 2002), 28.

5 Cited in Mary Riddell, 'Irvine Welsh interview', *New Statesman* (3 May 1999), 23.

6 Cited in Alexander Laurence, 'Irvine Welsh: Scottish and still alive', *Free Williamsburg* 13, www.freewilliamsburg.com/july_2001/interviews.html (July 2001).

7 Drew Milne, 'The fiction of James Kelman and Irvine Welsh: accents, speech and writing' in Richard J. Lane et al., eds, *Contemporary British Fiction* (Oxford: Polity Press, 2003), 159.

8 Will Self, 'Carry on up the hypodermic', *Observer*, Review (11 Feb 1996), 6.

9 Cited in Jennifer Berman, 'An interview with Irvine Welsh', *Bomb Magazine* 56 (1996), 57.

10 John King, 'The boys are back in town: *Porno*', *New Statesman* (2 Sep 2002), 36.

11 Cited in Redhead, *Repetitive Beat Generation*, 146.

12 Michel Foucault, *Power/Knowledge Power/Knowledge: Selected Interviews and Other Writings, 1972–1977*. Ed. Colin Gordon. Trans. Colin Gordon, John Mepham and Kate Soper (Brighton: Harvester Wheatsheaf, 1980), 119.

13 Burhan Wazir, 'Sick Boy and the hangover', *Observer* (18 Aug 2002), 30.

14 Cited in Berman, 'An interview with Irvine Welsh', 59.

15 Cited in Kelly, 'Irvine Welsh in conversation with Aaron Kelly', 11.
16 Cited in Kelly, 'Irvine Welsh in conversation with Aaron Kelly', 11–12.
17 Fredric Jameson, *The Seeds of Time* (New York: Columbia University Press, 1994), 148.
18 King, 'The boys are back in town', 36.
19 King, 'The boys are back in town', 36.
20 King, 'The boys are back in town', 37.

Conclusion

Plotting against power or scheming against the working class?

For his detractors, places such as Muirhouse or Westerhailes are not the only schemes in Welsh's work: he is himself a Machiavellian schemer who cynically and opportunistically pursues commercial gain from his depictions of such places. Elspeth Findlay asserts that Welsh's fiction is better interpreted not as an active articulation of an underclass constituency but rather as a passive and packaged product that is riddled with bourgeois values:

> surely it is too simplistic to equate schemie subject matter and the use of dialect with a working class aesthetic? A closer look at Welsh's work suggests quite the reverse. It could be argued that these books rely on an assumed middle class reader, a reader who enjoys a bit of literary rough, a night of slumming it in the pages of a paperback, before returning to the responsibilities of middle class life in the morning . . . Welsh's plots win favour with those champions of bourgeois values, the Victorian moralists. Vice is lovingly depicted for the guilty voyeur, but usually punished in the end. Alan Venters of *Trainspotting* knowingly spreads HIV but his punishment is revealed in photographs of his son's murder. The gang rapist and football casual of *Marabou Stork Nightmares* is castrated by the girl he raped. The same melodramatic moralising produces moments of redemption. Roy, the football casual of *Marabou Stork Nightmares*, does not meet his gruesome fate before an epiphanic revelation that life can be gracious as well as bestial. Grace in this case comes not through the Bible but through the right drugs . . . The narrative language of melodrama is closely knit with middle class sensibility. The traditional bourgeois vision incorporates a bargain. The exercise of self-help and self-denial is rewarded by self-improvement. This exchange leaves an unsatisfied appetite for self-indulgence, for the reckless contempt for security and the future. Melodrama lets the middle class reader indulge temporarily, before restoring order by pun-

ishment and redemption. It is an essentially hypocritical form of narrative . . . Welsh's fiction also recalls an earlier genre beloved of bourgeois
readers, the gothic novel. His books stop the reader's breath and force
the reader's fingers to turn the page by playing on irrational fears of a
violent, amoral underclass . . . the reader can enact irrational fears in the
safe environment of a novel.[1]

This study has indicated that Welsh's most recent fiction has
employed figures who offer mediatory vantage points through which
to retrieve a milieu that is increasingly distant to its author – Kathryn
Joyner in *Glue*, Nikki in *Porno*, or even Bruce Robertson in *Filth* who
patrols and regulates the schemie terrain – and it can be argued that
such liminal, insider-outsider figures are present in Welsh's very first
fiction. Alan Sinfield comments that: 'Renton affords something of a
bridge to the liberal, middle-class reader. He was at university for a
year, is thoughtful and likes books (he steals them because he wants
to read them); he uses quite a few long words and can carry on a conversation about Brecht'.[2] However, the allusion to Bizet's *Carmen* in
Trainspotting suggests a self-awareness in Welsh that a middle-class
audience will read and indulge his work. Indeed, as Renton points out
in *Trainspotting*, in a comment that also intimates Welsh's sense of
the hegemony of the dominant order of society, 'society invents a spurious convoluted logic tae absorb and change people whae's behaviour is outside its mainstream' (*T* 187). Similarly, Welsh recognises
that the most strategic means by which hegemony functions is
through the annexation and neutralisation of resistance in the terms
of the dominant culture:

> while a well-funded cultural system exists to spew out ruling-class cul-
> ture, any culture, art and history promoted outside of this system relies
> largely on concerned maverick groups or individuals. The society is only
> 'liberal' or 'pluralist' to the extent that it tolerates those different voices
> which are generally let in to spice up the mainstream only when it
> becomes intolerably bland. In the meantime, we lose so much of our
> culture'.[3]

So in Welsh's case, has dissidence been shelved in two senses: dispensed with as an interventionist force and yet also packaged and
marketed in bookshops? Mary Riddell admonishes: 'Any working-
class Scot who finds himself in the society columns of *Elle* must worry
less about media prurience than the risk that he is writing himself out
of his own plot'.[4] But it is hardly Welsh's own fault that he is now

famous. And his fame should not be regarded as a by-product of easy commercialism or selling out. Welsh stringently asserts that no one should read his work because it is hip or because they feel obliged to do so. It is notable that *Trainspotting*'s vaunted anti-establishment credentials were boosted by the fact that Donald Dewar, the late New Labour politician who became the inaugural First Minister of the newly devolved Scottish parliament, refused to read it. However, Welsh respects that decision entirely:

> I hate all that stuff, that you've got to fucking read this cause it's so fucking hip – do you fuck. Dewar went massively up in my esteem for not reading it. Nobody has to do anything – least of all because it's meant be fucking cool. A lot of people that have read *Trainspotting* have read it for all the wrong fucking reasons. I just wanted to write a little fucking book about where I came from, and what I was up to, what everyone was up to. When that book sold 3000 copies – the first printing – all the boys in Edinburgh came up and were like, 'Well done Welshy, ya cunt, good on ye'. One hundred thousand copies, it was like, 'You've made a bit of money out of that now ya cunt, eh?' A million copies and it was just: 'Fucking cunt'. It's the same book, the same fucking book.[5]

Willy Maley contends that 'Welsh's work is not just cult fiction, but diffi-cult fiction. It questions commitment, redefines radicalism'.[6] Both the content of Welsh's work and its marketing illustrate the interrelations of culture and commerce in contemporary society. Malcolm Bradbury considers Welsh 'the Sir Walter Scott of postmodern grunge,'[7] replacing older sets of romantic stereotypes about Scotland with equally stereotypical and touristic voyages through a dark and dangerously alluring theme park. On this note, Welsh does profess an admiration for Scott's marketing skill: '*Ivanhoe* was Scott making a play for the English market. One thing that Scott did understand more than any other novelist of his time – and probably any other novelist since – was the importance of marketing and PR. He really understood that he had to get to a bigger market'.[8] However, just as Renton steals books to read and to educate himself, Welsh's work, which has encouraged many people to engage with literature who were previously alienated from it, also affirms the emancipating power of literature, reading and thinking for constituencies of people outwith the ready-made bourgeois audience for culture. Welsh's work affirms his own point that 'culture is there for everybody'.[9]

With regard to culture and political emancipation, Antonio Gramsci's theory of the 'organic' intellectual is illuminating.[10] Gramsci argues that it is difficult for working-class people to become intellectuals and yet remain organically linked to their social class purely because the inequalities of society ensure that most of the working classes are denied access to higher education, whereas middle- and upper-class intellectuals readily voice the concerns of their respective constituencies because education and access to learning, political power and social influence are constitutive attributes of those classes. The working-class intellectual often gains access to privileges systemically withheld from the rest of their class so that a fissure is opened up between the intellectual and their class. It is not a question of intelligence, as Welsh's many thoughtful and indeed intellectual working-class characters demonstrate, but of opportunity. Welsh is aware that his social experiences as a famous writer are inaccessible to most of his characters. He freely admits, for example, that now 'travelling has become my drug. It's real freedom. It's something I've always aspired to. Thought I never would, though'.[11] However, he also maintains that he retains an organic attachment to the milieu of his work:

> When your talking about voyeurism you really need to talk about the voyeurism in yourself first. And there's no way around it, there's no doubt about it, there is an element of voyeurism, there's an element of voyeurism in everything. But it's like, has John Grisham done all these cases as a lawyer, has Ian Rankin murdered people? I write about where I'm coming from. I may not have done as many legal cases as John Grisham but I've murdered more people than Ian Rankin [*laughs*]. Naw, but I met this wee guy a couple of years ago on Leith Walk and he goes, 'You were a junky for fucking eighteen months; I was a fucking junky for fucking thirty-five years and *you've* written a fucking book about it.' But, I mean, away and fucking learn to write and then come back you cunt, know what I mean? But I've never felt I was on the outside looking in; I've always felt I was a part of everything I've ever fucking seen or experienced.[12]

Welsh states further that: 'There are two kinds of working-class philosophies, a radical or revolutionary one that sees the middle and upper classes as enemies; and another more individualistic desire to escape from the working and assimilate into the upper classes. That antagonism is always going on in a working-class head. It's wanting to be in a different situation'.[13] His work offers profuse examples of the individualistic, assimilative mindset – most obviously Sick Boy and even Renton – but it also details a more radical and politicised awakening that circumvents internecine myopia by turning its rage upon power and the state, which culminates in Spud's reclaimed history of Leith in *Porno*. Ultimately, for Willy Maley, 'like Zola, Welsh is on the side of the vanquished'.[14] The importance of Welsh's dissenting recoup of lost or suppressed voices swells when it is considered that those banished to the margins of society are not represented – either politically or in culture – by the dominant institutions of society. Welsh posits:

> there is no real opposition within the mainstream, the Labour Party has become the Tory Party because all the left have been kicked out of it, the unions don't have any power any more. Even the radicals and the churches, that side of religion, that's been blunted. So it's basically people who are outside the system that have got any sort of radicalism: you're either right outside society or you're exploited.[15]

Welsh's allegiance to those written out of history and society can be gleaned by his review of Arthur Herman's study, *Scottish Enlightenment: The Scots' Invention of the Modern World*, for the *Guardian* newspaper. Therein Welsh acknowledges the positives of the Scottish Enlightenment and its facilitation of a democratic education system. Yet he also considers the negatives of Scottish culture such as racism, intolerance, slavery, imperialism and class inequality. Welsh pertinently refuses to rationalise these negatives, such as the Highland clearances, as necessary side-products of an over-arching progress:

> The Highland clearances are a shameful element of Scotland's history, and can't be glossed over in this manner. That such atrocities took place at the same time as a sanitised tartan-kitsch modern tourist industry was being created by Walter Scott for the patronage of the bloated, foppish, alcoholic English king only renders them all the more obscene. The problem with this notion of 'a price of progress' is that it becomes self-serving by failing to take into account the non-enfranchisement and marginalisation of the people at the receiving end.[16]

The direct importance of a commitment to the voices of the vanquished in contemporary Britain resides in the fact that the 'Third Way' economics of the New Labour government proposes a progressive capitalism in which class divisions are no longer important since everyone is a stakeholder who may share equally society's benefits. The current dominant ruling and managerial classes, even their most well-intentioned proponents, in contemporary Britain are embarked upon the misconceived project of using capitalism as the ameliorative remedy for the ills of society when it is precisely that very economic system which is structurally responsible for those inequities in the first place. At its best, Welsh's work demonstrates that poverty, inequality and suffering exist not because capitalism is not working properly but rather because that is precisely how capitalism does work. Welsh's fiction gives the lie to this hegemonic and market-driven doctrine of progress and benign commerce by depicting and giving voice to those who are excluded from such mainstream narratives and are on the receiving end of its effects. Welsh's work attests that working-class identity has undergone profound shifts and transformations and it simultaneously acknowledges tensions and ruptures within those identities. But it also retains a perception of the continued oppressions, disenfranchisements and inequalities of class in an epoch that complacently proclaims a 'classless society'. As Ian Haywood affirms: 'So long as capitalism requires the existence of a working class, there will be a working-class literature'.[17]

Notes

1 Elspeth Findlay, 'The bourgeois values of Irvine Welsh', *Cencrastus* 71 (2002), 5–6.
2 Alan Sinfield, *Literature, Politics and Culture in Postwar Britain* (London: Athlone Press, 1997), xiii.
3 Irvine Welsh, 'Foreword', to Phil Vasili, *The First Black Footballer, Arthur Wharton 1865–1930: An Absence of Memory* (London: Frank Cass, 1998), xii.
4 Mary Riddell, 'Irvine Welsh interview', *New Statesman* (3 May 1999), 23.
5 Cited in Aaron Kelly, 'Irvine Welsh in conversation with Aaron Kelly', *Edinburgh Review* 113 (2004), 14.
6 Willy Maley, 'Subversion and squirrility in Irvine Welsh's shorter fiction' in Dermot Cavanagh and Tim Kirk, eds, *Subversion and Scurrility: Popular Discourse in Europe from 1500 to the Present* (Aldershot: Ashgate, 2000), 199.
7 Malcolm Bradbury, 'Forth man', *Sunday Times*, Travel Section (25 Oct 1998), 1.
8 *The Story of the Novel*. Channel 4. Broadcast 20 July 2003.
9 Cited in Jennifer Berman, 'An interview with Irvine Welsh', *Bomb Magazine* 56 (1996), 57.
10 See Antonio Gramsci, *Selections from the Prison Notebooks*. Ed. and trans. Quintin Hoare and Geoffrey Nowell Smith (London: Lawrence and Wishart, 1996), 6, 12, 15–16, 60, 330.
11 Cited in Francis Gilbert, 'Where there's muck', *The Times*, Metro Section (25 July 1998), 16.

12 Cited in Kelly, 'Irvine Welsh in conversation with Aaron Kelly', 10–11.

13 Cited in Berman, 'An interview with Irvine Welsh', 56.

14 Maley, 'Subversion and squirrility in Irvine Welsh's shorter fiction', 193.

15 Cited in Steve Redhead, *Repetitive Beat Generation* (Edinburgh: Rebel Inc, 2000), 144.

16 Irvine Welsh, 'The flowers of Scotland', *Guardian* (19 Jan 2002), 28.

17 Ian Haywood, *Working-Class Fiction from Chartism to Trainspotting* (Plymouth: Northcote, 1997), 160.

Select bibliography

Fiction and drama by Irvine Welsh

Trainspotting (London: Secker and Warburg, 1993).
The Acid House (London: Jonathan Cape, 1994).
Marabou Stork Nightmares (London: Jonathan Cape, 1995).
Ecstasy (London: Jonathan Cape, 1996).
Trainspotting and Headstate: Playscripts (London: Minerva, 1996).
Filth (London: Jonathan Cape, 1998).
You'll Have Had Your Hole (London: Methuen, 1998).
4–Play: Trainspotting, Marabou Stork Nightmares, Ecstasy, Filth (London: Vintage, 2001).
Glue (London: Jonathan Cape, 2001).
Porno (London: Jonathan Cape, 2002).

Articles and essays by Irvine Welsh

'City tripper', *Guardian*, G2 (16 Feb 1996), 4.
'Welcome to the working class', *Guardian*, G2T (13 Sep 1996), 4.
'Foreword', to Phil Vasili, *The First Black Footballer, Arthur Wharton 1865–1930: An Absence of Memory* (London: Frank Cass, 1998), xi–xiii.
'The flowers of Scotland', *Guardian* (19 Jan 2002), 28.
'From America', *Daily Telegraph* (31 Mar 2003), accessed at www.telegraph.co.uk (Apr 2003).
'Flower of Scotland', *Guardian*, Review (23 Aug 2003), 14.

Official website

www.irvinewelsh.com

Other sources

Adams, Tim, 'Just say no', *Observer*, Review (2 June 1996), 14.

Adams, Tim, 'Peter panned', *Observer* (7 Dec 1997), 30.

Alberge, Dalya (1999), 'Boring theatre gives author the needle', *The Times* (6 Feb 1999), 3.

Arlidge, John, 'Return of the angry young men', *Observer* (23 June 1996), 14.

Ashcroft, Bill, Gareth Griffiths and Helen Tiffin, *The Empire Writes Back: Theory and Practice in Post-Colonial Literatures* (London: Routledge, 2002).

Baker, Phil, 'An unfair cop', *Sunday Times* (2 Aug 1998), 8.

Bakhtin, M. M., *Rabelais and His World*. Trans. Hélène Iswolsky (Cambridge, Mass: MIT Press, 1968).

Bakhtin, M. M., *The Dialogic Imagination: Four Essays*. Ed. Michael Holquist. Trans. Caryl Emerson and Michael Holquist (Austin: University of Texas Press, 1981).

Barnes, Hugh, '*The Acid House*', *Independent on Sunday* (3 Apr 1994), 31.

Baudrillard, Jean, *Selected Writings* (Cambridge: Polity Press, 2001).

Beckett, Andy, 'The myth of the cool', *Guardian*, G2 (5 May 1998), 2–3.

Beckett, Andy, 'Irvine Welsh: the ecstasy and the agony', *Guardian* (25 July 1998), 6.

Bell, Ian, 'Last exit to Leith', *Observer* (15 Aug 1993), 47.

Bell, Ian, 'How Scotland got the write stuff', *Observer* (19 Nov 1995), 17.

Berman, Jennifer, 'An interview with Irvine Welsh', *Bomb Magazine* 56 (1996), 56–61.

Beveridge, Craig and Ronald Turnbull, *The Eclipse of Scottish Culture: Inferiorism and the Intellectuals* (Edinburgh: Polygon, 1989).

Bhabha, Homi K., *The Location of Culture* (London: Routledge, 1994).

Birch, Helen, 'Meeting God down the pub: *The Acid House*', *Independent*, Weekend Supplement (16 Apr 1994), 29.

Bracewell, Michael, 'Farewell to the nineties', *Independent on Sunday* (28 Nov 1999), 11.

Bracewell, Michael, 'Review of *Repetitive Beat Generation*', *Independent* (4 Mar 2000), 10.

Bradbury, Malcolm, 'Forth man', *Sunday Times*, Travel Section (25 Oct 1998), 1.

Bradfield, Scott, 'A touch too Scotological', *The Times* (30 July 1998), 39.

Braid, Mary, 'Irvine Welsh: addicted to mischief', *Independent* (28 Apr 2001), 24.

Bresnark, Robin, 'An interview with Irvine Welsh', *Melody Maker* (16 Jan 1999), 12.

Brockington, Michael, 'Poisoned haggis', *Vancouver Review* (Fall/Winter 1995), www.sfu.ca/~brocking/writing/phaggis.html (Aug 2003).

Brodie, John, 'Off-kilter', *Premiere* 11: 3 (1 Nov 1997), 118.

Brown, Geoff, 'Set your phrases to mildly stun', *The Times* (31 Dec 1998), 37.

Brüggernmeier, Martin and Horst W. Drescher, 'A subculture and its characterization in Irvine Welsh's *Trainspotting*', *Anglistik & Englischuntterict* 63 (Winter 2000), 135–169.

Burroughs, William S., *Junky* (London: Penguin, 1977).

Callahan, Maureen, 'Heroin chic: angry young cinema', *New York* 29: 27 (15 July 1996), 36.

Callinicos, Alex, *Against Postmodernism: A Marxist Critique* (Oxford: Polity Press, 1992).

Campbell, James, 'Scratch 'n' sniff', *Guardian*, Review (28 Apr 2001), 14.

Cannadine, David, *Class in Britain* (London: Yale University Press, 1998).

Cardullo, Burt, 'Fiction into film, or, bringing Welsh to a Boyle', *Literature/Film Quarterly* 25: 3 (1997), 158–162.

Cavenett, Wendy, 'A star is bored', *Independent* (11 July 1998), 20–21.

Coe, Jonathan, 'Where authors fear to tread', *Sunday Times* (13 Mar 1994), 7, 13.

Collin, Matthew, *Altered State: The Story of Ecstasy Culture and Acid House* (London: Serpent's Tail, 1998).

Cooper, Neil, '*Filth*', *The Times* (21 Sep 1999), 44.

Cowley, Jason, 'Prickly flower of Scotland', *The Times* (13 Mar 1997), 33.

Craig, Cairns, *Out of History: Narrative Paradigms in Scottish and British Culture* (Edinburgh: Polygon, 1996).

Craig, Cairns, *The Modern Scottish Novel: Narrative and the National Imagination* (Edinburgh: Edinburgh University Press, 1999).

Craig, Cairns, 'Constituting Scotland', *Irish Review* 28 (2001), 1–27.

Crawford, Robert, *Devolving English Literature* (Edinburgh: Edinburgh University Press, 2000).

Cullingford, Martin, 'Our novel way of speaking', *The Times* (20 July 1999), 15.

Curtis, Nick, 'Drug-fuelled romances: Scottish fiction', *Financial Times* (8 June 1996), 12.

Davie, George E., *The Democratic Intellect: Scotland and Her Universities in the Nineteenth Century* (Edinburgh: Edinburgh University Press, 1961).

Davie, George E., *The Scottish Enlightenment and Other Essays* (Edinburgh: Polygon, 1991).

Davison, John, 'Heroin UK: how heroin chic culture came to the high street', *Independent* (11 May 1999), 41.

Dixon, Keith, 'Making sense of ourselves: nation and community in modern Scottish writing', *Forum for Modern Language Studies* 29: 4 (1993), 359–368.

Downer, Lesley, 'The beats of Edinburgh', *New York Times Magazine* (15 Mar 1996), 42–45.

Eagleton, Terry, *The Ideology of the Aesthetic* (Oxford: Basil Blackwell, 1990).

Fane, Charlotte, 'Football hooligans take bookstores by storm', *The Times* (16 June 1998), 19.

Fanon, Frantz, *The Wretched of the Earth*. Trans. Constance Farrington (Harmondsworth: Penguin, 1967).

Farquarson, Kenny, 'Through the eye of a needle', *Scotland on Sunday* (8 Aug 1993), 4.

Findlay, Elspeth, 'The bourgeois values of Irvine Welsh', *Cencrastus* 71 (2002), 5–7.

Fisher, Mark, 'Talking 'bout E's generation', *Observer*, Review (9 Oct 1994), 6.

Freeman, Alan, 'Ghosts in sunny Leith: Irvine Welsh's *Trainspotting*' in Susanne Hagemann, ed., *Studies in Scottish Fiction: 1945 to the Present* (Frankfurt am Main: Peter Lang, 1996), 251–262.

Freeman, Alan, 'Ourselves as others: *Marabou Stork Nightmares*', *Edinburgh Review* 95 (1996), 135–141.

Frith, Simon, 'Art ideology and pop practice' in Cary Nelson and Lawrence Grossberg, eds, *Marxism and the Interpretation of Culture* (Chicago: University of Illinois Press, 1988), 461–475.

Gardiner, Michael, 'Democracy and Scotland's postcoloniality', *Scotlands* 3: 2 (1996), 24–41.

Gardiner, Michael, 'British territory: Irvine Welsh in English and Japanese', *Textual Practice* 17: 1 (2003), 101–117.

Gardner, Lyn, 'Heartless laughter of the damned', *Guardian*, G2T (5 Apr 1995), 4.

Giddens, Anthony, *The Third Way: The Renewal of Social Democracy* (Cambridge: Polity Press, 1998).

Gilbert, Francis, 'Where there's muck', *The Times*, Metro Section (25 July 1998), 16.

Gilbert, Francis, 'Mainstream consciousness – review of *Repetitive Beat Generation*', *The Times*, Metro Section (26 Feb 2000), 17.

Gilroy, Paul, *There Ain't No Black in the Union Jack: The Cultural Politics of Race and Nation* (London: Routledge, 2002).

Gordon, Giles, 'Pandering to the English view of Scotland the drugged', *The Scotsman* (13 June 1997), 19.

Graham, Colin, *Deconstructing Ireland* (Edinburgh: Edinburgh University Press, 2001).

Gramsci, Antonio, *Selections from the Prison Notebooks*. Ed. and trans. Quintin Hoare and Geoffrey Nowell Smith (London: Lawrence and Wishart, 1996).

Grant, Iain, 'Dealing out the capital punishment', *Sunday Times* (5 Sep 1993), 14.

Hallam, Julia, 'Film, class and national identity: re-imagining communities in the age of devolution' in Justine Ashby and Andrew Higson, eds, *British Cinema, Past and Present* (London: Routledge, 2000), 261–273.

Harold, Christine L., 'The rhetorical function of the abject body: transgressive corporeality in *Trainspotting*', *JAC: The Journal of Composition Theory* 20: 4 (Spring 2000), 865–887.

Harvie, Christopher, 'The folly of our fable: getting Scottish history wrong', *Scottish Studies Review* 1: 1 (Winter 2000), 99–105.

Haywood, Ian, *Working-Class Fiction from Chartism to Trainspotting* (Plymouth: Northcote, 1997).

Hemming, Sarah, 'Grim wit in a drug wasteland', *Financial Times* (21 Dec 1995), 11.

Herbrechter, Stefan, 'From *Trainspotting* to *Filth*: masculinity and cultural politics in Irvine Welsh's writings' in Russell West and Frank Lay, eds, *Subverting Masculinity: Hegemonic and Alternative Versions of Masculinity in Contemporary Culture* (Amsterdam: Rodopi, 2000), 109–127.

Higginbottom, Adam, 'Irvine Welsh: a man of substance?', *Independent on Sunday* (29 Apr 2001), 20.

Hill, John, *British Cinema in the 1980s* (Oxford: Oxford University Press, 1999).

Hodge, John, *Trainspotting and Shallow Grave: The Screenplays* (London: Faber, 1996).

Hornby, Nick, '*Marabou Stork Nightmares*', *TLS* 4804 (28 Apr 1995), 23.

Horrocks, Roger, *Masculinity in Crisis: Myths, Fantasies, Realities* (Houndmills: Macmillan, 1994).

Horton, Patricia, '*Trainspotting*: a topography of the masculine abject', *English: The Journal of the English Association* 50 (Autumn 2001), 219–234.

Howard, Jennifer, 'Fiction in a different vein', *Washington Post*, Book World (8 Sep 1996), 1, 9.

Hughes-Hallett, Lucy, 'Cruising for a bruising', *Sunday Times* (15 Aug 1993), 6–8.

In Your Face. Irvine Welsh: Condemn More, Understand Less. BBC2. Broadcast 27 Nov 1995.

Jackson, Alan, 'Cold call interview: Irvine Welsh', *The Times Magazine* (30 Jan 1999), 9.

Jackson, Ellen-Raïssa and Willy Maley, 'Birds of a feather? A postcolonial reading of Irvine Welsh's *Marabou Stork Nightmares*', *Revista Canaria de Estudios Ingleses* 41 (2000), 187–196.

Jackson, Rosemary, *Fantasy: The Literature of Subversion* (London: Routledge, 1988).

Jameson, Fredric, *Postmodernism, or, the Cultural Logic of Late Capitalism* (London: Verso, 1991).

Jamieson, Gill, 'Fixing the city: arterial and other spaces in Irvine Welsh's fiction' in Glenda Norquay and Gerry Smyth, eds, *Space and Place: The Geographies of Literature* (Liverpool: Liverpool University Press, 1998), 217–226.

Jones, Oliver, 'Shoot me up, Scotty', *Premiere* 9: 11 (1 July 1996), 60.

Kakutani, Michiko, 'Slumming', *New York Times Magazine* (26 Mar 1996), 16.

Kane, Pat, 'Me tartan, you chained to the past', *Guardian*, G2T (18 May 1995), 12.

Kane, Pat, 'Fatal knowledge of an inescapable masculinity', *Scotland on Sunday* (16 July 1995), 12.

Kane, Pat, 'Infernal desires: *Ecstasy*', *New Statesman* (7 June 1996), 37–38.

Kaufmann, Stanley, 'Scotland now, England then', *New Republic* (19–26 Aug 1996), 38–39.

Kelly, Aaron, 'Irvine Welsh in conversation with Aaron Kelly', *Edinburgh Review* 113 (2004), 7–17.

Kenyon, Meb and Phyllis Nagy, 'Season of lad tidings', *Guardian*, G2 (4 Dec 1995), 7.

Kermode, Mark, 'End notes', *Sight and Sound* 6: 3 (1996), 62–63.

Kimmel, Michael, 'Masculinity as homophobia: fear, shame, and silence in the construction of gender identity' in Harry Brod and Michael Kaufman, eds, *Theorizing Masculinities* (London: Sage, 1994), 119–141.

King, John, 'The boys are back in town: *Porno*', *New Statesman* (2 Sep 2002), 36–37.

Kingston, Jeremy, 'Violent but fair: *Filth*', *The Times* (8 Feb 1999), 17.

Klein, Naomi, *No Logo: No Space, No Choice, No Jobs* (London: Flamingo, 2001).

Landy, Marcia, 'The other side of paradise: British cinema from an American perspective' in Justine Ashby and Andrew Higson, eds, *British Cinema, Past and Present* (London: Routledge, 2000), 63–79.

Lasdun, James, 'A smart cunt', *Village Voice* (23 July 1996), 74.

Laurence, Alexander, 'Irvine Welsh: Scottish and still alive', *Free Williamsburg* 13, www.freewilliamsburg.com/july_2001/interviews/html (July 2001).

Leonard, Mark, *BritainTM: Renewing Our Identity* (London: Demos, 1997).

Lezard, Nicola, 'Junk and the big trigger: *Trainspotting*', *Independent on Sunday*, Sunday Review (29 Aug 1993), 28.

Lister, David, 'Welsh attacks elitist theatres', *Independent* (5 Feb 1999), 7.

Luckett, Moya, 'Image and nation in 1990s British cinema' in Robert Murphy, ed., *British Cinema of the 1990s* (London: BFI Publishing, 2000), 88–99.

Lury, Karen, 'Here and then: space, place and nostalgia in British youth cinema' in Robert Murphy, ed., *British Cinema of the 1990s* (London: BFI Publishing, 2000), 100–108.

Lyotard, Jean-François, *The Postmodern Condition: A Report on Knowledge*. Trans. Geoff Bennington and Brian Massumi. Foreword by Fredric Jameson (Manchester: Manchester University Press, 1996).

Macaulay, Alastair, 'Dramatic shape-ups offstage and on', *Financial Times* (15 Mar 1996), 17.

MacDonald, Kevin, 'Postcards from the edge', *Independent on Sunday* (28 Jan 1996), 18.

MacDonald, Laura, '100% uncut: Irvine Welsh on *The Acid House*', www.indiewire.com/film/interviews/int_Welsh_Irvine_990804.html (Aug 2003).

Mackay, Fiona, *The Case of Zero Tolerance: Women's Politics in Action?* (Edinburgh: Waverley Papers, 1995).

Maconie, Stuart, 'Fool Britannia', *The Times*, Metro Section (26 Dec 1998), 24.

Maley, Willy, 'Denizens, citizens, tourists, and others: marginality and mobility in the writings of James Kelman and Irvine Welsh' in David Bell and Azzedine Haddour, eds, *City Visions* (Harlow: Prentice Hall, 2000), 60–72.

Maley, Willy, 'Subversion and squirrility in Irvine Welsh's shorter fiction' in Dermot Cavanagh and Tim Kirk, eds, *Subversion and Scurrility: Popular Discourse in Europe from 1500 to the Present* (Aldershot: Ashgate, 2000), 190–204.

Maley, Willy, 'You'll have had your theatre', *Spike Magazine*, www.spikemagazine.com/0199welshplay.htm (Mar 2003).

March, Cristie L., *Rewriting Scotland: Welsh, McLean, Warner, Banks, Galloway and Kennedy* (Manchester: Manchester University Press, 2002).

Mars-Jones, Adam, 'Stick whingers: *Glue*', *Observer* (6 May 2001), 22.

Massie, Allan, 'Sir Walter Scott's literati', *Scotland on Sunday* (16 June 2002), 23.

McCann, Paul, 'Screen writers help Liverpool's striking dockers to tell all', *Independent* (2 July 1999), 4.

McCarron, Kevin, 'The disenchanted circle: slave narratives and junk narratives', *Dionysus: The Journal of Literature and Addiction* 8: 1 (Winter 1998), 5–14.

McCracken, Scott, *Pulp: Reading Popular Fiction* (Manchester: Manchester University Press, 1998).

McCrone, David, *Understanding Scotland: The Sociology of a Stateless Nation* (London: Routledge, 1992).

McIlvanney, Liam, '*Filth*', *Scottish Literary Journal* 26: 1 (June 1999), 145–148.

McKay, Ron, 'Would the real Irvine Welsh shoot up?', *Observer*, Review (4 Feb 1996), 9.

McLean, Duncan, *Ahead of Its Time: A Clocktower Press Anthology* (London: Jonathan Cape, 1997).

McMillan, Neil, 'Junked exiles, exiled junk: Irvine Welsh and Alexander Trocchi' in Glenda Norquay and Gerry Smyth, eds, *Space and Place: The Geographies of Literature* (Liverpool: Liverpool University Press, 1998), 239–256.

McNab, Geoffrey, 'Geoffrey McNab talks to the team that made *Trainspotting*', *Sight and Sound* 6: 2 (Feb 1996), 8–11.

Mendelsohn, Jane, 'Needles and sins: *Trainspotting*', *New Republic* (2 Sep

1996), 31–33.

Milne, Drew, 'The fiction of James Kelman and Irvine Welsh: accents, speech and writing' in Richard J. Lane et al., eds, *Contemporary British Fiction* (Oxford: Polity Press, 2003), 158–173.

Mitchell, Chris, 'Love is a many splintered thing', www.spikemagazine. com/spikeecs.htm (Jan 2000)

Molloy, Deirdre, 'Scotland the brave', *Observer* (12 Nov 1995), 8.

Monk, Claire, 'Underbelly UK: the 1990s underclass film, masculinity, and the ideologies of "New Britannia"' in Justine Ashby and Andrew Higson, eds, *British Cinema: Past and Present* (London: Routledge, 2000), 274–287.

Monnickendam, Andrew, 'Lost causes: national identity and postmodernism', *Etudes Ecossaises* 3 (1996), 105–115.

Monnickendam, Andrew, 'Literary voices and the projection of cultural failure in modern Scottish literature' in T. Hoenselaars and Maruis Buning, eds, *English Literature and the Other Languages* (Amsterdam: Rodopi, 1999), 231–242.

Mooney, Bel, 'Shakespeare is better than studying Irvine Welsh', *The Times* (10 Aug 1999), 36.

Morace, Robert A., *Trainspotting: A Reader's Guide* (London: Continuum, 2001).

Muir, Edwin, *Scott and Scotland: The Predicament of the Scottish Writer* (London: Folcroft Library Editions, 1971).

Muir, Edwin, *Scottish Journey* (Edinburgh: Mainstream, 1979).

Mulholland, John, 'Acid wit', *Guardian*, G2T (30 Mar 1995), 8.

Nairn, Tom, *The Break-Up of Britain: Crisis and Neo-Nationalism* (London: Verso, 1981).

Neubauer, Jürgen, 'Critical media literacy and the representation of youth in *Trainspotting*', *Anglistik und Englischunterricht* 63 (Winter 2000), 135–150.

Nightingale, Benedict, 'What a load of hybrid interplay', *The Times* (26 Feb 1998), 37.

O'Brien, Sean, 'Schemies, soapdodgers and huns', *TLS* (1 Oct 1993), 20.

O'Hagan, Andrew, 'Scotland's fine mess', *Guardian*, Weekend Section (23 July 1994), 24.

O'Hagan, Andrew, 'Smack aleck of the beat generation', *Observer*, Review (10 Dec 1995), 15.

O'Hagan, Andrew, '*Trainspotting*: the boys are back in town' in Ginette Vincendeau, ed., *Film/Literature/Heritage: A Sight and Sound Reader* (London: BFI Publishing, 2001), 223–227.

Oliver, Fiona, 'The self-debasement of Scotland's postcolonial bodies', *SPAN: Journal of the South Pacific Association for Commonwealth Literature and Language Study* 42–43 (1996), 114–121.

O'Toole, Fintan, 'Imagining Scotland', *Granta* 56 (Winter 1996), 70–71.

Paget, Derek, 'Speaking out: the transformations of *Trainspotting*' in Deborah

Cartmell and Imelda Whelehan, eds, *Adaptations: From Text to Screen, Screen to Text* (London: Routledge, 2002), 128–140.

Peter, John, 'The theatre of excess', *Sunday Times* (1 Mar 1998), 14.

Pittin-Hédon, Marie-Odile, 'Postmodern fantasy: the supernatural in Gray's *Comedy of the White Dog* and Welsh's *Granton Star Cause*', *Etudes Ecossaises* 7 (2001), 61–74.

Pittock, Murray, *Celtic Identity and the British Image* (Manchester: Manchester University Press, 1999).

Porlock, Harvey, 'Critical list', *Sunday Times*, Bookmark (9 June 1996), 2.

Powers, John, '*Trainspotting*', *Vogue* (Jul 1996), 25.

Private Eye, Literary Review No.1061 (23 Aug–5 Sep 2002), 24.

Punter, David, 'E-textuality: authenticity after the postmodern', *Critical Quarterly* 43: 2 (Summer 2001), 68–91.

'Q & A: *Trainspotting* author Irvine Welsh on cops and drugs', *Time Magazine* (28 Sep 1998), 92–94.

Redhead, Steve, ed., *The Passion and the Fashion: Football Fandom in the New Europe* (Aldershot: Avebury, 1993).

Redhead, Steve, *Post-Fandom and the Millennial Blues: The Transformation of Soccer Culture* (London: Routledge, 1997).

Redhead, Steve, ed., *Rave Off: Politics and Deviance in Contemporary Youth Culture* (Aldershot: Ashgate, 1999).

Redhead, Steve, *Repetitive Beat Generation* (Edinburgh: Rebel Inc, 2000).

Reynolds, Simon, *Energy Flash: A Journey through Rave Music and Dance Culture* (London: Macmillan, 1998).

Riddell, Mary, 'Irvine Welsh interview', *New Statesman* (3 May 1999), 22–23.

Rietveld, Hillegonda, 'Repetitive beats: free parties and the politics of contemporary DiY dance culture in Britain' in George McKay, ed., *DiY Culture: Party and Protest in Nineties Britain* (London: Verso, 1998), 243–267.

Roberts, Rex, 'Is it ecstasy or existentialism?', *Insight on the News* (16 Sep 1996), 34.

Romney, Jonathan, '*The Acid House* – bleak house' *Guardian* (1 Jan 1999), 7.

Roper, Michael and John Tosh, *Manful Assertions: Masculinities in Britain Since 1991* (London: Routledge, 1991).

Samuel, Raphael, Barbara Bloomfield and Guy Boanas, *The Enemy Within: Pit Villages and the Miners' Strike 1984–5* (London: Routledge and Kegan Paul, 1986).

Savage King, Chris, 'Voices from the edge', *Sunday Times* (16 Apr 1995), 9, 12.

Scruton, Roger, 'Modernists and monsters', *The Times* (10 Dec 1998), 41.

Schoene, Berthold, 'The union and Jack: British masculinities, pomophobia, and the post-nation' in Glenda Norquay and Gerry Smyth, eds, *Across the Margins: Cultural Identity and Change in the Atlantic Archipelago* (Manchester: Manchester University Press, 2002), 83–98.

Schoene, Berthold, 'Nervous men, mobile nation: masculinity and psychopathology in Irvine Welsh's *Filth* and *Glue*' in Eleanor Bell and Gavin Miller, eds, *Scotland in Theory* (Amsterdam: Rodopi, 2004), 121–145.

Schoene-Harwood, Berthold, '"Emerging as the others of ourselves": Scottish multiculturalism and the challenge of the body in the postcolonial condition', *Scottish Literary Journal* 25: 1 (1998), 54–72.

Schoene-Harwood, Berthold, *Writing Men: Literary Masculinities from Frankenstein to the New Man* (Edinburgh: Edinburgh University Press, 2000).

Self, Will, 'Carry on up the hypodermic', *Observer*, Review (11 Feb 1996), 6.

Sierz, A., 'Cool Britannia? In-yer-face writing in the British theatre today', *New Theatre Quarterly* 14: 56 (Nov 1998), 324–333.

Sinfield, Alan, *Literature, Politics and Culture in Postwar Britain* (London: Athlone Press, 1997).

Skinner, John, 'Contemporary Scottish novelists and the stepmother tongue' in T. Hoenselaars and Maruis Buning, eds, *English Literature and the Other Languages* (Amsterdam: Rodopi, 1999), 211–220.

Smith, Andrew, 'Irvine changes trains', *Sunday Times*, Culture Supplement (1 Feb 1998), 6.

Smith, Murray, *Trainspotting* (London: BFI Publishing, 2002).

Spin Magazine, 'Scots, drugs and rock'n'roll: an interview with Irvine Welsh', www.spin.com/new/poplife/author.html (Sep 2002).

Spinks, Lee, '*Ecstasy*', *Scottish Literary Journal* 47 (Autumn 1997), 80–82.

Spittal, Robin, '*Trainspotting*: A new Scottish icon?', *Etudes Ecossaises* 5 (1998), 195–205.

Stallybrass, Peter and Allon White, *The Politics and Poetics of Transgression* (London: Methuen, 1986).

Stephenson, William, 'Scoring Ecstasy: MDMA, consumerism and spirituality in the early fiction of Irvine Welsh', *Cultural Value* 7: 2 (2003), 147–163.

Strachan, Zoë, 'Queerspotting', *Spike Magazine*, www.spikemagazine.com/0599queerspotting.htm (Aug 2003).

Swann, Paul, 'The British culture industries and the mythology of the American market: cultural policy and cultural exports in the 1940s and 1990s', *Cinema Journal* 39: 4 (2000), 27–42.

Taubin, Amy, 'Making tracks', *Village Voice* (23 July 1996), 66.

Taylor, Alan, 'Thieving, rape, drugs. And that's just the police', *Observer* (9 Aug 1998), 34.

Taylor, Alan, 'My kind of century', *Scotland on Sunday* (21 Feb 1999), 7, 12.

The Story of the Novel, Channel 4. Broadcast 20 July 2003.

Thompson, Be, 'The interview: Irvine Welsh', *Independent on Sunday* (2 June 1996), 14.

Thorne, Matt, 'Fanny peculiar – review of *Glue*', *Independent on Sunday* (6 May 2001), 12.

Thornton, Phil, *Casuals: Football, Fighting and Fashion – The Story of a Terrace Cult* (Lytham: Milo Books, 2003).

Thornton, Sarah, *Club Cultures: Music, Media and Subcultural Capital* (Oxford: Polity Press, 1995).

Tonkin, Boyd, 'A wee Hades: *Marabou Stork Nightmares*', *Observer*, Review (23 Apr 1995), 20.

Turner, Jenny, 'Sick boys', *London Review of Books* (2 Dec 1993), 10.

Turner, Jenny, 'Love's chemistry', *Guardian*, G2T (31 May 1996), 17.

Unpop Dotcom, 'An exclusive interview with author Irvine Welsh', www.unpop.com/features/art/welsh.html (Sep 2003).

Wakefield, Neville, *Postmodernism: The Twilight of the Real* (London: Pluto, 1990).

Walsh, John, 'The not-so-shady past of Irvine Welsh', *Independent*, Weekend Section (15 Apr 1995), 25.

Watson, Jeremy and Gillian McCormack, 'Posh Welshie cannae dae the voices nae mair', *Scotland on Sunday* (14 Apr 2002), 28.

Watson, Roderick, 'Postcolonial subjects? Language, narrative authority and class in contemporary Scottish culture', *Hungarian Journal of English and American Studies* 4: 1–2 (1998), 21–38.

Wazir, Burhan, 'The trend spotter', *Observer* (11 Aug 2002), 5.

Wazir, Burhan, 'Sick Boy and the hangover', *Observer* (18 Aug 2002), 30.

Welch, Dave, 'Irvine Welsh', www.powells.com/authors/welsh.html (Sep 2002).

Whyte, Christopher, ed. and intro, *Gendering the Nation: Studies in Modern Scottish Literature* (Edinburgh: Edinburgh University Press, 1995).

Whyte, Christopher, 'Masculinities in contemporary Scottish fiction', *Forum for Modern Language Studies* 34: 3 (1998), 274–285.

Williams, Nicholas M., 'The dialect of authenticity: the case of Irvine Welsh's *Trainspotting*' in T. Hoenselaars and Maruis Buning, eds, *English Literature and the Other Languages* (Amsterdam: Rodopi, 1999), 221–230.

Williamson, Kevin, *Drugs and the Party Line* (Edinburgh: Rebel Inc, 1997).

Wishart, K., 'Drugs and art meet on campus', *Times Higher Education Supplement* (30 May 1997), 18.

Wroe, Martin, 'Hard drugs and heroine addiction', *Observer* (10 Mar 1996), 13.

Young, Elizabeth, 'Blood on the tracks', *Guardian* (14 Aug 1993), 33.

Young Elizabeth, 'Grubby faces', *Guardian*, G2T (8 Mar 1994), 14.

Žižek, Slavoj, *Looking Awry: An Introduction to Jacques Lacan through Popular Culture* (London: MIT Press, 1991).

Index